Talking
with
Serial Killers

**SLEEPING WITH
PSYCHOPATHS**

Born in 1948 in Winchester, Hampshire, **Christopher Berry-Dee** is descended from Dr John Dee, Court Astrologer to Queen Elizabeth I, and is the founder and former Director of the Criminology Research Institute (CRI), and former publisher and Editor-in-Chief of *The Criminologist*, a highly respected journal on matters concerning all aspects of criminology from law enforcement to forensic psychology.

Christopher has interviewed and interrogated over thirty of the world's most notorious killers – serial, mass and one-off – including Peter Sutcliffe, Ted Bundy, Aileen Wuornos, Dennis Nilsen and Joanna Dennehy. He was co-producer/interviewer for the acclaimed twelve-part TV documentary series *The Serial Killers*, and has appeared on television as a consultant on serial homicide, and, in the series *Born to Kill?*, on the cases of Fred and Rose West, the 'Moors Murderers' and Dr Harold Shipman. He has also assisted in criminal investigations as far afield as Russia and the United States.

Notable book successes include: *Monster* (the basis for the movie of the same title, about Aileen Wuornos); *Dad Help Me Please*, about the tragic Derek Bentley, hanged for a murder he did not commit (subsequently subject of the film *Let Him Have It*); and *Talking with Serial Killers*, Christopher's international bestseller, now, with its sequel, *Talking with Serial Killers: World's Most Evil*, required reading at the FBI Behavioral Analysis Unit Academy at Quantico, Virginia. His *Talking with Psychopaths and Savages: A Journey Into the Evil Mind*, was the UK's bestselling true-crime title of 2017; its successor volume, *Talking with Psychopaths and Savages: Beyond Evil*, was published in the autumn of 2019. In 2020 a new edition of his *Talking with Serial Killers: Dead Men Talking* appeared, and he has since published *Talking with Serial Killers: Stalkers* and *Talking with Psychopaths and Savages: Mass Murderers and Spree Killers*.

https://www.christopherberrydee.com/

Christopher Berry-Dee

Talking
with
Serial Killers

SLEEPING WITH
PSYCHOPATHS

A chilling study of the innocent
lovers of savage murderers

jb

First published in the UK by John Blake Publishing
an imprint of Bonnier Books UK
4th Floor, Victoria House
Bloomsbury Square
London WC1B 4DA
England

Owned by Bonnier Books
Sveavägen 56, Stockholm, Sweden

www.facebook.com/johnblakebooks 🅕
twitter.com/jblakebooks 🅣

First published in paperback in 2021

Paperback ISBN: 978-1-78946-561-7
Trade paperback: 978-1-78946-428-3
Ebook ISBN: 978-1-78946-429-0
Audiobook ISBN: 978-1-78946-564-8

British Library Cataloguing-in-Publication Data:

A catalogue record for this book is available from the British Library.

Design by www.envydesign.co.uk

Printed and bound in Great Britain by Clays Ltd, Elcograf S.p.A

5 7 9 10 8 6 4

John Blake Publishing is an imprint of Bonnier Books UK
www.bonnierbooks.co.uk

For Claire

PICTURE CREDITS

Acknowledgements

Oh, how do I thank thee ... is an issue that many authors should address when completing a book – 'thee', of course, being the many family, friends, colleagues, and never the sundry ne'er-do-wells, the latter one happenchance comes across occasionally along the way.

Sometimes, I write a voluminous set of acknowledgements, other times those I thank are included in the body text proper; then there are the briefest of acknowledgements, maybe a page and a bit, just to show willing, and to kick off with, I thank all of my readers past and present, for without you we authors would never get a book into print and publishers would soon go out of business.

My writing career started way back in 1990. It has been a long literary road, and I am indebted to my previous publishers: W.H. Allen; Smith Gryphon; John Blake Publishing, now an imprint of Bonnier Books UK; and more recently Ad Lib, for all of the support, encouragement, the many editors, the marketing folk and the lawyers, who have guided me through thick and thin. Therefore, I am extremely mindful of this, so thank you all very much indeed.

The great true-crime writer and historian, Robin Odell, was my mentor. Dearest friend, John Blake, has been my loyal publisher for some seventeen years, adding, of course, my present editor-in-chief, Toby Buchan, who has the patience of a saint and his own richly embroidered literary bloodline stretching back to his grandfather, John Buchan, first Baron Tweedsmuir, GCMG, GCVO, CH, author of the famous spy novel *The Thirty-Nine Steps*.

So, that's the acknowledgements done and dusted once again – well, I did say I can be brief – so Praise the Lord, and off we go.

Contents

Prologue

Introduction

There is an odd synchronicity in the way parallel lives
veer to touch one another, change direction and then
come close again and again until they connect and hold
for whatever it was that fate intended to happen.
ANN RAE RULE, AMERICAN TRUE-CRIME WRITER
(1931–2015)

This book is largely about distress with, I must add, many humorous moments to lighten the load, for every single grim date throughout the black history of true crime is painted bright crimson; the colour of the blood spilt by thousands of innocent men, women, youngsters, and children, who have been murdered by every possible means known to mankind. Therefore, before we begin, our hearts must go out to their families, their next-of-kin, their friends, and their colleagues who mourn the losses, for death is tangible, grief less so.

I vividly recall many years ago, while writing with Robin Odell my book *Ladykiller* – later retitled *Prime Suspect* – concerning the life and crimes of the emerging, if not already a fully emerged British serial killer, John David Guise Cannan – the poignant, tearful words of one of his victims, survivor Sharon Major (name changed for legal reasons):

> *I know what John did to me was wicked but there is a good side to John which is desperately trying to get out. He almost killed me and I still live in terror of him today but one has to learn to forgive and that I have done.*
>
> Sharon Major: an interview with
> the author in Bristol, 1992

John Cannan – who *is* the prime suspect for the unsolved 1986 murders of Suzy Lamplugh in South London, and Sandra Court, at Poole, Dorset – is now serving a life sentence. At the time of writing, he is locked up in HMP Full Sutton, York, yet this sexual psychopath's legacy of brutal rape and homicide still haunts his surviving victims to this very day. We will return to Sharon Major soon enough, for her story will turn you cold – as bitterly chilly as a wintery day.

I have been studying and writing about murder most foul for some three decades. Face-to-face I have interviewed and/or corresponded at length with around thirty serial killers, mass murderers, spree killers and one-off wanton takers of human life. It is a matter for public record that I have helped clear up a few cold cases, specifically in Texas, Connecticut and Rochester, New York State, so I know a thing or two about serial killers and monsters, this much I *can* confirm.

Moreover, during my long journey along 'Murder Road', I have met the grieving families of lost loved ones. I have witnessed the tears of those innocent women and some men, who have unknowingly lived and slept with a monster beside them – the beast is snoring and they can smell his breath, totally unaware that their husband, partner or lover, even this one-night stand, is one of the most sick and twisted psychopaths alive: a terrifying example of the *very worst* of humankind.

This book is about those women and men who have already slept with monsters – please consider the 1991 movie *Sleeping with the Enemy*, starring Julia Roberts and Patrick Bergin, for these killers, all of whom wear masks of normality, are society's enemies too. However, in real life the character of Julia Roberts's psychopathic husband would be a nightmare come true ... and in real life this type of terrifying scenario *does* come true every week of every year for hundreds of innocent women who wake up to frantically realise that they have been sleeping with a man whose secret God-awful perverted life has been hidden behind a false façade, in some cases for decades.

Therefore, this book plunges the reader into real–life nightmares from which there can be no peaceful awakening in one's warm bed. No! The racket on this dawn-breaking morning is the homicide police smashing in the front door and the kids are terrified.

Yes, you have been reading in the press; it's been all over the TV news about the serial killer ... the slasher/rapist. You've heard about the killer known as 'BTK' who was finally arrested and identified as Dennis Lynn Rader who roamed at large between 1974 and 1991. With up to forty victims, maybe even more, he was happily married with two adoring children and his wife, Paula, never suspected a thing. Then think about Peter Sutcliffe, the 'Yorkshire Ripper'. Twenty-two victims in total. Nine were injured with thirteen murdered – oh, how ironic that he died on Friday the 13th of November 2020, his last words being: 'I'm not going to make it.' As we will see later, this weasel's wife, Sonia, never suspected a thing either. But now, yes RIGHT NOW, police with guns drawn haul *your* husband – 'Mr Bible Thumper', or 'Mr Lorry Driver', or 'Mr Extreme Narcissist' – out of *your* bed and drag him away protesting his innocence. Hours later, your head still reeling in shock, you learn that your husband has been charged with multiple sex slayings – now try to get your head around that!

Countless in number, wives and partners are being deceived day after day, having cereal for breakfast with a spouse who might have come home the previous night after an unexplained absence ... bullshit excuses as to where he's been ... his jeans torn at the crotch ... he was not smelling quite right, and even this morning he snaps at you and the kids because he's in a foul mood. Fact: he's a depraved serial killer, *that's* what he is. And, guess what – you didn't have a clue! Moreover, the wives, the partners and the parents of such beasts are almost as much victims as the lives destroyed; innocent people now reduced to scattered ashes or rotting corpses buried deep in their graves with the sides falling in, and, of course, the lives of the grieving next-of-kin who remain behind ... forever broken-hearted ... we should never forget their mental suffering, either.

Yet, here is something that you will probably *already* know: there are thousands of women and men who court these monsters caged behind bars. We call them 'murder groupies', people of all ages who become besotted and fall in love with these human scum who often have scores of female fans writing sexually explicit garbage to them week in, week out. In one instance, the serial murderer, Keith Hunter Jesperson, aka 'the Happy Face Killer', wrote one of his scores of letters to me and enclosed a letter from a female fan. He boasted: 'Christopher, see that red kiss mark, that's not lipstick, it's menstrual blood, and she's young and pretty too.'

When I visited with my film crew the bookish-looking Connecticut serial killer Michael Bruce Ross (1959–2005) in his brown-painted cell on death row at Somers Prison (now known as Osborn Correctional Institution), he held aloft bundles of letters from his female fans, and laughed: 'Look, Christopher, love, love, love everywhere. Some are so sexy I masturbate to them at least forty times a day.' He paused, to add sheepishly, 'Um, but I do get sores on my penis, though,' before giggling hysterically once again. Perhaps these adoring 'fans' had done their homework yet they were in love with a monster who had killed seven young females, three of whom were schoolgirls; two of them, fourteen-year-olds April Brunais and Leslie Shelley, were abducted, raped then strangled out near Beach Pond, a vast expanse of water with a dam holding back the Pachaus River, which separates the states of Rhode Island and Connecticut. Indeed, during my interview with the since-executed Ross, he admitted for the first time that he had anally penetrated April post-mortem. He also admitted that he had returned to the decomposing bodies several times to masturbate. When I spoke to his prison counsellor, a young woman named Anne Cournoyer, she confirmed Ross's priapic and compulsive masturbation, and of her he gloated, 'Yes, if it was the wrong time for her and the right time for me, I'd rape and kill Anne too.' Furthermore, in one of my books there is a photo of me talking to Ross through his death row cell door. Look at the smug grin on that monster's bespectacled face, yet, while at large he looked like the 'All-American Boy', one you might have had living next door to you or even dating your daughter.

In this book I am going to make my own mark as we focus in on the women and men who have slept with the *real* enemy ... their exclusive, first-hand accounts that will break your heart ... and let the Devil take the hindmost, because I also expose the 'murder groupies' and examine their own warped upside-down, utterly amoral mindsets; these people who fantasise about having a child with a kiddie-killing psychopath.

> *How do I love thee? Let me count the ways.*
> Elizabeth Barrett Browning (1806–61):
> Sonnet 43

As my own writing style has developed, so has my knowledge of the human mind; it is as if I have been on a long journey often into dark places where sits the completely unknown – the abyss. Therefore, in this book, as in quite a few previous titles, I try to bring readers along with me, this time into not only the minds of the killers, but also how the women and men must have felt upon suddenly learning of the cold-blooded truth – that a real life Grim Reaper has been intimately close to them for more time than one might have dared dream of, to be sure.

Furthermore, I will attempt to make each chapter author/ reader interactive, insofar as we can examine these cases together, to agree or to disagree with each other, to try and see how these monsters successfully mask themselves, until the day comes when the stone-cold truth is finally revealed.

CHRISTOPHER BERRY–DEE

UK AND EL NIDO, PHILIPPINES

Sharon Major v. John David Guise Cannan (UK)

False face must hide what the false heart doth know.
WILLIAM SHAKESPEARE: *MACBETH* (1606)
ACT I, SC. 7, I. 82

If anyone was a real monster, come and meet John David Guise Cannan and learn what he did to Sharon Major. Perhaps then people who plead mitigation for such killers will change their minds; better still, it may open some blinkered eyes, because this might have happened to *you*.

Getting to interview Sharon was no easy task, for she knew that I was writing a definitive book about Cannan and that he was writing to me, so she was rightly nervous and trembling from head to foot when eventually, after several months of correspondence bonding throughout 1992, we had a waterfront lunch in Bristol. Mostly women, and some men, have suffered terribly at the hands of sex-crazed monsters only

1

to have had their once peaceful and decent lives turned upside down and inside out, with the physical and mental trauma quite often lasting for the remainder of their lives. Therefore, thank you Sharon because thousands of women and men will read your story and hopefully heed your words. God bless you from all of us, too.

Of Sharon – I'd say about 5ft 5in tall, slim not petite, smartly dressed, longish fair hair framing an open friendly face; indeed, it was not difficult to see immediately why the smooth-talking, bullshitting 'Billy Liar' John Cannan, took a 'fancy' to her way back in 1980, when she had just turned thirty-two, for that's when her tragic story began.

Cannan's full life story of crime, his narrative stretching way back to his formative years, can be found in my book *Prime Suspect*, and there is quite a bit about him on the Internet. However, by the end of 1979 he had effectively deserted his wife and daughter. Then aged twenty-six, a lower-ranking car salesman and a heavy social drinker, he considered himself to be God's gift to any young woman, but his drinking, supported by a few thefts, had brought him spiralling downhill into alcoholism and thus down on his uppers.

> *He [John] was the best looking man I'd ever met and immediately I had a physical attraction towards him … we laughed and joked and agreed to meet up after work.*
>
> Sharon Major: to the author.

On Valentine's Day, in February 1980, Cannan thought his fortunes had changed for the better when he strolled nonchalantly into a Sutton Coldfield off-licence on the pretext of buying a case of wine. A case of wine my foot, for he didn't have a pot to piss in! Knowing Cannan's well-established modi operandi (MO), I strongly suspect that he had earlier noticed Sharon when passing by the shop, where she worked; had taken a liking to her and then used this not-unique ploy to chat her up. After they'd hit it off, using another of his seduction techniques he followed up by sending Sharon roses at the shop and she was won over by his charm – she was smitten. The roses? I omitted to say that he had got the money for the flowers by robbing a service station a few days beforehand.

It sounds a bit of a *Fifty Shades of Grey*-ish opener, does it not? Nevertheless, during their first date Sharon explained to John that she was married with two children and on the verge of separating from her husband, although they still continued to share the same house with hubby soon to move out. For his part, this well-dressed Pinocchio said that he was divorced from his wife June (a claim that was untrue at that time), and that he worked as a 'sales manager' at a local car show-room, which was not accurate either because his main task was to wash the cars, generally tidy the place up, and make the coffee and tea.

When Cannan's father – who *did* manage the car dealership – learned of his son's extramarital liaison, he took an uncompromising moral line, one that John described to me in a letter as: 'supercilious'. There was a showdown in the showroom. John left his job, and he left his wife and child in the lurch. Of course we all know that a car on a sales forecourt may look all shiny and new, but quite often when its new owner gleefully drives away it falls apart, and this is *precisely* what would happen to Sharon Major's life soon after she met the shiny new John Cannan, for inside he was falling apart at the seams.

Nevertheless, John packed his bags and checked in at Sutton House in Chester Road, Erdington. He had stayed at this place before with several of his 'conquests' from the 'hot spots of Birmingham', although which specific 'hot spots' he failed to elaborate in his expansive correspondence with me, during which he also described his technique: ' ... buy 'em a drink, tell 'em I love them, tell 'em they were the best thing since sliced bread then take them to Sutton House where their legs opened faster than a mousetrap snaps shut and a cheap night of easily forgettable passion.'

Thank you for that, John – duly noted!

Notwithstanding John's expansive guide to his seduction techniques, despite his present low state he and Sharon hit it off and became regular companions. In April 1980 he left Sutton House and went to live with her and her children, for by this time her husband had left home to make room for a cuckoo in the nest. So here he is, the boastful 'Mr Flash' ... the self-proclaimed car showroom manager ... oops, he has not even a half-decent place of his own, so being a leech, he shifts his stuff along with his loads of bullshit baggage, into Sharon's home, all too soon to start sponging off her.

So, already we find in Cannan, a loser soon to be an abuser. Nevertheless, to all intents and outward appearances for the next six months or so their relationship *seemed* to prosper.

Conveniently for John Cannan, he had acquired a roof above his over-inflated ego; a ready-made family with Sharon's two youngsters: a boy aged four and a daughter aged six; his meals cooked for him and a warm bed waiting.

John, you have it made. This was a great opportunity for you to get back on your feet so please ... I am begging you, don't screw things up. Okay?

'I took very seriously my role as their surrogate Dad,' he wrote to me. 'I occasionally bought them toys and took the little boy to his first football game, Aston Villa *v.* Birmingham City ... we sat munching hamburgers, and I taught him how to call the referee a "a pillock".' Of the little girl, he recollected that she was ' ... backward for her age, and me and Sharon took her to see a specialist at a children's hospital ...

' ... and, Chris, we went on trips as a family, including a visit to Blackpool and to Sharon's parents at Ilfracombe, but as all dads, surrogate or otherwise, know entertaining children is expensive,' he wistfully recalled before adding festively, ' ... but I bought them secondhand bicycles for Christmas 1980. I painted them up, because funds would not run to new ones.'

Yes, yes, John. Just like the funds, I expect the bikes didn't run to much either ... bearing in mind my readers haven't got all day to listen to you, can we please get down to the nitty-gritty: you tell us why you raped and almost beat Sharon to death. I expect you are going to tell us that it was all Sharon's fault when the relationship fell apart, just like you told Mr Justice Drake before he locked you up for ever and a day – at once ordering the Home Office to throw away the key.

But the vast expense of buying the two secondhand kiddie bikes was merely the start of his financial woes. While Sharon had a job, John lost his when he drove off in a car without authority from the car firm employing him at the time. Nice one, John – losing two car sales jobs in as many years was *quite* good going, and just about as good as you will ever get because Sharon was twigging to your true nature by then.

Perhaps a little late in the day, but nevertheless by accident, Sharon bumped into his allegedly divorced wife, June. Whoopsie-daisy for now the proverbial was about to hit the fan where it would stubbornly stick, for Sharon encountered Mrs June Cannan in the local Safeway store where she explained that she was still married to John. And she had baby Louise with her in a pushchair. However, Sharon did not immediately challenge John about this discrepancy in his story as he was 'busy looking for another job', but she now had a new slant on his character. She later described him as 'extremely plausible and convincing', which are two of the most common, deep-seated psychopathological traits to be found in extreme narcissists and sociopaths. Nevertheless, their sexual relationship was described by Sharon as at first being: 'normal, healthy and active', regarding him as ' ... a demanding lover who varied his technique'.

After the affair had finished, Sharon said that: ' ... although John was a very physical lover, we never used sexual aids and bondage was never employed.' However, later she was to alter this previous account by stating that he was no great shakes in bed. Harsh words and accusations would later be voiced about the use of 'prosthetics', as John liked to call sexual aids, and of attempts to commit anal intercourse. But, by then their relationship had long been over.

So, perhaps now is an opportune moment to look a little

more closely at John Cannan, for *if* he was an 'attentive lover', he was also a jealous one, and it is here that we see yet another typical trait of the narcissistic sociopath/psychopath – that of blaming one's own faults and transferring them onto other people – and we will see this behaviour exhibited in other killers as we march on through this book. John claimed that he became fed up with other men calling at the house when he was out – the implication being that Sharon possessed loose moral values, which was, and *is*, utterly untrue. Indeed, he said that one evening he became so incensed when a male acquaintance phoned Sharon from The Belfry golf club lounge, that he leapt into his car and drove off to confront him.

But according to John, when he arrived at the golf club and called out the man's name, he was told, most inconveniently for him, that the chap had left. To embroider this story even further, John told me in correspondence that the man turned up at the house the following evening and a row between them ensued in the street. No blows were exchanged but John says that he had done enough to demonstrate that, as he put it, 'I was the Master of the House, so Sharon could not have her cake and eat it too.'

Yeah, John, you tell her. Except that you didn't have a car at the time because you had just lost your job, and you have never played golf, not even pitch-and-putt at a fair. Moreover, you were potless as well. Indeed, during my research for *Ladykiller*, I discovered that he never had a 'row' outside of the house, or any house, at all. It's a cock-and-bull story: a pure invention, one which is further supported in that while he was brave enough to kidnap, rape, rob and kill helpless women, this gutless loser would never have faced up to a man

– he was too keen to keep his teeth intact and protect his self-admiring, constantly mirror-groomed good looks, to risk any of that stuff.

In one of his letters written from prison, Cannan talked of his 'strong desire to keep the family together' because he claimed to be a 'family man'. I rather think that Mrs June Cannan might well disagree with this simply because her devoted husband was out and about most nights, half-cut and trying to knock off anyone whose name began with Miss, Ms or Mrs. 'I wanted to forge a more constructive future for us all,' he claimed. But the odds were not running – just like his finances, nor the two kiddies' bikes – in his favour, so he took a job with a car firm in Bideford, Devon, which Sharon believed was in expectation of her moving to live near her parents in Ilfracombe. Indeed, John did spend some of his weekday nights with her parents then commuted to Sutton Coldfield at weekends. Very occasionally he stayed with his mother in order to see his wife and daughter. Nevertheless, the financial implications of sustaining this complicated existence were crippling him. He was, in effect, trying to support two families while living apart from both at the same time. He described it as 'Pressure with a capital P'. Something had to give and cracks began to widen in his relationship with Sharon.

John says that he was besotted with Sharon because her maturity appealed to him. He was frank to me about his drinking but he lied to her over his finances. 'She was, or seemed to be, the answer to a prayer,' he said describing things when he first moved in with her in April 1980. But, as his financial situation deteriorated, so his drinking accelerated.

He claimed he was paying maintenance to June (a lie), supplementing Sharon's income when he was paying rent on a cottage in Devon in the hope of moving with Sharon and her children (a lie). 'Financially, I was trying to do the impossible. My income was falling considerably short of my outgoings and every month my bank overdraft was getting bigger.' Nevertheless, in addition to this self-imposed burden, John had to finance his drinking, which now amounted to a bottle of Scotch a day. It was lucky Sharon worked in an off-licence, wouldn't you agree? Cutting to the chase, these unfortunate circumstances took a toll on their relationship. They argued about the slightest thing and he was jealous of Sharon's other relationships with her friends. On one occasion he gave her a black eye, and she began to realise that while John could be loving and caring (when it suited his purpose, I hasten to add), he also had another more sinister side to his character, which frightened her. 'I realised that there was an extremely evil streak in him,' she said later. Sharon, by this time, wanted their relationship to finish but she did not know how to go about it, saying: 'One part of me still wanted to be with him but common sense told me it had to end.'

Matters came to a head with the approach of the festive season. There was an argument because Sharon's husband was coming to the house to visit his children on Christmas Day and Boxing Day. 'He wasn't going to stay at my house,' Sharon explained to me, 'just visit'. John took exception to the idea that Sharon's husband, who, as the bigoted John Cannan saw it, had walked out and left the family then had decided to spend the Christmas holiday with his two children. Talk about calling the kettle black, with John saying, 'That

I *strongly objected* to,' adding that he pleaded with Sharon to make a clean break with her estranged husband and not allow him to see his own kids ever again. After much argument, he lost his case and, as he later described it, ' ... the upshot was that I spent Christmas alone in a small hotel in Erdington.'

Sharon did not see John again until he turned up with a bottle of wine at the house in the early afternoon of 30 December. So can the reader see him using his standard, cheap, wooing method again? – it's all so pathetically fake, even plastic, isn't it? She recalled that John suggested: ' ... that as we'd always had such a lovely time together and been so close to each other ... that we have one more time in bed.'

Yes, the controlling nature of this extreme narcissist is unraveling. Cannan's insecurities, his utterly weak psycho-pathology, his over-inflated ego so often flying high above on a very fine string, is about to burst. His psychological infrastructure is like a house built on shifting sands; his shallowness, his own weaknesses are staring him straight back into his face. We can see this in the way he threw his toys out of his cot when Sharon's husband wanted to see her and his two children over Christmas. This self-proclaimed 'Master of the House' (he had no title to the property anyway), this '... I'll teach Sharon she can't have her cake and eat it, too', flim-flam man, has lost control and his bubble world is primed to burst. It will take just one more puff and John's bravado will come tumbling down.

However, Cannan inevitably tells us a different story. 'She yielded and I opened the bottle. She was crying and begging me to come back. Sharon didn't want our relationship to end ... it was me who had alluded to splitting up but eventually I agreed. We went to bed and tried to patch up our differences,' says John, adding, ' ... we'd both been drinking and started to argue. She said the wrong thing (transferring blame) and suddenly I snapped.'

What followed was later to become the subject of much bitterness and recrimination. Sharon's account was that during intercourse, John put his hands around her neck so that she had trouble breathing. 'I told him to stop, saying, "Don't, you'll kill me doing that." He said, "I mean to kill you. I'm going to kill you. You've hurt me so badly, I'm going to hurt you too."' Sharon was terrified by the fierce expression on John's face. She tried to get off the bed but he held her down by placing his body across hers. She reacted by screaming and punching him about the head; and she pleaded with him to stop and think about her children. 'I don't give a fuck about them,' was his menacing reply.

Sharon's recollection was that John then reached for the plastic bag he had brought with him into the bedroom and emptied the contents onto the bed. 'There was a vibrator,' she said, ' ... a gun and a pair of black rubber pants with a false male penis fitted to it'.

John picked up the gun, pointed it at her face and said 'This is loaded'. Sharon was now convinced that he intended to kill her. She struggled to seize hold of the weapon and direct it away from her. 'Between us,' she said, 'we pulled the trigger'. As a result the gun fired an air pellet which lodged in the wall. Sharon recognised the weapon as an air pistol, which they had used during the summer to shoot at targets in the garden. 'I knew that it fired one pellet at a time,' she would later tell police.

After Sharon had managed to throw the gun onto the floor, John tried a different tactic. 'I'm going to screw your backside,' he shouted. He failed in his attempts because she struggled furiously but he did succeed in twice penetrating her vagina with a vibrator. She began to bleed heavily, but undeterred, he had sexual intercourse with her wearing the false penis. 'He made extremely violent love to me with this thing which hurt me a great deal,' she claimed in her statement to police. Her neighbours heard Sharon's screams but they turned up their record player to drown out the noise.

* * *

At this point, perhaps we should take a breather and look at what we have so far where John Cannan is concerned, and I am very sure that most readers will by now have summed up this horrible man. I say this because *most* women have a sense about these types of men – in other words they can smell a rat like Cannan a mile away. However, with this being said, the first dizzy blossom of love can often cloud good judgement and this is what happened with Sharon Major. She was on the verge of her marriage breaking up, her husband seemingly quite amiable about it all, and he was doing the fatherly thing by wanting to see her and his children over that Christmas.

At first blush, John must have seemed heaven-sent for Sharon. Romantic, tall, well built, well dressed, some say handsome, others not. His other interesting feature, if one can call it 'interesting', was that his eyebrows met in the middle. I am informed that this is called a 'unibrow' (or jacco brow or monobrow; called synophrys in medicine) – how about

12

that for a freebie bit of info – but individuals who possess this eyebrow may fight to possess a palpable feeling of balance or stability in life. Nevertheless, he may have been charming – he spoke with a put-on worldly upper class accent – but we know that all that glitters is not always gold. Moreover, there may be a few readers who will suggest that Sharon was embellishing her part of this story. I say otherwise because all that she has told us thus far would be reenacted again and again in Cannan's future crimes: the same wooing tactics – wine, champagne and flowers – the plausible 'Billy Liar' façade; bullshit-layered-upon-bullshit; the same threatening to strangle several of his conquests – one of them the ice skater Jilly Paige. A firearm, albeit a replica pistol, was used by him in his robberies and abductions, and sex aids were employed by him over and over. It is almost as if the way he treated Sharon Major was to become his criminal blueprint, one thereafter from which he rarely strayed thereafter.

Cannan's psychopatholgy is one of classic extreme narcissism, a description that fits him like a glove. These types of people are extremely manipulative. They use people for their own selfish ends. They physically and emotionally suck their partners dry. They are bullies and control freaks and *never* at fault themselves. However, Sharon saw through Cannan, as if she had seen flashy goods in a jeweller's window and entered to find that the shop sold nothing but cheap crap. That, I think, sums up Cannan to a tee.

The other point I make here is that extreme narcissism is borderline sociopathy, in more serious cases fully emerged psychopathy. And this is why I have used the example of Sharon Major *v*. John Cannan as being something of a keynote chapter in this book. As we shall see in a moment, Sharon Major was extremely fortunate to have escaped with her life, while several other women would later suffer a terrifying and dreadful fate at the hands of this real-life monster.

* * *

We rejoin the grim struggle between Major and Cannan with Sharon several times trying to get off the bed. She was bleeding internally, from the mouth and nose where he had struck her in the face. She grabbed his testicles to try and stop his continuous attack, ' ... but that just made him more violent than ever ... John was so evil, looking almost possessed,' she said. At one point she lost consciousness and remembered coming to with him slapping her face and saying 'I haven't finished with you yet'. He called her a whore and a bitch and he renewed his attempts to achieve anal intercourse.

By now this sexual assault had gone far beyond rape because the attack was bearing the hallmark of sexual sadism. He was visiting upon Sharon all of his own social failures and inadequacies, and she had become the helpless repository for everything he despised himself for being. He was enjoying treating her like a cat playing with a mouse. He was denigrating her, blaming her for his own shortcomings, but nevertheless, after two hours trying to fend him off, a near-exhausted Sharon consented to his demands provided she could use a lubricant. 'Let me get some Vaseline,' she said. This was a ploy to get out of the bedroom in the hope of dashing down the stairs ... to get out of the house into the street ... to get help.

'With one arm across my neck and a hand holding my arm behind her back, John frog-marched me towards the other bedroom,' said Sharon. She found the Vaseline and he began to manoeuvre her back to the main bedroom.

Now knowing that he was going to kill her, or at least subject her to further disgusting sexual abuse and physical attacks, Sharon made her move at the head of the stairs. She would say afterwards, 'I'd be better off dead or paralysed than to face going back into the bedroom.'

Sharon pushed John, causing him to lose balance, and they both tumbled down the stairwell where she hurt her back. 'I couldn't have fought with him anymore. I was so physically drained,' she says. At this point, she later recalled John reverting to 'his old self'. He was caring and full of apologies. 'Oh, my God,' he said. 'What have I done? I'm sorry.' While he telephoned for an ambulance, Sharon tried to stand up, thinking he was still going to kill her – then she blacked out. The reader might now be asking, why John's sudden switch to apparent normality? Indeed, this is a very interesting part of the narcissist/sociopath/psychopathic personality. One might call this is a type of 'Dr Jekyll *v*. Mr Hyde' syndrome – a mind splitting, as if there is one boxer fighting himself in the same ring. Indeed, this is not an easy issue to get our own heads around. However, I have witnessed the same 'mind switching' in many of the serial killers I have interviewed over the years. One moment they are simmering with fury, eyeballing you and one senses that they are about to explode into uncontrollable violence, then, seconds later it vanishes like a fart in the wind, and the beast inside the killer is contained ... at least for the time being.

As a slight digression, I was interviewing 'The Monster of the Rivers' – the New York State serial killer and paedophile, Arthur John Shawcross. I was with my film crew sitting within inches of this man in a small room at the Sullivan Correctional Facility, NY, when I pressed him on the murder of a schoolboy, Jack Blake. This was a subject 'Art' had warned me *not* to mention. 'I won't fucking go there ... DO YOU FUCKIN' UNDERSTAND?' he had previously snarled, but I needed to because it was an important matter for Jack's next-of-kin. Shawcross had never admitted this murder to anyone, Jack's sister wanted 'closure', and I wanted a confession from this overweight, disgusting lump of humanity sitting there boiling away.

All the physical signs of an instant explosion of violence were right before my very eyes: he started to sweat profusely; his facial skin whitened and tightened as taut as bat skin or fabric over a biplane's wing. His eyes zeroed in on me. His massive unshackled hands clenched and unclenched as his emotions rose high and higher ... He could have easily ripped my head off in an instant. The guards were outside. Only my wetting-their-pants film crew were with me, but then, with a smile, I leaned forward right into *his* face and said quietly: 'Arthur, your girlfriend, Clara, is waiting outside the prison. She loves you very much. She tells me you are getting married ... that *you* want *me* to be the Best Man at your wedding. She wants *you* to tell me the truth about Jack ... ' Then, putting my hand on his knee, I raised my voice, with: 'Now ARTHUR, Don't you FUCK up or Clara is gonna be real pissed off with you!'

Like all cowardly psychopathic killers, this sort of 'back into their face' response and physical touch sends all of the little lights and wiring inside of their heads into billions of sparks of confusion. Of course this takes place in milliseconds … it's like a voice inside their minds saying: 'Hey, bro, this guy has just fucked ya. I'd revert to the factory default position if I were you and act dumb.'

So, Shawcross switched back to something almost normal. Without wishing to over-dramatise this, I had, for a short time, exorcised the beast, and he gave me a full confession all captured on camera. Yes, I *had* promised Arthur and Clara that I would *love* to be his Best Man at his wedding. I had told him that it would be an honour … that I'd willingly fly thousands of miles to the prison … bring gifts and money for dearest sweet Clara … but I'll tell any pack of lies to get what I want from a sadosexual serial killer. As for Clara waiting outside of the prison … um, nope! She was about thirty miles away.

On a more everyday domestic level many women sometimes witness their partners losing their tempers over some small real or imagined slight, and they cannot figure out why. In extreme cases, the men explode into a violent rage for no apparent reason whatsoever, and this commonly happens when the man is in drink. Afterwards, he feels contrite, apologises profusely and the next minute he's washing the dishes, has managed to find a vacuum cleaner which he didn't know existed, and in very extreme cases he zips down to a florist to buy a huge bunch of flowers with the word 'sorry' now tattooed on his forehead.

Therefore, if we knit something along the lines of 'The Shawcross Experience' with a domestic example, we can see John Cannan, the arch manipulator, post-rape shutting away the monster inside his head and replacing it with a pseudo caring and loving man. With that said, on her way to hospital in the ambulance, Sharon asked John, 'You really did mean to kill me didn't you?' 'Yes I did,' he replied. She was treated in the casualty department and John remained with her until just before the police arrived. She gave him the keys to her house and told him to remove all of his things. She phoned a female friend who drove to the hospital and took her home. By then, fearful that the police would be soon arresting him, Cannan had collected up his stuff, including the sordid contents of his plastic bag, and left his set of house keys behind. The cowardly bully had scarpered.

Sharon had been battered and bruised with now a swollen face and two black eyes. Her facial injuries necessitated dental treatment on her front teeth, and Cannan had pulled out so much of her hair 'that you could have made a wig with what had come out,' she said. Her parents travelled up from Ilfracombe to look after her and the children. 'I told both of them about the physical attack,' she told me, 'but I omitted to tell them about the sexual side of the assault,' Her father was shocked and hardly recognised her, such was the battering she'd received at the hands of John David Guise Cannan.

Putting yourself into Sharon's frame of mind following this near-death attack, you might understand why she didn't at first make a formal complaint against Cannan to the police. She told me that her first reason was that she had no faith in the legal system, for back then police were more, shall we say unsympathetically lax in the way such complaints were handled. She knew that she had only just escaped being killed, that if she lodged a complaint against John ' ... he might get only a few years' imprisonment' and might 'track me down and finish off what he had started,' she said still shaking all over as she relived it all over again. Sharon's second reason was that she was afraid he would try to get her through the children. 'I was absolutely terrified of John.' She regarded the day of the attack as the end of the relationship and resisted Cannan's narcissistically desperate and whining attempts at reconciliation. Better late than never, God bless her.

* * *

Here it will be instructive to learn what Cannan told me in his correspondence, bearing in mind that Sharon's account of the stormy and conclusion of her affair with John Cannan came seven years after the event. At the time he was in police custody charged with many more serious sex-related offences including homicide, for we all know in even the most minor of lovers' tiffs, partners will disagree over the circumstances. Nevertheless, this far more serious encounter was to prove no exception and John's account, as one might expect, differed substantially – enter stage right 'Narcissist and Sadosexual Psychopath: John David Guise Cannan'. So, John, you have just stepped into the limelight ... umm, let us all hear what *you* have to say.

In correspondence, and there was a lot of it, neatly written, grammatically correct on blue or white lined prison notepaper, he referred on many occasions to the 'assault' on Sharon Major, repeatedly denying that he had made a 'sexual attack' on her. To water this down a bit, he admitted making what he called a 'serious sexual assault' – but 'attack', no way he would ever have attacked her, because, 'I adored her too much for that.' Yet, he freely acknowledged using what he called 'sexual prosthetics in the course of love-making', which he thought, 'probably accounted for the difficulties she subsequently encountered with her vaginal coil.' So, just think about that uncalled-for comment – the blame game ... it was Sharon's fault ... what a disgusting man Cannan truly is.

Moreover, quite why Cannan chose to associate 'prosthetics' with sexual devices is anyone's guess. It describes the branch of surgery concerned with prosthesis, the replacement of a missing body part with an artificial substitute. Now this is interesting, because we have previously noted that amongst John's sexual accoutrements was a black, strap-on penis.

John claimed that these 'prosthetics' were left at Sharon's home by a 'man friend' who was, 'the producer of porno-graphic video films', in which they were used as 'props'. 'The truth is,' he alleged, 'she was an instructive, older and enthusiastic partner ... ' Well, how lucky he was in hooking up with an 'instructive, older and enthusiastic partner' who worked in an off-licence, of all places. Nevertheless, despite his alleged adoration of Sharon, this did not prevent him from calling her version of events 'utter tripe', and maintained that she suffered 'terrible emotional insecurity and [sought] acceptance and comfort from as many people as possible, especially men, which tend[ed] largely to make her stray', adding, ' ... she wasn't sugar and spice and all things nice ... but a devious and calculating woman, who frankly couldn't be trusted.'

This, of course – and as most psychiatrists and psychologists will be bound to agree – is sociopathic John Cannan mirroring his own shortcomings and displacing them onto Sharon Major, in a 'Not me, guv, it was all her fault' sort of way. He also maintained that her failure to report the sexual assault to the police in 1981 was because ' ... no offence had occurred'.

Uh, just wait a second John. A few lines up you admitted committing a serious sexual assault. You can't have it both ways.

John's version of events was that he had been incensed over Sharon's decision to have her husband home at Christmas, and this must have really pricked this ego. He was turfed out of the nest while Mr Major sat down to a roast dinner wearing a paper-mâché party hat to merrily pull crackers with his loving children while our highly-strung crackerjack, Cannan, had to piss off and find someplace else to stay. And then John reminded me in a letter that ' ... she had been a little more than just a friend to another male acquaintance, too. Never have I been so angry,' he said, 'I really slagged her off ... I told her *our* affair is over. The one thing I can't stand is a cheating partner. I can't stand slags. We shouted at each other and blows were struck. I hit her and I hit her hard ... I wanted to hurt her, I did hurt her.'

He continued: ' ... and she exaggerated her injuries and I *never* pulled her hair out. So serious were her facial injuries,' he said sarcastically, 'that neither the ambulance man, the hospital doctor or her doctor had any recollection of her condition.'

So you spoke to the hospital doctor and Sharon's own GP and the ambulance man did you, John? I don't quite get when this all could have happened because by then you had hightailed it and the cops might have arrested you at any minute.

But if anything, John never learns to shut his big mouth. He continues: ' ... she has told a tissue of lies and made herself sound and look extremely silly. Anybody with a modicum of common sense and experience of both people and life could not fail to deduce her malice and spitefulness ... '

But John, *I have seen* Sharon's medical file. Jesus Christ, you beat the living daylights out of her. She didn't rip out all that hair by herself, or knock her own front teeth out, either!

However, just to politely remind the reader, these recollections of events came in letters written by John from prison ten years afterwards and while he was facing the prospect of serving a life sentence. He blamed Sharon for precipitating the end of the affair which 'occurred against the background of considerable provocation'. Yet despite all of the above being alleged against this 'malicious', 'spiteful', 'silly', 'devious, 'calculating full of tripe', 'never sugar and spice', and a woman of loose moral values, and the fact that it was *he* who wanted to terminate the relationship, he says: 'I tried to repair the relationship, using what little money I had to hire a car to drive down to Ilfracombe to find Sharon. I wanted to apologise and get us back as a family again'. Sadly for John Cannan he might as well have saved what little money he had and stayed where he was, for upon his arrival in Ilfracombe she wasn't there.

In February 1981, he says that he returned to her house in Sutton Coldfield. 'We sat in the kitchen and I begged Sharon to forgive me for hitting her, I was truly sorry,' which is just another of his outrageous lies, for after his almost murderous attack she would never talk to him again.

When interviewing face to face any convicted serial sex offender or, even at some time during lengthy correspondence, as sure as night follows day they will revert to type, unable to resist bringing up the subject of sex again and again. John would prove no exception when he kicked off by playing the sexually naïve card, claiming that that he was 'sexually inexperienced' but that Sharon introduced him to 'things I'd never known before'. I think that he must have been biting his tongue when he penned that yarn, or, he had forgotten that earlier he had bragged about his earlier sexual techniques, *inter alia*: ' ... buy 'em a drink, tell 'em I love them, tell 'em they were the best thing since sliced bread then take them to Sutton House where their legs opened faster than a mousetrap snaps shut and a cheap night of easily forgettable passion.'

He also alleged that, to avoid any trouble with Sharon's husband – and so considerate is John – he'd agreed to store the sexual aids at his rented flat where they were later discovered by the police concealed in the attic along with a large assortment of pornographic videos and magazines. A large collection of 'do it yourself', publications along some 'sex self-help' video tuition – in other words, hard porn.

He also denied that anal intercourse had ever played a part in their relationship. Sharon had claimed that he had asked her for anal sex on one occasion earlier in their relationship which she'd refused and apparently he did not press the issue again until the day he sexually attacked her. She recalled that 'there was something quite different about him on that occasion'. She sensed in his demeanour that something was wrong. He was more physical than usual during the sex which preceded the attack. She consented to what she thought would be the final time together before the relationship ended. But from the moment he tried to strangle her, and in every act that followed, she said John was behaving totally against her wishes. 'There was no way I'd consent to that sort of treatment from *any* man,' she later told the police.

I find more than a ring of truth in what Sharon is telling us, for once again we see the sudden mental switch from the normal suave John Cannan into a sex fiend, and as I mentioned earlier, this switching back and forth is atypical of the narcissistic antisocial/psychopathic individual. We find it in so many serial killers who approach their intended prey using guile, cunning and charm, in their efforts to entice their vulnerable victim into a situation where they have total control and the true nature of the beast emerges. With Cannan, we know from his letters quoted above that he thought of Sharon as a whore; therefore, once this evil monster had Sharon where he wanted her he could vent all of his anger and his fury, and visit upon her all of the punishment he felt that she deserved.

Knowing John Cannan as well as any person can – in truth probably much better than he knows himself – I can *totally agree* with Sharon's assessment of his character when she says that he was ' ... really in love with himself.' He was 'always looking into a mirror', was vain about his appearance and always well groomed. In fact some women have described Cannan as being 'too pretty'. Sharon described him as a complete loner, 'very deep, with no friends at all, male or female'. He was a person who lived in a world of his own, but the things he said 'were so plausible and with a degree of truth in them ... I didn't know what to believe in the end,' she said despairingly.

Sharon's assessment of John is spot-on, and it applies to thousands of other men who have this fantasy-driven psychopathology, for indeed they really *do* live in their own, lonely little world where elephants fly, lead balls bounce and sexy fairies reign supreme. And, like others of Cannan's ilk, I suggest that his vanity was an outward sign of his inner emptiness and feelings of discontent. There is a constant pathological preening of one's outer self in vainglorious efforts to present a socially acceptable mask to others, when consciously, even subconsciously, they know that what lies within is nothing but rotten to the very core.

So, let's now look at another materialistic side to Cannan because, in fact, on reflection I recall seeing his black entry model BMW after police in Bristol impounded it following his later attempted robbery in Leamington Spa. There it was sitting all shiny with its skinny wheels and cheap retreads. You will know the sorts of flash guys who buy these mobile badges just to be able to boast: 'Hi, hun ... I own a Bimmer' – of course, and at that very instant the branded key fob inadvertently slips from his fingers onto the bar. However, the moment one opened the boot of John's car, the clutter and crap it held filled two large plastic bin liners. This also precisely sums up his psychopathology.

Beauty may be only skin deep, but Cannan's self-obsession was also clearly indicated in subsequent interviews with detectives. Sharon denied having any other men friends during the time she spent with John. 'I was too scared and frightened of him to do that,' which fits perfectly with the controlling and manipulating narcissistic personality, a personality type that mirrored Cannan exactly. She said that John was always eager to go out when he was with her whether he had money or not. In simple terms, he was over-jealous and possessive, and he didn't want to see his prize catch hooked by someone else – thus revealing a weakness in his own shallow character and his permanent inner sense of insecurity topped up with a bucketful of inner low self-esteem. Sharon paid her share of the expenses and said that she never saw him with large amounts of money. Whether or not this *is* a fault I cannot say because most people notice that I never have large amounts of money myself!

Of his moods, Sharon claimed, 'As long as everything was going his way he was nice and charming. He could sell sand to the Arabs, he had that much confidence' – although his work history as a car salesman would give lie to this part of her assessment. What jobs he did get at dealerships were soon terminated. His father sacked him because he was bone idle and didn't wash the cars which was actually his main task. Another dealer fired him because he drove off in one of their cars without permission. Yet another company fired him on the spot after a husband spotted Cannan chatting up his wife who was looking for a new motor, and complained to the boss. Finally, he was sacked from a place because the police called looking for him in relation to a rape offence.

Sharon would also explain that when things were against John Cannan he changed. 'The evil side of him showed through,' she said. 'He used to flick from one mood to another.' She clearly understood John's mercurial temperament and had been subjected to a demonstration of what happened when he completely lost any self-control.

* * *

On 14 March 1981, some three months after Cannan's horrifying assault on Sharon, he was detained at Sutton Coldfield police station in connection with an attempted robbery. While there he was first officially questioned about the attack in an interview with Detective Sergeant (DS) Barry Butler and Detective Constable Brock Harrison, to whom he admitted having had 'a terrible argument' with Sharon, 'finishing up with us having an awful fight … I admit I went a bit too far and hurt her.' DS Butler told him that a letter had been found in his flat during a police search. It was addressed to him by Sharon and was dated 26 February 1981. She referred to the incident on 30 December of the previous year and described John's conduct as 'evil, wicked, brutal and depraved'. 'From enquiries we have made,' said DS Butler, 'we believe that you forced Sharon to have sex with you in various positions. Is that right?' John replied, 'Well, it's not quite as simple as that, let me explain?'

As always, this was John trying to blow smoke, ducking and diving and trying to wrest control of the situation from the police. He did much the same when being interviewed by homicide detectives in Bristol, 'We were having a great time in bed when Sharon brought up the subject of her other men friends,' he blustered, when it was he who had brought up the subject of other men when he viciously accused her of being a whore. 'She did this to try and upset me,' he said. The result was he lost his temper and hit her about the head and body.

'I just lost control and went stupid,' adding meekly: 'Looking back now I am ashamed of it and it seems that although it was me, that it was someone else.'

Oh, yes, and haven't we heard this lame excuse before, this weak attempt at trying to mitigate one's own criminal behaviour time and again? It is a half-hearted split personality ploy, one designed to invite some sympathy, even a mitigatory defence, one which, I might add, *never* works. Nevertheless, this was a significant admission which, at face value, was simply a convenient way of making himself remote from the attack. But perpetrators of serial violence are known to 'allegedly' experience such feelings. Ted Bundy the US serial murderer talked about his victims as if he were watching a film. Michael Bruce Ross, the Connecticut serial killer (now executed) told me during an interview at Somers Prison that it was like he was watching someone else doing the rapes and killings, and that he could not remember any of the faces at all.

Detective Constable (DC) Harrison asked Cannan if he was saying that after losing his temper he assaulted Sharon and forced her to have intercourse against her will and that she objected strongly. Almost with a slip of his tongue, the now garrulous Cannan said, 'Yes, she was shouting and hysterical. I just tried to hurt her as she's hurt me.' DS Butler leaned forward then asked: 'You are clearly admitting then *that you raped her, aren't you?*' In a clear acknowledgement of his actions, John blandly replied, 'Yes. I suppose it amounts to that, she upset me so much ... do you think I might have a cup of tea?'

It would be over six years before John Cannan was

questioned again about his assault on Sharon Major. After his arrest in Leamington Spa on Thursday, 29 October 1987, he was taken to Bristol and held in custody on suspicion of abducting Shirley Banks, whom he *had* murdered. Sharon Major made a statement to the police regarding her former boyfriend in which she said, 'I won't be happy until I know he's locked up and I'm safe forever from him and his evil ways.'

> *It was like a struggle between the mongoose and the snake.*
>
> Detective Chief Inspector Bryan Saunders:
> while questioning Cannan about the murder of
> Shirley Banks and the rape of Sharon Major, to the
> author at Filton Police Station.

During a long series of tape-recorded interviews carried out in Filton, Bristol, John was questioned by DCI Saunders of the Avon and Somerset Constabulary about the assault on Sharon. This was part of a marathon contest between John and the police. His attitude was confrontational and certainly far from contrite. He always had an alternative explanation for the events on the tip of his tongue and showed flashes of one of his strongest personality traits: he thought he was never wrong about anything.

Incidentally, although the Avon and Somerset Constabulary later destroyed their own copies of these interviews, I had already obtained copies from his solicitor, Jim Moriarty, and was able to supply them to DCI Jim Dickie and DI Stuart Ault of SOII MetPol. They in turn used them to formulate an interview strategy when many years afterwards they arrested Cannan at HMP Wakefield, and brought him to Buckingham Palace Road Police Station in London, where he was cautioned and interrogated about the missing estate agent, Suzy Lamplugh. Furthermore, John's letters to me also gave the police other vital intelligence about Suzy's murder, and that of the killing of twenty-seven-year-old Sandra Court in Bournemouth, Dorset, on Saturday, 3 May 1986.

* * *

In conclusion to the matter of Sharon Major *v.* John Cannan, I feel that all of my readers will wish to thank Sharon for her bravery, and for her plucking up the courage in coming forward to be interviewed by me for a book. She would have been well aware that, had her true name slipped out, it might have revealed to the world her relationship with John Cannan, warts and all. It is one thing to give it up to police during interviews all of which she could have declined to do, as were her legal rights. It is fair to add that Sharon has never been interviewed by a reporter from the national press either. Furthermore, at *no* time during my discussions with Sharon did she *ever*, for one moment, think that her story would help other women in trying to understand what it's like to suddenly realise that the man she fell totally in love with, supported and doted upon, could ever metamorphose into such an evil creature. For my part, I just think that Sharon wanted to say what she felt she *needed* to say, then slip back into obscurity where she lives very happily right now.

Sharon Major, we thank you from the bottom of our hearts. But I want to add one further point. There is much written about narcissistic partners and domestic abuse on the Internet these days, and in John Cannan we find perhaps a very extreme, unedifying example. Nevertheless, any male narcissists are, I reiterate *are*, weak to their very core. They are nothing more than cowardly bullies, so if you are in the unfortunate position of having a 'Mr Narcissistic Flash' giving you the runaround, drop him like a hot brick and *never* take him back because a leopard never, *ever*, changes its spots.

Here endeth the lesson!

Kelli Kae Boyd v. Kenneth Alessio Bianchi (USA)

Oh what a tangled web we weave, when first we practise to deceive.
SIR WALTER SCOTT, FIRST BARONET
(1771–1832), MARMION

In her own words, Sharon Major has given *us* a valuable life's lesson; it being what it's like to suddenly learn that love can be fleeting, plunging from champagne and roses and all things nice into a Stephen King-style nightmare story coming true. There are those who might suggest that if Sharon had been more astute she would have sensed very quickly that something was wrong with the vain and arrogant John Cannan, but as we all know, the first blossom of love can be romantically infectious – we are inclined to seek the best in someone for we, as compassionate humans, do not enter into relationships to seek out the worst.

John Cannan was mega vain, so maybe car mirrors were

invented just for him and not for road-safety after all. But there is a vast difference between wanting to present oneself smartly and excessive vanity – the latter of which 'Pretty Boy Cannan' had in abundance. He was oily and slick with his affected English speech; nevertheless, he was able to sweep some women off their feet. He was a 'lady killer' in every sense of the word. Furthermore, we quite often find that narcissists can be vanity driven almost to a pathological degree. This was John Cannan to a tee. So if any reader has one of these types in their home, just watch for the red flags that cropped up in Sharon's relationship with Cannan – because this is exactly who he thought he was, and God's gift to all women thrown in for good measure.

Narcissism was John Cannan's pursuit of gratification from his vanity, his egotism; his admiration of his own idealised self-image and attributes. We can see all of this throughout Sharon's appraisal of his character; indeed, we only have to read his own words to see how he loved self-flattery, perfectionism and being arrogant. So if you have the mind for heady reading, try Sigmund Freud's essay 'On Narcissism', while you will find the condition Narcissistic Personality Disorder (NPD) included in the Cluster B personality disorders in the *Diagnostic and Statistical Manual of Mental Disorders* (*DSM*).

I pointed out from the outset that this book is about distress. Well, if you want to get *really* distressed, try reading the *DSM*, then take some Valium and go and see a shrink, because you will certainly need one after even a few pages.

KELLI KAE BOYD V. KENNETH ALESSIO BIANCHI (USA)

Their robotic cruelty reflected dehumanization, stunted conscience, and inability to empathize. They are usually smooth, verbose, glossy, neat, artificial – both controlled and controlling. Behind a 'mask of sanity', they lived superficial and often destructive lives.

Richard Kraus

One might also categorise the likes of Peter Sutcliffe, Ted Bundy and Kenneth Bianchi as exploitative, displaced sadosexual serial killers, and these three psychopaths were 'exploitative' in that their sexual behaviour was that of men always on the prowl for women to exploit sexually, to force women to submit sexually with no care for their welfare at all.

They were 'displaced' in that their sexual behaviour was an expression of anger and rage: the cumulative backlog of experienced and imagined insults from many people they had met over the preceding years, all of which continually chipped away at their self-esteem and fragile egos. Indeed, it was Bianchi's mother, Frances Piccione, who told me during a radio interview: 'It seemed that whenever Ken had a fight with a girlfriend, or had problems, he went out and raped and killed someone.'

I had corresponded with Bianchi for several years before he granted me an 'audience' at the Washington State Penitentiary, Walla Walla, Washington State. In another of my books, I have fully documented his narrative from cradle to the present day, therefore, there is no repeat of that to be found here. Besides, this book is about women who have slept with savages such as Bianchi and those 'working girls' whom he abducted, raped, tortured and murdered, often in collaboration with his sidekick and cousin, Angelo Buono. Two of their victims were the schoolgirls Dolores 'Dolly' Cepeda (aged twelve) and Sonja Johnson (aged fourteen).

Without wishing to labour the issue, I spent much time with homicide cops in LA and Bellingham, Washington, while researching a TV documentary on 'the Hillside Stranglers'. I visited all of the crime scenes and rather sadly I had to look at the scenes-of-crimes photographs to be able to fully understand the horrific gravity of Bianchi and Buono's activities. So, before we meet Kelli Kae Boyd, who became Bianchi's common-law-wife, let's look at Dolly and Sonja.

The murders of Sonja and Dolly, and the violence and brutality they suffered, shocked everyone involved in the hunt for the men who had been dubbed 'Hillside Stranglers' by the media. Sonja and Dolly were two little innocents who happened to be in the wrong place at the wrong time.

All of Bianchi's rape and torture homicides were sickening and stomach-churning, but without doubt, Kelli had no clue when she met Bianchi that he had also killed two little girls. Moreover, there is strong evidence that he had murdered three schoolgirls years previously, in Rochester, New York, in what have been known as the 'Alphabet Murders' or 'Double Initial Killings'.

Before any eagle-eyed reader jumps down my throat to argue vehemently that it was proven that someone *other* than Bianchi had committed these Rochester homicides – which he'd committed suicide to avoid arrest – and that it's documented on the Internet, let me say that while this may seem highly plausible, it isn't. I say this because the circumstantial evidence against Bianchi is pretty much overwhelming, and if the cops were to be honest – and many of them do agree with me – Bianchi is still the prime suspect, whether he likes or not.

Dolly and Sonja were both pupils at the Saint Ignatius School in Highland Park, LA. They were last seen alive on Sunday, 13 November 1977, boarding a bus at the Eagle Plaza stop, which was just a quarter-mile from Angelo Buono's home in Glendale, LA. Bianchi and Buono followed the bus and, when the girls alighted near their home, Bianchi approached them, posing as a police officer, and accused them of shoplifting. They were taken 'downtown', and as Bianchi finally told me in correspondence, they were 'interviewed' in Angelo's house.

The following account is not for the faint-hearted. Sonja was raped and murdered in a bedroom by Buono, while Dolly sat outside with Bianchi.

'Where's my friend?' asked Dolly when Buono came out alone. 'Oh, don't worry,' said Bianchi, 'you'll be seeing her in a minute.' The last thing that Dolly saw was the dead face of Sonja beside her on a mattress stained with blood, semen and faecal matter, as Bianchi raped, sodomised and then strangled the terrified child to death.

Children playing on a rubbish tip at Landa and Stadium Way found the girls' naked bodies at 4 p.m. on Sunday, 20 November. The scenes-of-crime photographs showed Dolly and Sonja sprawled out amongst discarded beer bottles and tin cans and other trash. Sonja rests on her right side, her left hand tucked up under her breasts, the hand nudging her chin. The right arm hand gripped tight in a death spasm is outstretched and underneath her right side. The legs are almost straight, the left foot draped over the neck of Dolly who was on her stomach. Her torso slightly crooked and leaning to the right of her legs, which were parted. Dolly's left arm is also tucked underneath her body, her hand covering her mouth as if to stifle a scream. Can you envisage this now, because you can see her right arm bent at the elbow, it is outstretched? There are set of deep human bite marks on her buttock and both girls are covered with ants. Close by is a sign. It reads: 'NO TRASH TO BE DUMPED HERE'.

I visited this dreaded place one rainy afternoon with former LAPD lead homicide detective Leroy Orozco. He parked his car at the bottom of a long uphill trek to where the girls had been found. Over in the distance was LA city proper. It was shrouded in mist. Directly below a flood canal and a freeway. We both stood silently with my TV film crew and said a quiet prayer.

Very occasionally, I revisit the Hillside Stranglers crime scene photos to say another prayer, for when one sees such terrible things *only then* can one understand the true, evil nature of monsters like Kenneth Bianchi and the human destruction that beasts like him cause ... it is heartbreaking, nothing less.

Naturally, honest, churchgoing Kelli Kae Boyd hadn't a clue about the true nature of her intended – just like Sharon Major, she had no idea at all. There were, of course, red flags popping up all over the place, but so besotted was Kelli with Kenny that she couldn't see the wood for the trees.

The public were just as outraged that we, as law enforcement officers, could not do anything to stop these

brutal murders. Especially the single women in this city
who went to work at nights, going to markets, going to
see their families. They were petrified.

Detective Richard Crotsley, LAPD:

to the author at interview

At a 1976/77 New Year's party, Bianchi met Kelli Kae Boyd who worked at the head office of real-estate agents Cal Land. In Sheila Isenberg's book *Women Who Love Men Who Kill,* Kelli was described by Detective Frank Salerno — somewhat unfairly in my opinion — as an as an 'overweight, short and plain young woman'. In addition, Bianchi later accused Kelli of giving him gonorrhea after falsely telling him that she had been raped. The fact that he had caught gonorrhea from a sex worker whom he then killed seemed to have slipped his mind. Isenberg's book title, however, implies that Kelli was in love with a man *whom she knew* to be a killer when this was not the case, or am I misreading something here? But so what if Kelli (now deceased) was not tall and was a bit conservative in her dress and decent in morality? — she *was* an innocent party throughout.

Very much as Sharon Major did with John Cannan, Kelli fell for Bianchi's smooth line of chatter (insert 'bullshit' here) and they dated for a month before she decided to ditch him because of his immaturity and insecurity. 'He was very possessive, and he always wanted to know where I was going and whom I was doing it with, and I didn't really like that very well,' she later told Detective McNeil of the Bellingham Police Department, Washington State.

Snubbed by Kelli, but at least with enough cash to find

a place of his own, Bianchi rented rooms at Tamarind Apartments, 1950 Tamarind Avenue, and no sooner had he shut the door then he picked up a telephone and started wooing Kelli again. Just like John Cannan, as was Ken's practice with previous girlfriends – one of whom he had recently murdered – he sent Kelli bunches of flowers and, before long, he was treating her at the most expensive restaurants he could afford. Now, to put this into some perspective, the most expensive restaurants *he could afford* were not pricey by LA jet-setting standards at all. We are probably talking about a Denny's or cheapo taco joint, so let us put it out of our minds that this egotistical narcissist was flush with money because, like Cannan, he was not. So, bless her cotton socks and cream button-up blouse, Kelli fell for his renewed patter. They moved in under the same roof – a place that Kelli had rented – and at the beginning of May 1977 she announced that she was pregnant with his child. She was to give birth to their son Ryan on Thursday, 23 February 1978.

Life with Bianchi was always going to be a rough ride – well, it would be, if unbeknownst to you, your 'Man about the House' was out at all hours running a stable of sex workers, killing some of them and preying on little girls – but Kelli, in total ignorance, imagined that she had finally found her 'Mr Right'. However, the couple still argued frequently; more than once she turned him out, and each time he either returned to Angelo Buono's place where he slept on the floor, or he would call his own mother who, at her wit's end, mediated reconciliation, while this lowlife was out raping and killing again.

Throughout all this, although she was heavily pregnant, to her credit Kelli still worked at Cal Land. She was frugal with her money, while Bianchi, who earned considerably less than her, would fritter his wages away. Even when he was promoted to 'Assistant Title Officer', he still needed more cash, so he decided to earn more on the side. He would reinvent himself as 'Dr Bianchi' with a doctorate in Psychology. (For more on the history of Bianchi's life and his crimes, see my book *Talking with Serial Killers: World's Most Evil*, or another of my titles, *Emissaries of Satan*.)

The straw that finally broke Kelli's back came when she had kicked him out yet again, and almost instantly he was on the phone telling her that he had terminal cancer. In my one and only brief interview with Kelli, she explained that 'Ken was Ryan's dad. Looking back he wasn't a good dad, I suppose, but he was Ryan's dad. I felt so sorry for Kenneth. Even his mom was convinced that he was really dying.' Kelli went on: 'I took him for a medical appointment at Verdugo Hills Hospital. I wanted to go in with him but he told me to wait in the car. He never came out.' And, the final straw was this: after a long and patient wait, a concerned Kelli went into the hospital to learn that a Mr Kenneth Bianchi was unknown to the doctors. They had had never heard of him. In fact, posing as a doctor himself, he had pilfered a whole lot of medical supplies and cleared off out of a back door. NOTE: These medical supplies were later found when the Bellingham PD raided his home some time later. Nonetheless, upon learning of Bianchi's fake terminal cancer, the dime finally dropped. Kelli upped sticks with her son, to travel north to the small seaport town of

Bellingham, Washington State, where she would be much closer to her parents.

Job done and dusted ... umm, maybe not. By now, readers will probably have guessed that, yes, once again Kelli took her Kenny back. So, what was that all about? – especially since Bianchi's photofit had been published in the media by just about every law-enforcement agency throughout the US of A? It's not a good thing to speak ill of the dead, but surely it was more than time for Kelli to wake up, wasn't it?

Having been accepted back by Kelli, who took him him into the rented Bellingham home that *she* was paying for, Bianchi first found employment as a security officer at a Fred Myer department store out on Interstate 5. Here, he supplemented his income by stealing thousands of dollars worth of electrical appliances and tools. These, like the medical supplies, were also found by police when they searched the basement in Kelli's home.

Then he started work as a security officer with the Whatcom Security Agency (WSA) – one of those outfits who provide security for homes, businesses and industries. Soon, and unbeknownst to his employers, he had self-promoted himself to 'Capt. Kenneth Bianchi', with a phony business card to support his alleged credentials. He even applied to join the local police department. He attended a few classes with the Sheriff's Reserves before a couple of young women told the cops that he was a sexual deviant. He had told Susan Bird, Angie Kinneberg and Margie Lager that he was single, and a professional photographer with top-level connections to the porn industry back in LA. He told them that they could earn really good money as sex workers and that he had clients for them. However, after a few auditions during which Bianchi was more interested in the couch type of interview, one of the girls picked up on the fact that Kenneth was of the philosophy, that: 'If it flew, floated or fucked, it's best to rent it'. In addition, another of the girls suddenly learned that Kenneth had a child and a common-law wife named Kelli Kae Boyd. She reported this to the sheriff, who chucked Bianchi out of his classes and who also advised the boss of WSA that they were employing a rotten apple. Now further very belated background checks had to be carried out and it was soon only a matter of time before Bianchi would finally come unglued ... but before he did, he killed two other young women: university students, Karen Mandic and Diane Wilder.

> *I hate confrontations. People only have their whereabouts checked when they are suspected of doing something wrong. So, knowing I hadn't done anything wrong, and nothing to hide, I had given the original, short answer, about going to the Sheriff's Reserve Class. That was simpler than the longer, true explanation. Besides, if I had killed those girls, I would have remembered it. I didn't, and that's what I kept telling the police.*
>
> Kenneth Bianchi: trying to alibi himself up for the Mandic-Wilder homicides in correspondence with the author.

Twenty-two-year-old co-ed Karen Mandic and her room-mate, twenty-seven-year-old Diane Wilder, both studied at the Western Washington University. Karen was last seen alive at 7 p.m. on Thursday, 11 January 1979, when leaving the Fred Myer store where she worked as a part-time cashier. She told her manager that she would return to cash up at 9 p.m. Earlier in the week she had told two friends, Steve Hardwick and Bill Bryant, that a man who'd recently asked her for a date had now offered her a house-sitting job for that Thursday evening and it paid $100 an hour. In fact, he had asked her out several times, giving his name as 'Captain Alessio Bianchi'; he had explained to Karen that his company provided mobile and static security patrols within a fifty-mile radius of Bellingham and that this was an ideal opportunity for the co-ed to earn some extra cash. She was thrilled.

Upon hearing this, her boyfriend Steve Hardwick was deeply suspicious from the outset; $100 an hour was unheard of for a job like this and he advised Karen not to accept Bianchi's offer. For her part, Karen insisted that WSA was a highly respectable company so everything would be okay. 'It is a Doctor Catlow's house,' she said, adding, 'It's 302 Bayside. The doctor is away with his wife.'

Although Hardwick knew WSA, he pressed Karen further. 'Don't worry,' she snapped back, 'I'm taking Diane with me. Besides, Ken has given my name to the insurance company who are paying the bill. I can't change anything now.'

The two young women were never seen alive again.

At 4.40 p.m. the next day, Karen Mandic's green Mercury Bobcat was found, just a mile from the Bayside address, in a vacant cul-de-sac in Willow Drive. The car contained the fully clothed bodies of Karen and Diane. At autopsy, it was determined that both co-eds had been raped and strangled with a ligature.

During my visit to Bellingham, I went to 302 Bayside and the now developed cul-de-sac where the girls' bodies were found. I interviewed the police involved, and Robert Knudsen, SOCO for the Bellingham PD, told me this:

> *The car was locked; however the passenger door was only on the first catch and so I had no trouble getting into the vehicle that way. I opened both doors, and took a closer look, and the bodies of two young ladies had been tossed in like two sacks of potatoes, one thrown on top of the other.*

With this grim discovery, an order went out for Bianchi's immediate arrest, with the help of his employer, Randy Moa. Knowing that he might be armed and considered dangerous, Moa radioed Bianchi and told him to check out a disused guard shack at the south terminal, a remote area of the docks. Detective Terry Wight was brandishing a pistol when he arrested him. Bianchi would never be a free man again.

> *They were told to lay face down and then they were separated, tied up and, individually, one by one, untied, undressed and I had sex with them. Then they were both dressed again. Then I killed them separately. I believe, ah, Diane Wilder was the first and Karen Mandic second. Then they were carried out and put in the back of the car and driven to the cul-de-sac.*
>
> Kenneth Bianchi: confessing to the author at interview at the Washington State Penitentiary.

Kelli Kae Boyd was at home when the police turned up with a search warrant and to explain that Kenneth had been arrested on suspicion of double homicide. She almost collapsed in shock. Detectives Nolte and McNeill and Field Investigator Moore conducted a thorough search of the property where, in the bedroom, they picked up a pair of blue uniform trousers. The crotch had been ripped and Kelli confirmed that they were the pants that her common-law husband had been wearing the previous evening. She also pointed to a red plaid shirt and there was an identical one lying underneath it. Kelli said that Ken had been wearing one of the shirts the night before, and fibres identical in every respect to those of these shirts were later found on the stairs leading to the basement in Dr Catlow's home. The officers also took possession of a pair of cowboy boots, and they soon matched the sole tread pattern with snowy imprints found at both Willow Drive and Bayside.

Hanging in the bedroom closet was a .357-calibre Smith & Wesson Highway Patrolman revolver, complete with a standard Sam Browne belt and holster. Again, in the same closet Nolte discovered a shoulder holster and several cameras. The firearm was legally owned by Bianchi and in extremely good condition. The cameras and photographic equipment were of professional quality, and this added veracity to the claims of the three women whom Bianchi had wanted to photograph.

Your Ken is a fuckin' magpie.
Detective McNeil: to Kelli Kae Boyd.

With a stunned Kelli looking on, the officers now turned their attention to her dressing table where they found a quantity of jewellery and seven watches. She explained that Ken had given her most of these items as presents – in fact, these had been taken from former Hillside Strangler victims. They were his 'trophies' from the crimes.

Kelli's home was now searched from top to bottom. In the basement cops found several thousand dollars' worth of brand-new tools, all in their original boxes without price tags or sales receipts. It was soon discovered that this treasure trove had been stolen from the Fred Myer store where Bianchi had previously worked as a security guard. However, the stash of stolen booty didn't end with the tools, for on one shelf there was a large quantity of medical supplies – enough to fill a doctor's surgery. Bianchi had stolen it all from the Verdugo Hills Hospital in Los Angeles. And, when Detective Moore made the mistake of prising open a cupboard, he was literally buried under scores of tins of crabmeat that tumbled out. Ken had taken the hoard from a cold storage company where WSA had assigned him as a guard. Finally, a box full of brand-new jackets and touch-tone telephones was opened. These had been stolen from the Uniflite Corporation, whose offices were at the dock's south terminal.

Well, if you cannot trust a security guard, then whom can you trust?

* * *

If John Cannan was manipulative, he doesn't hold a candle to Kenneth Bianchi, who threw not only the psychiatric profession into utter confusion but the US judicial system too. But what about Kelli Kae Boyd?

Any reader might wonder what on earth was Kelli doing in taking Ken back so many times, because she was a sensible, hardworking, Christian woman and nobody's fool by a long chalk. She was as honest as the day is long, so what possessed her? Was it her love for her common-law husband that made up for all of his irresponsible ways, his mood swings, and his unexplained absences way back in Los Angeles? Surely, so many red flags had been raised in LA that it seems inconceivable that she hadn't got rid of the man long ago, but she didn't. The answer to me seems almost obvious: he was, *and he still is*, one of the most cunning, devious, controlling, manipulative narcissistic criminal psychopaths in the history of serial murder. Even his mother told me: 'Christopher, you catch Ken out in lies and he argues till eventually you start to believe that he is right and you are wrong, and then when he senses that you are starting to believe him he shows a face that almost makes you want to apologise and say that you are sorry for distrusting him. That's how manipulative my son is.'

There is no doubt that Ken's mother adored Kelli Kae Boyd, so perhaps it was Frances's love for 'Kenny' that helped Kelli to forgive. That said, however, I still have one problem and it is this: surely Kelli Kae Boyd must have become very suspicious when Bianchi started to bring all of the stolen property back to their small home and stash it away? How does one explain away dozens of tins of crabmeat; thousands of dollars' worth of brand-new tools still in their boxes; very expensive, professional camera equipment; new jackets and touch-tone phones; enough medical supplies to fill a doctor's surgery, when for the better part of the time Kenneth was skint and she knew it? He had always been short of money since she first met him, and the seven watches and jewellery that he had given to her as 'gifts' had all been taken from the dead bodies of those whom he, with Angelo Buono, had abducted, raped, tortured and killed, with their naked bodies dumped around the hills of Los Angeles like so much garbage. One of these women had caustic cleaning fluid injected into her veins while she desperately clung on to precious life in abject agony before death mercifully supervened. Another young woman had a plastic bag placed over her head then coal gas piped into it. While she suffocated, Bianchi raped and then strangled her to death. What sort of man could do all of this then calmly take away the victim's jewellery and present it as a 'gift' to any woman – a wife, a common-law-wife, or even a girlfriend, come to that?

One might have thought that at long last in Bellingham, Kelli Kae Boyd would have cottoned on that Bianchi was, at the very least, a compulsive thief, for *she must have known* that all of this stuff had been stolen. I mean, how does one explain that away? Was her love so deep that, like Bianchi's mother Frances, she was able to forgive him for everything to constantly live in denial? The answer to that question will never be known, for Kelli, bless her, has since passed away.

For his part, Bianchi will never be released from prison, yet even today he attracts scores of 'murder groupies' and they send him money in return for saucy letters. He has been married then divorced behind bars, but frankly, I have lost count of how many times and I no longer care. So, while we can probably understand a little of Kelli Kae Boyd's mindset and, post-mortem, forgive her for any 'oversight' on her part, there can be *no* forgiving the stupid, brain-dead women who still court this monster, for Bianchi's horrendous crimes are well documented on the Internet along with many of the God-awful crime scene photographs as well. To quote Detective Charles Ritter, who said to me: 'The Devil spat against a shithouse wall and that motherfucker Bianchi hatched out in the sun ...

Several days later, I was looking into the distance towards the Mount Baker recreational area, to then gaze wistfully at the most magnificent vista in the locality – the pine-clad slopes of San Juan, the Vancouver Islands and the Strait of Juan de Fuca. It was now 1996. The whole state was wrapped in an icy coat, a typical winter in those parts. In a few days time I would be fishing for steelhead at Gig Harbor. My mind travelled back to January 1979 when Karen Mandic and Diane Wilder were killed.

I would like to say that I felt a lump in my throat, that I shed a tear, but I didn't. Instead, I gleefully went and bought a scenic postcard. On the back I wrote: 'Hi, Kenny, you murdering scumbag, I bet you wish you were here. I'm enjoying this view, what's your view like today? Ya'll have a nice day, ya'll hear. Your friend, Christopher.' I was later told that when Bianchi received my card he flipped and threw a plastic cup at a correctional officer who told him to shut up as he was being thrown in the hole for a month. What I don't get, however, is that I have methodically written to him several times since – always on postcards you understand

– the most recent sent from the sugar sand beaches under the swaying palms at the Casa Kalaw resort, El Nido, Palawan, Philippines, but our Kenny *never* replies. I wonder why?

Postcards? Umm, well this is the least I can do in memory of *all* of Bianchi's victims – I only wish I could have done more, may they rest in peace.

Teena Sams v. Michael Benneman Sams (UK)

I cannot fault Teena, the former wife of one-legged kidnapper and killer Michael Benneman Sams who is now serving a life sentence within the walls of HMP Full Sutton, near York. In fact, she was very generous to me while I was researching and writing my book *Unmasking Mr Kipper,* published in 1996. Generous, you might ask? Well, yes, Teena most certainly *was* for she gave me two very special 'gifts': the orange Austin Metro car that Michael had driven during his abductions and his Suzuki scooter which he rode when extorting money during a kidnapping/ransom bid. I mean, for a criminologist, what could be better than that?

With a little effort, the car and the moped were transported to my then home in the sleepy Hampshire village of Wickham, and here I parked them up on my land and a few yards away from my two goats who kept the grass down.

Built along an ancient Roman road, Wickham is one of

those rural places where crime should not exist. We had a nosy-parker 'Neighbourhood Watch' scheme; a village square; a mill; the obligatory Co-op; a tea shop that sold cream teas; a few half-decent pubs dotted about where drinkers played shove ha'penny; St Nicholas's Episcopal church that I never once visited; a solicitor who misappropriated half-a-zillion pounds from his clients and then upped sticks and absconded to Switzerland with a local stable girl thirty years younger than he – and a police constable by the name of Brian Woodcock who wore a tall hat – a jolly nice chap, indeed, with a surname entirely appropriate for rural England.

PC Woodcock once spotted your author zipping around the area in the aforementioned orange Metro – formerly the property of Mr Sams. He flagged me down to note that I wasn't wearing a seatbelt.

'But, Brian ... ' I protested, ' ... your mates cut the seatbelts out for forensic testing. Look, they even messed up half the paintwork and the windows are covered with this grey fingerprinting dust. It won't come off.'

Brian then did what all coppers do when stopping a car – he walked slowly around it with some umms and ahhhs, then he was on his radio for what I think they call these days a 'PNC check', or something like that. 'So, Christopher,' he said, finally noting the small moped crammed into the back of the Metro, ' ... you have changed your name by deed poll to Michael Sams, have you? ... but Michael Sams is locked up in prison ... But *here* he is on MY ROAD!'

Clearly, PC Woodcock was confused. He then did another thing that policemen *always* do when pulling over a motor vehicle – he took out his notebook, poised to write something with the well-sucked end of a lead pencil. Then he paused. 'This car isn't taxed ... *and* it has *no* MOT and *no* insurance ... ' Sheepishly, albeit with tongue-in-cheek, I replied: 'Yes, officer you are correct. Hey, I can't insure and tax this thing in prison, can I? ... and I can't get it MOT'd because they won't let me out for the day ... I'm serving life.'

Back then, a country bobby was just that, and the one thing I do like about them is that while they still wear tall hats they retain a sense of humour because they are dry country folk at heart. They have been around the field a few times and they know the locals like the hay on the land. Brian's response to me, with a smile was: 'I heard through the grapevine that *you* were out the other night *with* a shotgun. Pheasants, was it? My wife and me, well "Mr Sams", we like pheasant, so it would be nice if we could find a brace on our doorstep in the morning. I will pluck them ... no problems at all. My sergeant has a thing about rabbit.' Then he pedalled away.

PC Brian Woodcock got his pheasants and a rabbit. The rabbit? Well I shot it ten minutes after he cycled over the brow of a hill – and that *is* a true story.

* * *

For my readers who are in the know, you should know that Michael Sams was a kidnapper, blackmailer, killer and electronic tool repairman by profession, with his last workshop premises in Newark-upon-Trent. Again, there is no room in this book for a full account of Michael's 'narrative', but it is worth saying that during his first stint in prison, after perhaps being given far too much first-offender 'bird' for nicking a car and then clocking the speedometer, plus various related offences, he had a leg amputated below the knee.

To back up a bit, some time before he found himself in front of a court, Mr Sams had fallen from a ladder. He suffered a bad injury and doctors had prescribed strong painkillers to deaden the pain in his leg until all was fixed up again. But then Michael was put in prison ... and he was denied the painkillers ... so he suffered in agony ... which the prison doctors thought was malingering. So they didn't diagnose a very serious infection (it was cancer) until it was too late ... The upshot being: off with Michael's leg just above the right knee.

To put no finer point on it, oh, boy – was Michael Sams upset! Indeed, he wrote many notes in his prison journal. He was madder than Hell, and determined that once he was released it would *be* payback time, and give some payback he certainly did by becoming one of the 'Most Wanted' criminals in recent British criminal history. He was no slouch either. His criminal repertoire was varied indeed: attempting to derail an East Coast express train; blowing up department stores; leaving a so-called explosive device on a motorway; kidnapping for ransom; murdering; blackmailing; homicide x 1; unlawful imprisonment – the list goes on and on ... oh, and he rigged his workshop electric meter, too!

During his first spell in prison for his car theft offence, Sams reflected back over the years. He reasoned that he was an intelligent man. God only knew how hard he'd worked to make good. His first marriage to Susan had been on the rocks for years, and he had effectively lost his two sons and now his only brother had passed away.

If we had been a fly on his cell wall, we would have seen Michael metamorphose before our very eyes. Every brick of the prison reeked of disinfectant, urine and stale sweat. There was never a moment's peace, day or night, with cons screaming at each other across landings and wings. To Sams, although not a narcississt by any means, this was a human dustbin, a stinking warehouse storing only low life. Reality stared him in the face, for he was now one of them.

Yes, Michael had a grudge ... as in a mega grudge against society. Yet before he fell off a ladder he was a nice guy, but as they say: 'What goes up, must come down' – and Michael Sams came down in a very big way. His mind began to transform him into someone angry and bitter. One evening, racked with pain, he sat down to itemise his personal profit-and-loss account. I managed to get hold of the original document, and studying it allows us a rare glimpse into the mind of this emerging killer.

I have lost the following:
(1) Freedom for six months (with parole).
(2) A wife, 2 children and our £20,000 home (£7,000 was her share of the house).
(3) £500 I paid for the first car.
(4) £100 I paid for the second car (both cars were recovered by the police).
(5) £600 I have lost through having to sell my present car while in detention. [This car was the orange Austin Metro mentioned above.]
(6) A total loss of £8,000.

Sams had not finished his accounts just yet, however:

> But now consider the loss to others ... over the next five years we have:
>
> (1) Loss to 100 customers £300,000 (an average of £300 for each customer whose central heating would break down when I am unable to service it).
>
> (2) Loss of money owing by me to my suppliers, whom I will not be able to pay whcn my firm collapses £4,500.
>
> (3) Loss of my tax to the Inland Revenue, plus loss of VAT to Customs & Excise over the next five years £10,000.
>
> (4) Cost to the Government for my imprisonment for 6 months, £35 pw I am told = £875.
>
> (5) Supplementary Benefit I will have to be paid when I am released as I do not forsee [sic] employment in the next 5 years £7,250.
>
> A total loss to the Government and others of over £322,625. (Government departments will directly lose or have to pay out £22,625).
>
> Add to this the loss to myself and you have a staggering loss of over £300,000. All for the loss of one motor vehicle to a young lady for 5–6 weeks.
>
> By the time my release comes in October [1978], I should be a very bitter person ... SOCIETY OWES me and I will be repaid.

And perhaps Michael had a point. He had entered prison a small-time crook, but in the eyes of the law, up until then Sams had not committed a single criminal offence – had received not so much as a parking ticket – until he became involved in the theft of a car.

Quite what punishment Sams would have recommended for himself is unclear. But one thing is sure: once his right leg was amputated above the knee the bitterness would grow into become an all-consuming hatred. What price would he place on that? So, was he malingering? No. A visual examination of his leg would have shown clearly that there was something seriously wrong. Sams's medical notes – to which I have had access – confirm that he was prescribed large quantities of pain-relieving drugs and sleeping tablets right up to the week of his incarceration – immediately *after* which these drugs were withdrawn. So, here *we must* ask ourselves, why should these medical problems be of interest when studying the mind of Michael Sams? How does a swollen knee and unrelenting pain assist us in attempting to unravel his thought processes?

Part of the answer lies with the fact that Michael Sams had cancer and it was spreading fast. If his sentence had been a few months longer, he might have died in the prison hospital. Deep down, Sams felt that he was going to die, and ultimately the delay in treatment cost him dearly. The man who had once been a proud and determined champion runner for the Bingley Harriers would never run again.

I am not suggesting that here we find some mitigation for Michael's future crimes, of course I am not! However, as previously mentioned, I did have access to his medical file and

I showed it to a number of eminent doctors who specialise in this area. Each of them stated categorically that whoever treated Sams in prison was incompetent and should have been sued for abject negligence. Indeed, if this sort of malpractice had occurred more recently, Sams would have had a queue of lawyers waiting to represent him in the European Court of Human Rights.

When Michael was released from prison, he was referred back to his own physician, a Mr Norton. On Friday, 10 November 1978, the surgeon picked up his surgical saw and severed half of Sams' right leg. Although this operation undoubtedly saved the man's life, it did little to improve his state of mind, for he believed that, had the leg been treated much earlier it might have been saved. Nonetheless, just before Christmas, he was seen again by Mr Norton, who wrote in his notes that his patient was 'making excellent progress', adding, 'He has a sound stump.' Sams was not exactly buoyed up by these comments, having to come to terms with a lifelong handicap. When he remarried a few months later, his wedding photographs portrayed a gaunt, frail, grey-faced ghost putting on a brave show for the guests.

* * *

While in prison on remand, Sams spent much time studying history and writing letters to a woman he'd met while awaiting sentencing. Despite grieving the loss of wife Susan to her hairstylist Alfonso Grillo, he was always scouring 'Lonely Hearts' columns for prospective lovers. He met Jane Marks (*nee* Hammond) after replying to her advertisement in the *Yorkshire Post*. Aged thirty-seven, she had been married twice before and came from the seaside town of Cleethorpes on South Humberside.

Susan Sams – now Mrs Grillo – had won the legal dispute for overdue maintenance payments owed by her former husband, and their former home, 'Oakfield' – where he had fallen from the ladder – had been taken by bailiffs. So, with no roof over his head, Sams moved in with Jane at her house in Norman Row, Leeds. He was unemployed for the first time in his life, and still hobbling around on wooden crutches waiting for an artificial limb to be fitted. This, however, did not prevent him from driving a car. He often used to brag about how he'd fooled the law by illegally using a crutch to work the accelerator and brake pedals.

The couple had only been wed a very short time when Jane realised that she'd married the wrong man yet again. I really don't understand why a longer courtship would not have been a better idea after her first two marriages had failed, but each to their own.. Nonetheless, Sams had now become a listless, argumentative millstone around her neck. They started to row, and she went completely off sex. Sams later agreed that he did change for the worse, but as usual he has a convenient explanation. He would lay the blame for his behaviour at the feet of others. In a letter to me, he wrote:

> *Jane saw this change and told me. But I didn't believe her, or didn't want to believe her. To my mind I loved all women and wouldn't harm any woman. I certainly never did anything violently towards Jane. It was the reverse.*

Sams went on to allege:

> *She often pushed me over and had a go at me. But even though Jane kept telling me I had changed, I didn't believe her. The crash came when we were turned down for adopting due to the fact that I had only recently been released from prison.*

Sometimes, it bewilders even me as to how stupid these types of people are. Here we have Jane, divorced twice only to marry an ex-con after meeting him through a lonely-hearts column; he of course with one-and-a-half legs, no employment nor any prospects for the distant future – and they want to adopt a child? I don't know whether Jane had any kids, but Michael had two lads and he could not even pay for their maintenance.

In reality, Sams knew that this second marriage was going the same way as his first, but a damn sight faster. He resorted to threats and intimidation to prevent Jane from leaving him, going as far as saying that he would get a pistol and shoot her dead. Whether Michael had access to a firearm is unknown – I suspect not – nevertheless, the threat so terrified Jane that she forced him out onto the street then slammed and locked the front door. She had been reduced to a quivering wreck, which gives the lie to Sams's letter to me that she was the violent one, not he. However, there had been something evil in her new husband's eyes, and his quiet, soft voice had carried sinister undertones. If this was, indeed, true, she must have asked herself, 'What if he does come back to shoot me?'

In a statement Jane later made to police, she claimed in a state bordering on hysteria she fled that same evening to stay with a friend. The following morning she returned with a hired van and hired help, and removed as many of her possessions as the truck could carry. After their divorce, Michael Sams would never see Jane again.

The degree of loss that he claims he suffered at losing wife No. 2 can be gauged by a statement he made to me in 1992: 'Once more I surrounded myself with beautiful girls.' These 'beautiful girls' were of course sex workers whom he met in public houses in Bradford. He was using the red-light districts of the North to trawl for nightly sex.

On Tuesday, 20 November 1979, Michael Sams answered an advertisement he'd seen in the *Yorkshire Evening Post*, placed by the tool-making firm Black & Decker, based in Leeds. A search by me through the firm's personnel records revealed that Sams commenced work with the company on Wednesday, 2 January 1980, in the position of 'workshop repairman'.

During the next two years, he lived first at 1 Neville Mount, then at 16 Woodview Mount – both in Leeds. However, just before Christmas 1981, he was asked if he would move to the company's workshop in Birmingham. Sams had obviously impressed this famous firm with his dedication to hard and precise work, so he accepted the offer with the proviso that Black & Decker contributed towards his relocation costs, which they did.

He moved on Monday, 4 January 1982, taking up residence in a modest new property at 139 South Road. Then, came what I believe was an amazing burst of property speculation worthy of any serious Monopoly player: he sold 139 South Road to purchase 57 Short Heath Road, within a stone's throw of Witton Lakes and the Leak Hill recreation ground. It was while here that he met the woman who was fated to become wife No. 3.

He was very kind and considerate. We went out nearly every night. I would either visit him at Short Heath Road or he would come to my house.
                    Teena Sams: at interview with the author

Slim and quite tall, with short hair, Teena Sams was welcoming when I visited her in her Birmingham semi-detached, and made a pot of tea and opened a packet of digestive biscuits. Out front was parked the orange Metro car covered with a wet, blue tarpaulin. Teena also seemed to like graves, too. Alongside the kitchen window, among some wilting flowers were a number of pet graves with little white crosses, as I recall. She had a neurotic budgie or a canary, although I can't remember what sort of bird it was because it had plucked out most of its plumage. Actually, I somewhat doubt that even the bird could remember either, because its reflection in its mirror looked as though it had been sucked through a spinning fan.

But later, after tea and biscuits, what Teena also served up was a cunning plan: a plot that would enable me to meet and interview her husband in prison. I told Teena that this would be impossible because Michael was Category A – only close relatives allowed to visit. The reader will have to refer to my book, *Unmasking Mr Kipper*, to learn exactly how I managed to get a Visiting Order (VO) and then a two-hour sit-down talk with Michael Sams in HMP Full Sutton, but I did. And, more to the point, he revealed something that leads us directly towards part of his MO: trains.

Michael loved train sets; he was a train nerd; he collected train and railway memorabilia. He even stole signs, such as one from London's Paddington station – he had half-inched it in broad daylight and then scrubbed it up clean. Others he filched from the Honourable Artillery Company and countless more, all of which all pointed directly to the terminus that is Sams's psychopathology: he was an avid train spotter.

Michael was of this mainline breed of stalwarts, and Teena loved him all the more for it. He was the provider. He had mostly rebuilt their house. He was quiet. He was a devoted husband. He could not have hurt a fly, for how could he when he only had one leg – although the artificial leg did creak a bit when he limped to and fro.

If the truth were known, Teena told me that she didn't have much choice other than to like him. Their later beautiful whitewashed walled home, Eaves Cottage in Sutton-on-Trent, was jam-packed with Michael's railway stuff and Teena touched any of it at her peril. 'If a signal was up when he went to work and it was down when he came home, it was like a Spanish Inquisition', she whispered, while looking over her shoulder as if this was a secret that should never be known. She continued: 'But, Michael *was* a good man ... a bit quiet at times ... but they all are, these trainspotters ... they do live in a world of their own,' before going on to talk about more everyday matters.

At this point, I was really starting to like Michael Sams,

even more so when Teena left the sitting room to return with a large envelope in which were some beautiful watercolour paintings of railway scenes. They were magnificent – the detail so carefully precise that only a talented artist with a deep knowledge of railways could have achieved it with such perfection. In my hands were hundreds of hours of research and delicate brushwork, and it now became perfectly clear to me that I was looking into the mind of the *real* Michael Benneman Sams. His artwork conveyed to me his MO: everything he did when planning his crimes was carried out meticulously, with no room for mistakes, for unlike an oil painter, who can over-paint or scratch off, a watercolourist has no leeway for sloppy work. Except that Michael made one small, fatal mistake – his attention to precision eventually caused him to come unstuck.

But who is Teena Sams?

* * *

Teena Sheila Aston was born Tuesday, 31 May 1949. Her father, Robert Christopher Aston, had been a well-decorated soldier, having served with valour in the Rifle Brigade throughout the Second World War. Teena's mother, Elsie, had worked at a children's home before taking up long-term employment with Elbies, a handbag manufacturer.

Like Michael Sams's previous wife, Jane, Teena had already been married twice when she fell in with him. Again, like Jane, both of Teena's attempts at marital bliss had ended in dismal failure.

On Tuesday, 5 November 1968, nineteen-year-old Teena had given birth to a son, Paul. She was then living with her parents in Yardley Wood Road, Birmingham. Six months later, she married the baby's father, William James Hegarty. This marriage lasted a mere fifteen months. Thereafter, for a few years Teena brought up Paul alone in a flat in Sisefield Road, Birmingham. Then she met her second husband, Graham Cooper, who, by all accounts, was a reasonable man who worked as a painter and decorator for the local council. This marriage *might* have lasted but for Graham's interest in Teena's very pretty niece, Denise. While Teena readily admitted to me that she could be a little 'dim' at times, perhaps it is more correct to say that she was naïve. This marriage of two years came to an end when she discovered that her randy husband was enjoying a full-blooded affair with Denise, who had just left school. (They later married.) However, if both of her marriages had brought Teena sadness, there was the consolation that Graham had at least left her with some security in the form of bricks and mortar: 818 Yardley Wood Road, just down the street from her parents' house. She now had a home of her own.

Sometime in early 1982, Teena placed an advertisement in the lonely-hearts column of the *Birmingham Evening Mail*, and guess what, she received twenty replies so she had the pick of quite a few good apples. Sadly, she picked a wrong 'un. As luck would have it, one of the potential suitors was none other than Michael Benneman Sams. He sent her a photograph, she rang him, she liked his soft quiet voice – they agreed to meet.

The couple frequented the Billesley Hotel, which, in those days, had a singles' club. They didn't drink or smoke to excess, and friends reckoned that they were marriage material.

Therefore, it came as no surprise when they became engaged eighteen-months after first meeting. They would marry in November 1988, after living together for about six years. Thus, all seemed tickety-boo thus far, but, it wasn't long before the rot set in.

Teena and Michael started to argue about the most trivial of issues. However, the spark that ignited most of the blazing rows was unwittingly caused by Black & Decker, who had asked Sams to move once again, this time to their Coventry workshop. Teena put her foot down, refusing to let him go. Surprisingly, he acceded to her demands and accepted voluntary redundancy, with a pay-off of £3,590.60. So, with over three grand in his pocket, Sams started up on his own. Black & Decker had taught him how to service power tools, so he looked around for suitable premises comprising a shop and workplace. The ideal place proved to be 42 Oundle Road in Peterborough, for it included a small flat above a shop. Sams leased the building, which he transformed into Peterborough Power Tools Ltd. He opened a trading account with Black & Decker, and within weeks he was repairing all manner of electrical equipment – not only those made by his former employer, but also Bosch and Skil products. Just as before, Sams did most of the work in between travelling to and from London where he frequented trade exhibitions. The paperwork? Well, he listed his accounts in a scruffy, oil-stained notebook, which Teena would later transcribe into something more legible.

* * *

At this point in the proceedings, it would appear to us that Michael Sams had forgotten about his pledge to get back at society and his desire to seek revenge seems to have evaporated. He was with Teena. He had started his own business, which was flourishing, so that any reasonable person might have said 'Well done, Michael!' Indeed, Sams quickly purchased another property, 10 Orchard Street, which he refurbished and rented out. Then came 22 Jubilee Street and 29 New Road. It seemed as if he were buying up half of Peterborough.

Teena was also in the property market, albeit not on the scale of Michael. She tried to sell 818 Yardley Wood Road in Birmingham, while taking out a mortgage on 215 Oundle Road. She and Sams moved in, and eventually, at some serious financial loss to herself, Teena disposed of both houses before moving into the flat above Peterborough Power Tools Ltd.

Quite how many properties they owned or rented between them remains a mystery: if the taxman never figured it out, neither can I. On the surface it appeared that having learned something from his previous mistakes, Sams had settled down. However, a study of his Inland Revenue records paints another picture. When investigators finally tracked him down years later they discovered that his personal finances had been in dire straits, and Peterborough Power Tools Ltd had fared no better. Given access to an Inland Revenue document, I noted this comment:

From records we can say that Peterborough Power Tools Ltd, throughout the period of trading, made negligible profits, indeed, in some years had substantiated losses.

We can also say that the remuneration drawn by both directors – Mr and Mrs Sams – was consistently low, supporting the belief that the company was not a very profitable concern.

Given that bland assessment, and the fact that the couple owned and leased many properties from which they drew rent, it is obvious that Michael Sams had been fiddling his taxes. In my exclusive interview with him at HMP Full Sutton, I touched upon this subject, and when I did he leaned towards me, smiled, and in his soft voice said that having been ripped off by the 'system' far too often, he'd enjoyed doing the same to the taxman. Michael Sams had certainly not forgotten that society owed him big time, for we recall this: 'By the time my release comes in October [1978], I should be a very bitter person ... SOCIETY OWES me and I will be repaid.'

Having yet again taken the self-destructive plunge into seemingly financial ruin, Sams was becoming violent and abusive towards Teena. Like the proverbial lemming, he was teetering on the edge of the abyss. And there was something else worrying Teena during those fretful months. The causes for concern were her husband's frequent trips to London and his secretive digging in the garden of 29 New Road, Peterborough. Sams always welcomed Teena to see any renovation work he carried out, but she told me that he almost forcibly kept her away from this address. Her recollection – seemingly untainted by the passage of time – is that Sams excavated a large hole in the garden which he then processed to fill in with rubble. This was no mean feat for someone with his disability – the effort required must have been enormous – and with just a third of the work done, he contracted some labourers to finish the job with hard core and top soil several metres deep. But maybe there is an ominous twist to this: nine years later, the police half-heartedly scooped out a well in the garden of 29 New Road in their search for the body of the missing London estate agent Suzy Lamplugh. But, well, *the* well was the wrong place to look. Perhaps they should have dug someplace else in that garden – and a lot deeper?

* * *

Michael Benneman Sams's narrative is, at once long, complicated, fascinating, and my book *Unmasking Mr Kipper* reveals a man whose mind is as equally complicated and fascinating too. One can also say that in many respects he suffered from an obsessive compulsive disorder (OCD) because he had a tendency towards excessive orderliness. This is evident from his watercolour paintings and the great attention to detail, and is further echoed in his work product and trainspotting and railway memorabilia collection too. But, herein lies the rub, for it was this overweening attention to detail that led to his downfall, so he has a very complicated psychopathology, indeed.

Without straying too far from the overall subject of this book – for it is the women, and some men, who have suffered at the hands of serial killers and monsters that is our *raison d'être* – some say that Michael Sams was a criminal psychopath; however, as much as others may disagree, I say that he wasn't. He is certainly no human beast such as John Cannan, nor is he a Ted Bundy or any of the other serial killers or otherwise

I have interviewed and corresponded with over the decades. He is not a Peter Sutcliffe either. Once again, I am not suggesting or even offering up any mitigation in defence of what he has done. That, for me, would be out of the question. Yes, Sams used sex workers, and yes he murdered one of them – Julie Dart. Sams kidnapped and killed Julie, not for sexual gratification nor out of a perverse hatred of women, as did Bundy or Sutcliffe and others of their disgusting ilk. He did it because he had kidnapped her in a botched ransom bid, not realising that neither the police, nor her family who were penniless, could ever have acceded to his demands. In a nutshell, and as crass as this may read, Julie Dart was hit over the head with a hammer, dying instantly from a single heavy blow, because there was no money to pay Sams off. It was for him a simple matter of expediency, for she had seen his face, she knew what his car looked like and if he'd freed her, all would have been lost in any event. With his later kidnapping of estate agent, Stephanie Slater, her firm paid up and she survived – he even drove her home, where he dropped her off, wishing her well as he drove away.

In light of this, I have to admit that in all of my experiences in dealing with and interviewing face-to-face cold-blooded sadosexual serial killers and mass murderers, I cannot envisage Sams as a monster. He could be very loving *at times*, as his three wives might have testified, and at other times he was compassionate. Caring, even doting … , and yes, he fiddled his taxes and rigged his electricity meter so that his workshop consumed so much electricity that even the utility company was confounded by the consumption. And he did have the wits to run the country's police ragged for months on end.

I will also admit that, setting aside all of his criminal enterprises and at times evilness, and comparing him to all of the other human pond scum I have interviewed, I liked Mike very much. Indeed, they should make a movie about him, for there is a lot of black humour to be found in this one-legged, soft-spoken killer's craftiness.

* * *

In September 1988, Teena's son Paul, who'd been training for a career as a nurse, died from viral infection meningitis. Devastated, Teena appeared to lose all interest in life and in the business for which Michael had worked so hard. She now begged him to agree to move away from Peterborough, and when he refused, she withdrew into a world of her own, which included rejecting all physical and sexual approaches from Sams. This led to many bitter arguments and nights when Teena slept in the spare bedroom – often because he told her to.

Sams now realised that he was in a no-win situation, so he decided to consider Teena's demands to leave Peterborough, the town that now held so many sad memories for her. For a start, he wasn't getting any sex, and this was driving him wild. Added to that, he no longer had Teena's cooperation in Peterborough Power Tools Ltd, so his accounts and general paperwork were in a terrible state. There was a growing list of irate creditors – if he were to survive in business, he would have to pay these suppliers off quickly, so this was when the idea of kidnapping for ransom and extortion started to formulate in his mind.

In the end, Michael decided to move his home and

business out of the area. If nothing else, that would resolve some of his domestic problems. In addition, at the age of forty-seven he finally married Teena, six years his junior, at the town's register office in November 1988. He promised that they would go house hunting. Furthermore, the idea of a move also appealed to his devious business mind: he could virtually dump Peterborough Power Tools Ltd. First, though, he would have to find other business premises close to his new home. The couple settled on the quiet Nottinghamshire village of Sutton-on-Trent for a home and the market town of Newark-on-Trent for a workshop. In a rare romantic mood, he decided to call the new firm 'T&M Tools' – 'Teena & Michael Tools'.

How Michael Sams obtained a mortgage for Eaves Cottage, Barrel Hill Road, Sutton-on-Trent, can only be described as: *via* deception. Reflecting on that period, Teena told me that she knew nothing of any of her husband's dealings with his mortgage adviser, Joseph Jennings, whom it is fair to say Michael duped – as in big time!

Nonetheless, as soon as contracts were exchanged, the couple drove up to their new home every weekend to decorate, ferrying paint and building materials back and forth in Sams's clapped-out Rover SD1. For a short while, Teena was in her element, and was 'thrilled to bits' to move into her 'dream cottage' with her Yorkshire terrier, Mimi and two German shepherds, Tara and Bonnie. For his part, Sams started to look for business premises. He found the ideal workshop advertised in the window of Richard Watkinson & Partners of 17 North Gate, Newark.

The Samses were back on the road again. All was looking

good when Michael secured a workshop, for £1,950 a year in Swan and Salmon Yard off Castle Gate in Newark. He went on to demand a rent-free period of three months, during which time of non-trading, he would, at *his* expense, renovate the unit for his purpose. Teena was in her element. At first she managed T&M Tools, where she spent much time eagerly painting the walls and generally tidying up the place. Sams would commute daily to Peterborough using his British Rail disabled-person pass. Yet, it seemed hardly a day went by without a County Court judgment dropping through the letterbox of his now almost-defunct business back in Peterborough. His properties were being repossessed, he was £16,000 in debt (not counting the mortgage and bridging loan for the newly purchased Eaves Cottage), unpaid suppliers were freezing his accounts, and two credit card companies were chasing him for money.

Notwithstanding this, when finally in residence at Swan and Salmon Yard, Sams built a counter and put up shelves that doubled as a partition to separate the sales area from his workshop at the rear of the building. However, high on his list of priorities was an alteration to the wiring. He intended to get his electricity supply free, and to do that he would have to bypass the meter.

In a scenario of 'DO NOT TRY THIS AT HOME', after cutting through the high-tensile wire to gain access to the terminals, he added an extra circuit breaker which was, in turn, connected to the live incoming cable set in the outside wall. He plugged the hole with an oily rag, so all this bright spark needed to make the connection was a cable clamp and a single piercing screw. Limping around in rubber boots –

a *very* sensible thing to do – Sams added a junction box to his illegal system, into which he could plug all manner of appliances. The extra circuit breaker was insurance just in case he overloaded his *gratis* supply and brought East Midlands Electricity engineers with confused expressions running from all directions.

The crooked ingenuity of Michael Sams knew no bounds, so we are obliged to give him credit for this much. However, in 1992 – after he was finally arrested for murder and kidnapping – one of these electric engineers examined his handiwork at the request of the police, who probably thought that, if he got away with murder they could at least nick him for stealing electricity. East Midlands Electricity Inspector, Stewart Hall, calculated that, over two years Sams had extracted an average of 5.8 units of juice a day – a miraculously low amount considering that this *was* an electrical tool repair shop!

* * *

Teena told me that during the early months of 1991, they argued frequently. Mike spent far too much time at work, leaving little time for her – which was all very reminiscent of his behaviour towards his first wife Susan. Teena also said that Sams, when he was at home, would often provoke an argument just to give himself an excuse to leave the cottage. He would storm out, often not returning for hours or even days. A friend recalled Sams saying that, if Teena didn't buck up, he'd drive to Leeds or Bradford to find a sex worker; moreover, he certainly knew where to look.

There are always two sides to a coin and they say that it 'takes two to tango', so we can imagine, even understand that

Teena was a sad figure at this time. Both she and Michael had carted a great deal of emotional baggage into this marriage, with four previous marriages between them and, to be fair, neither of them were about to change their spots. Plagued by memories of her deceased son Paul, she pulled out of the business. Sex with her husband was almost non-existent and she began thinking of leaving him, but she changed her mind when Sams agreed to their adopting of a child – even though they had been flatly turned down previously. Because Michael had had a vasectomy, the question of adoption had come up time and again – Teena longed for another child, and this route was the only possible solution. However, one must question why she would want another child?

Teena was now forty-two, her husband fifty. Two failed marriages each, with her having lost her beloved son, and with Michael unable to even pay the maintenance for his two growing boys. The couple were teetering on the edge of bankruptcy after a string of failed business ventures, with creditors chasing them for money and more County Court judgments against them that even they could count. Domestically, their already short marriage was pretty much on the rocks. Teena admitted to me that her husband was an ogre; a spouse with unpredictable mood swings and although she alleges that she knew nothing of his crooked ways at the workshop and his tax fiddling, and that he would not explain his absences away from home, it seems to me that she wanted a child for all the wrong reasons in much the same way as one might want a puppy. In other words, she wanted a child to replace what she had previously lost.

Nonetheless, to my way of thinking, adopting a child

was certainly *not* the way to patch up this quite obvious matrimonial disaster, and if Teena was that unhappy, then a divorce – the third no less – would have been the sensible way to go, however painful. Nevertheless, unfortunately for Teena – fortuitously for Michael – shortly after applying to the Social Services in Newark, Teena was forced to rescind the application, with the very real excuse of not being able to afford a child at this time because they were skint. They were informed that they could reapply later if things improved, but Michael must have been secretly rubbing his hands with glee.

With this bad news now adding to Teena's depressed plight, Michael decided that he would cheer *himself* up. He decided to scrap his Rover and buy another car – his perhaps selfish attitude being: 'I'm going enjoy myself even she won't.' He'd seen an orange Austin Metro on the forecourt of John Emmington's garage in Skellingthorpe. Despite having had a string of owners (and if you know anything about these 1990s Metros, you will understand why), it was advertised as: 'All previous owners have lavished loving care on this fine example of a colourful car.' With a genuine 40,000 miles on the clock it was legit, but that would soon change, I *can* tell you this much. Sams paid £1,800 for the Metro in hard cash.

His other means of transport was a plum-coloured Suzuki 'Love' scooter, a gift from Teena. Quite what he made of this gift, we may never know: the word 'love' was something almost alien to him and the colour – a sort of shade of darkish pink – probably not up every man's street. Nevertheless, this in partnership with the Metro car would be used to great effect when Sams came to kidnapping for ransom Birmingham estate agent Stephanie Slater.

Now, if readers now think that life wasn't exactly a bed of roses at this point in the Samses relationship ... hold your horses, because things have *only just started* to plunge south. With Teena clinically depressed and no longer working at T&M Tools – so let's be honest here, leaving Michael in the lurch – the business paperwork went undone, so inevitably everything started to spiral out of control once again. On the surface, however, Michael seemed calm and relaxed, a mask that provided quite an effective smokescreen for his ever-increasing despair and frustration. He was running up even larger accounts with new suppliers, which he could never hope to settle, his cash flow had dried up and a steady supply of customers had failed to materialise. It was almost like trying to bail out the sinking *Titanic* with a teaspoon.

Added to this was the substantial sum he owed his mother, Iris. During my interview with her – over yet another pot of tea and few digestive biscuits – this gracious lady told me that she had loaned her son £1,000 to help him set up Peterborough Power Tools Ltd, and had not seen a penny of it since. Notwithstanding this, in 1988 Iris cashed a bond for £8,000 to assist him in buying a property. He had only ever been able to repay the interest on his mum's loans, which amounted to £100 per month. He did, however, continue to meet that obligation until the week of his arrest on charges of kidnapping and murder. That Iris didn't get a penny more, he put down to the police for arresting him, so make of that one what you will.

As for the Samses' mortgage repayments, rent for the

workshop, purchases of stock, and general living expenses – not to mention his twin interests, model railways and trainspotting, on which he spent hundreds of pounds – all of these were weighty millstones around his neck. With Teena doing very little at all, he took over the household budget, allowing Teena only £40 a week to pay all food and domestic bills, and he monitored her every purchase like a hawk, demanding to see every receipt, which he merely glanced at then threw away.

Distressed, Teena most certainly was. She had become a prisoner in her dream cottage. Day after day, Sams would 'nit pick', constantly leaving sarcastic notes such as 'Fill up the kettle' and 'Don't move the cups.' He would force her to sleep in the spare bedroom – often bluntly saying: 'Spare bedroom tonight.' He even berated her in front of an elderly neighbour for not having his dinner on the table, although Teena hadn't a clue when he would arrive home from wherever he had been.

Teena explained that she was on the verge of a nervous breakdown, and no longer knew the difference between right and wrong. 'Try as I might,' she said, 'there was no pleasing this Dr Jekyll and Mr Hyde character.' Keeping the cottage spotless became her reason for living. But even as she tidied up and dusted, Sams claimed that it was done badly and constantly complained that his personal things were never put back in their right place. Although Teena said that Michael never actually struck her, it can be said that this was serious psychological spousal abuse.

In a further effort to resolve her troubles with her husband, and realising that T&M Tools was in dire financial straits,

Teena drew out what little money she had in her building society account and gave it to Michael. She might as well have thrown it down a toilet for the thanks she received; he snapped at her for keeping the savings a secret and accused her of deceiving him. Teena's diaries during this period (to which she allowed me access) make for depressing reading.

To ameliorate some of the financial problems that beset him, Sams came up with another cunning plan and signed on as unemployed – because he was allegedly unfit for work due to his disability – at Newark's Job Centre in Lombard Street. The manager, Pamela Little, helped him complete Form UB461. Ever the devious man, he made a false declaration, saying that he had merely been the service manager of Peterborough Power Tools Ltd when, in fact, he had been the proprietor and major shareholder. The fact that the T&M Tools workshop was a mere 500 yards away from Lombard Street seems to have slipped his mind. He made no reference to it at all.

Sams collected his first Giro cheque for £115.61 on Tuesday, 30 April 1991. An examination of his file shows that from then until his father's funeral on Monday, 17 February 1992, he illegally continued to draw state benefits totalling £5,086,84. And he also found Income Support a soft touch. While unlawfully saying he was unemployed, he convinced the Department of Social Security to pay the mortgage on Eaves Cottage, as well as the bridging loan he'd accumulated on the still unsold property at 29 New Road, Peterborough. I have often asked myself, why was Sams so keen to keep that property when all else had to go? Something to do with the hole he excavated in the garden? It might well be.

Newark isn't a big town by any stretch of the imagination, so obviously the DSS did not do their homework. For a stroll into Swan and Salmon Yard would have revealed the duplicitous and utterly brazen Mr Sams – unemployed due to disability – beavering away over a backlog of repairs, sending out statements of account to customers, including the local council who were a client, and filling in bank credit slips. Flipping the coin over, while Michael was quick to grab as much money as he could – legally or otherwise – he was extremely slow when it came to paying it out. He would employ all manner of subterfuges to avoid meeting even the smallest debt. He later used many of these ducking and diving tactics against the country's most experienced police officers and the Inland Revenue, whom he ran ragged along with every other creditor.

For example: take Beale Tools of Craywood, who had been one of Sams's suppliers since 1990. He now owed the firm several thousand pounds, and they had no intention of letting Peterborough Power Tools Ltd get away with the debt, so they continually pressed for payment. With County Court action looming, and knowing that his former supplier would force him into bankruptcy, Sams sent them a small cheque to buy time. With it, he enclosed a letter that ended cheekily: 'We thank you for you [sic] support, and you may rest assured you will continue to receive our custom.'

Sams was the last customer Beale Tools of Craywood needed, and the small reduction in his account failed to placate the company's solicitor. On Thursday, 11 April 1991 – the very month Sams signed on as unemployed – the company tracked him to T&M Tools and issued proceedings against the firm, in what was to be a futile effort to recover the remaining debt. This sparked Sams into trying one last time to prevent

Beale Power Tools ruining him. He typed another letter that was to become the prototype for all his future correspondence to creditors – indeed, if this was not such a serious business, one might even raise a smile:

> *It may be the case you have other communications with other suppliers who used Peterborough Power Tools Ltd, and they have told you that, I, out of my own pocket, paid their outstanding invoices. This was true. But this was done because they offered myself credit facilities on the understanding I did my best to secure monies for their outstanding invoices, it was therefore a goodwill gesture that I paid them out of my own funds, but I have no obligation to underwrite all outstanding invoices.*

Using the great gift of hindsight, one can see that Beale Power Tools were barking up the wrong tree, and one might have thought that their solicitor would have known better for they were suing a limited company that was, to all intents and purposes, already bankrupt, so they had no recourse against Sams, or T&M Tools, in any event. Nevertheless, while Sams's letter, full of magnanimous gestures, might have fooled someone, it didn't impress Beale's legal adviser. Although they pursued their action vigorously, they received not a penny more for their labours.

Things for Michael Sams were now building up a head of steam. The mental pressure was nearing breaking point and he had to find money through fair means or foul – and we can rule out 'fair' straight away. That April, he was trying to get the Inland Revenue off his back, so his first task was to distance himself totally from any involvement in 22 Jubilee Street and 29 York Road, Peterborough. He wrote a letter to the Inland Revenue, saying: 'Mrs Teena Sams has now handed the properties back to the building society. She will be living at Eaves Cottage until she finds a suitable property to rent.' This was an attempt to suggest that Teena owned the two houses in Peterborough, not him. Teena herself says she knew nothing of any repossession until 1994, when I showed her Michael's letter to the taxman. She had been under the impression that her husband had sold the houses and made a profit. Furthermore, to add insult to injury, this letter gave her another jolt: she was the co-owner of Eaves Cottage and had never intended to rent anything.

* * *

In June 1991, Sams sat down to think again about his money problems. Trying to kidnap a female estate agent seemed, to him, the only option. That summer at Crewe, he made a determined attempt to kidnap two women who, for legal reasons, cannot be named. Suffice it to say that the following will show the reader just how devious this man can be and why it was so easy for him to dupe Teena.

That June, Sams drove to Crewe and spent most of the day searching for estate agents and houses with vacant possession, eventually settling on 71 Westminster Street, which had rear access through an alleyway. His next stop was Derby where he posted two letters in unsealed white W.H. Smith window envelopes, addressed to himself in Newark. He needed a good impression of a Derby postmark.

A week later, on a Wednesday, he drove to Crewe, and just

after the staff left the office for the day, he pushed one of the envelopes through the letterbox of Swetenhams estate agency. The letter inside asked for a viewing of the Westminster Street address and gave instructions to phone him at a number in Ashbourne, Derbyshire, any day between 9.00 and 9.30 a.m. to confirm the details. Sams hoped that, the following day, the estate agents would think that the letter had been delayed in the mail and would ring the number immediately. He would be waiting for the call in a phone box in Ashbourne, and would arrange the viewing for later that day, when he would kidnap the estate agent – hopefully a female.

However, after Sams had posted the letter through the door, a policeman drove up and asked if he was all right. Lacking a disguise, Sams worried about going ahead with his plan in case the officer remembered him and his distinctive orange Metro car. Nevertheless, the following morning he drove to Ashbourne. When the phone failed to ring, he called Swetenhams himself and was told that they had only just received his letter. A viewing appointment was made for a fortnight's time.

Back in his workshop, Sams now reviewed his kidnap plans. He had constructed a chipboard box to contain his victim until a ransom was paid for the victim's release, and he laid out a length of chain. In a corner of the room, hidden from view under a grubby sheet, lay a set of false car number plates as well as two signs he would attach to the rear windows of his car: 'BLOCKED AND BROKEN DRAINS'. These would cover the windows entirely, giving the appearance of a small plumber's van.

His kidnapping kit consisted of two knives, rope and a gag,

while he would disguise himself by wearing a pair of Michael Caine-like heavy-rimmed glasses, dying his hair darker and attaching a few plastic warts to his face. He then sat down to go over his route for the kidnap proper.

Two weeks later, on Wednesday, 3 July 1991 (his day off work), Sams drove to Crewe for his 2 p.m. appointment at 71 Westminster Street. Disguised, he waited nervously outside the property. Then a man working on a nearby house walked up to him, offering his expertise should he decide to buy the property. This unwarranted interference may have saved the forty-one-year-old estate agent's life, for Sams was scared off by the persistent builder. When the woman arrived, accompanied by a schoolgirl on work experience, she was told that her potential client had gone.

Using the alias 'Lettin' – obviously a play on words – Sams made another attempt at the same address. This time a female colleague of the first estate agent booked the viewing. She later told the police about the builder who was annoying all of her potential clients. She also remembered a scruffy man wearing heavy-rimmed glasses walking towards her with a peculiar gait. Then he had suddenly changed direction and disappeared.

With two abysmal failures under his belt, Sams decided to pick an easier target: a sex worker. It was here in his careful scheming that he made a terrible mistake – he underestimated – although it has to be said that when all is said and done he knew as much about sex workers as he did about estate agents, the latter with whom he had come into contact through his property speculation exercises, the former simply for paid sex.

Sams drove to Leeds's red-light district where, without much difficulty, he zeroed in on a 'working girl' plying her trade. His plan was to kidnap her, drive her back to Newark; then after collecting £140,000 in ransom – which he naively believed the police would pay – he'd kill her and dump the body.

After striking a deal, the girl climbed into the orange Metro. Sams drove her to a nearby car park where she started to undress, and then within seconds he whipped out a knife and pushed it to her throat. With grim determination this feisty woman fought him off and, pushing him to one side she leapt from the car grabbing what clothes she could. Sams was half in and half out of the driver's door when a lump of house brick slammed into his windscreen (the damage was still visible when I took possession of the Metro). The woman stumbled off into the night leaving a stream of expletives in her wake, having had a miraculous escape, as this letter from Sams to me suggests:

> *Had either of these too [sic] had gone ahead then the captive would not have been allowed to go home. When the 3 July 1991 at Crewe failed, I have no explanation as to why I thought the police would pay a ransom for an unknown, everyday person (the prostitute). But I knew in my mind they would.*

A short time after this abortive kidnap attempt, Sams was again back in Leeds. This visit brought him into contact with eighteen-year-old sex worker Julie Anne Dart. Deploying exactly the same abduction method he had used previously, this time Sams succeeded.

We know that Sams drove Julie about seventy miles from

Leeds to Newark, where he arrived at about 1.45 a.m. He would have people believe that Julie entered his workshop as meek as a lamb, but there is strong evidence to suggest that she did not go willingly into that dark and cold place – in fact she put up quite a struggle.

David and Diana Maund's motor barge was berthed at Cuckstool Wharf, a mere seventy-five yards from the workshop, on the opposite bank of the slow-moving River Trent. They were both sitting in the lounge when they heard screaming, which David later described as 'hysterical'. He heard the words, 'Leave me alone! Leave me alone!' Later, Diana was to tell police that she had heard a man's voice say on a couple of occasions, 'You'll be all right now.' She also recalled hearing car doors slamming. The noises lasted about four minutes, but the Maunds did not investigate its source.

With Julie now chained and captive in a box in his workshop, Sams made several botched attempts to blackmail her parents and the police for ransom, all of which signally failed despite the police coming very close to catching him on several occasions. Sadly, the next time anyone saw Julie again was at 7.30 a.m. on Monday 8 July, by now reduced to decomposing corpse in Broadwalk Field, Lincolnshire:

I pulled into the entrance of the field, which is adjacent to the railway line. I immediately saw on my right a bundle under a tree. It was clearly visible, and there had been no attempt to hide it. At that time I presumed it was litter left by people using the lane. I went over to it and saw it was a white sheet with a pink stripe. The bundle was tied up very well with bluish rope. There appeared to be three wrappings around the bundle and one lengthways. It was very secure.

Farmer Robert Derek Skelton,
aged fifty: to police.

The body appeared to have been wrapped in a white sheet in such a way that the top and bottom ends of the sheet were situated at the head end, while the centre of the sheet covered the undersurface of the body, the buttocks and the back.

At the head end, the sheet was heavily soiled with blood and fluid from the putrefying body, [and the head] – which was flexed and tucked into the right shoulder region – was badly decomposed.

Numerous flies, occasional beetles and earwigs were present in the vicinity of the head end of the body. Numerous small larvae were present on the outside and inside of the opened sheet in the vicinity of the head.

Professor John Stephen Jones: Home Office
pathologist, Royal College of Pathologists

Following the safe release of estate agent Stephanie Slater in early 1992, for some weeks the police and the BBC had been putting together what Nick Ross, co-presenter of *Crimewatch UK*, called a 'considered package'. This included a profile of the offender; details of the orange Metro car, an artist's impressions of the kidnapper/extortionist/killer of Julie Dart/ kidnapper of Stephanie Slater; and more importantly, a tape recording of the Slater's kidnapper's voice which had been taped when he had called to book an appointment. There was also a distinctive railway badge on Michael's jacket that Stephanie remembered, and a sketch of this would also be shown on air.

The *Crimewatch UK* coverage of the case was screened at 9.30 on Thursday, 20 February 1992, but ITV's *News at Ten* the same evening would also feature the police's appeal to the public. The police felt that this was a last-ditch attempt to catch their man but also their best chance yet. Millions of viewers would tune in hoping to hear the voice of a person they knew so that they could claim the £175,000 reward for his capture.

Rehearsals had gone well. The principal investigator, Detective Chief Superintendent Tom Cook, who was to appear on the programme, had briefed the producer methodically, saying: 'If someone knows the face, knows the voice, knows the car, knows the location and it's within an area we are particularly interested in, then clearly that's going to score six out of six, and that will be given first-priority action. That's the way we are tackling it.'

Fifty telephone lines with an 088 number would trip through to three specifically adapted incident rooms in anticipation of a flood of calls. In front of each officer was a 'score sheet'; as the information came through, the calls eliciting the highest number of 'ticks' would be given top priority. For British Telecom, the company Sams had used so frequently in his blackmail and extortion schemes, it would be payback time: unbeknownst to Michael Sams the clock was ticking down for him too, for engineers had worked overtime fitting tape facilities in case the killer decided to ring in, and each line was linked to the digital tracing network.

Elsewhere, Sams's former wife Susan Oake was going

out that evening, and she set her video to record the programme while sons Charles and Robert would watch it live. Meanwhile, Sams had arrived at Eaves Cottage with chocolates and crisps. He was flush with the cash he'd successfully extorted during the Stephanie Slater kidnap-for-ransom job. He changed out of his overalls into a pair of tracksuit bottoms and a casual sweatshirt, and he was about to see, and hear, himself on television – smugly, he intended to be comfortable, thinking that now he was home and dry, the show would be a waste of time.

As the red battery-operated clock between the Georgian window and the bag of clothes pegs showed 8.30 p.m. Teena washed up in the neat little kitchen. She wiped the cream Formica worktops with a cloth, quietly moving the chrome chairs back under the table and watered her plants before joining her husband on the beige velvet sofa in the lounge. 'He seemed very quiet,' she told me. 'It was not like him at all. Normally he'd find something to complain about, but he was very quiet, just staring vacantly at an engine name-plate [Royal Tanks Corps] hanging above our stone fireplace.' The television's sound had been turned down for a moment and there was only the bubbling murmur of the fish tank next to it. 'Actually' Teena added, ' ... he poured himself a glass of wine, not me though. He always kept a rack of plonk in an alcove in the lounge in case visitors arrived. But no one ever did.'

I think I can picture this scene now, can you?

Teena, distracted, intently gazed at the scores of brass ornaments and horse brasses that she *had* to keep clean or risk facing Michael's wrath. Had she missed any of them, would

Michael notice a speck of dust? Can you see Teena now – almost a nervous wreck, watching her husband gorge on the chocolates and drink *his* wine? Then, as soon as *Crimewatch UK* came on air, he turned up the volume and settled back on the sofa. 'For the first time in months he held my hand ... ' she told me, with tears in eyes, ' ... it was *as if* he needed me.' Then Sams heard his own voice; he saw the artist's impression of him, heard an exact description of his orange Metro car, the strange gait and the railway badge – it was *HIM*!

Fifteen million people watched that programme and the switchboards simply couldn't cope. Charles and Robert Sams recognised their father immediately; both were stunned. But as Teena watched every minute of the programme and took in the description of a vicious killer – who was sitting right next to her, holding her hand – it still didn't cross her mind that Michael Benneman Sams was the man everyone was looking for – or did it? It seems almost inconceivable that Teena of all people didn't cotton on to the fact that her husband was the man being hunted nationwide by police. As I recall, when I met her she had excellent eyesight and was not hard of hearing, either.

When the programme finished, Sams got up to take Bonnie the German shepherd for a walk. Teena recalled: ' ... and as he closed the door behind him, he called out to me, "Don't be surprised if the police don't come around in about six months about the Metro."' They would certainly call about the Metro, but not in six months – they'd be at Eaves Cottage in the morning.

When Sams's former wife, Susan, returned home, switched on her television and watched the video recording of the

Crimewatch programme, she too heard her former husband's voice and recognised it immediately. 'I was entirely convinced it was *his* voice,' she soon told detectives. 'There was no doubt in my mind. Hearing it had such an effect on me that I became traumatised and suffered shock.' Then her two sons telephoned her to confirm what she knew by now. In a state bordering on hysteria, she rang the police.

The Julie Dart incident room's number hadn't been displayed on the programme, and Susan Oake's call came as something of a shock to DC Wayne Greenwood who wasn't expecting anything that evening, He recalled this in his evidence: 'At 11.15pm that evening I received a telephone call from a woman who sounded highly distressed and in a shocked condition.' The call lasted just a few moments and it is published here for the first time:

> *Susan: I've just heard a recording of his voice and I know who it is.*
> *DC Greenwood: Can you give his name, please?*
> *Susan: His name is Michael Sams. I've been married to him. You don't have to look any further.*
> *DC Greenwood: Can you give me your name please?*
> *Susan: Susan Oake. I live at Riddlesden, near Keighley. You've got to believe me, I know it's him.*

DC Greenwood then asked if Susan would like a police officer to visit her that evening and when she said that she would the police moved like lightning. Detective Superintendent Bob Taylor instructed DCs Dover and Newboult to call on Susan to obtain more information and within fifty-five minutes they were knocking on her door, to find her clearly distraught. She explained that her former husband, whom she called 'Mike', had a power-tool repair business in Newark, and that he was married to Teena with whom she shared a cottage in Barrel Hill Road, Sutton-on-Trent. Bit by bit, Susan slowly went through the links that had convinced her and her two sons that Sams was their man. He liked trains, he drove an orange car, the artist's impression of him was a great likeness, and the voice on the tape was definitely his.

'But he's got a limp,' she said. 'He had his right leg amputated years ago, he's got an artificial leg ... why hasn't someone mentioned the leg?' Months later, Susan would describe some of the moments of that interview as among the most frustrating of her life. 'I felt awful,' she said. 'Like I was betraying my family, my sons. This was their father.' However, that night, Sams's son Charles rang the West Midland's incident room. Stephanie had remembered her kidnapper's strange gait and the clicking as he walked. Only now would the West Yorkshire Police link Julie Dart's murder with the kidnapping of Stephanie Slater. It was like the domino effect – when one piece falls over the remainder follow. Moreover, with some 600 calls being received that night from people who were sure they knew whom the man was, it was not surprising to learn that Sams was low on the West Midland Police suspect list (primarily because they were told by Charles that Sams had only one leg), although Leeds put him down as No. 1. During the following days, over a thousand possible suspects were named, but only Susan and her sons got it right.

* * *

Sams spent his last night of freedom in a restless sleep. His leg was playing him up, and his mind was playing tricks on him. He knew the police could come for him at any moment, but he couldn't let Teena suspect anything, so although he needed her she would have to sleep in the spare bedroom once again. By dawn he was already awake so he made a cup of tea and a bowl of porridge.

He shouted goodbye to Teena, and looked for the last time at his Suzuki standing next to her own scooter in the utility room of Eaves Cottage. Even the walls in this part of the house were covered in railway memorabilia, including engine numbers and nameplates: 'The White Rose', 'The Talisman' and 'Yorkshire Pullman'. Only one item looked out of place: a white plastic plant box filled with damp earth. Sams had brought the dirt back after his walk with the dog. It would fill Teena's seed trays.

Earlier that morning, Bob Taylor had listened intently as DS Tim Grogan and DCs Greenwood and Dover briefed him about the previous day's events. (DC Newboult had the day off.) Taylor made a few short telephone calls to other officers, and despatched DS Grogan and DCs Paul Leach, Greenwood and Dover, to Sutton-on-Trent, where they arrived at 10.40 a.m. They were allowed entry into the cottage by a nervous Teena.

The presence of railway memorabilia in the cottage indicated a deep-seated interest in trains, but the Suzuki scooter meant nothing to the cops at that moment. The officers asked where Michael Sams was. Teena explained that he would be at his workshop, T&M Tools, in Newark. As they walked back to their car, Teena called out: 'He's probably expecting you. He said you might want to talk to him about his Metro. He'll be home at five o'clock.'

The detectives drove slowly up Barrel Hill then they drove like hell to Newark, where they arrived at 11.10 a.m. After a little searching, they found Swan and Salmon Yard and as they swung under the archway the first vehicle they spotted was Sams's orange Austin Metro, index no. VWG 386Y. It matched precisely the description given by an eagle-eyed car paint sprayer, Pervis Barnaby, who saw when Sams dropped estate agent Stephanie Slater off at her home after he had picked up the ransom money paid by her employers. Plus, the downward slope of the yard fitted the details given by Stephanie. Tim Grogan was moved to say, 'This is like driving down Wembley Way'.

At 11.20 a.m., the extremely excited detectives left their vehicle and entered the workshop via the heavy wooden sliding door on its metal runners. Inside was another door on which a sign indicated that the business was closed on Wednesdays. Smartly suited Tim Grogan called out, and Sams limped into the retail area from the rear of the place. 'What is it you want?' he asked abruptly. Grogan identified himself as a police officer, telling Sams that he was conducting enquiries into the murder of Julie Anne Dart. Walking past Sams, the officer noticed a long wooden beam in the roof running the width of the premises. 'I've been expecting you,' said Sams. 'My wife has just phoned me.'

DS Grogan noticed the hairs on the backs of Michael's hands – just as Stephanie had described. DC Leach saw the old-fashioned telephone, while DC Greenwood pointed to a number of stencils on a shelf. An old radio on another workshop shelf was playing music. DC Dover asked Sams: 'Can you tell me the station your radio is tuned to?' Sams replied: 'Radio Two. I have it on all day,' again as Stephanie Slater had described.

Grogan had seen more than enough. He led Sams to the shop counter. 'I am arresting you,' he said, following this with the traditional caution. Sams replied, 'You've got the wrong man. You're making a big mistake.' He was told to empty his pockets, and while DC Dover went to telephone Bob Taylor to tell him the news, the shop doorbell rang, sounding like the old-fashioned cash register that Stephanie had heard. Michael Sams was taken into Newark Police Station at precisely 11.40 a.m.

* * *

On Wednesday, 9 June 1993, the trial of Michael Benneman Sams was about to begin. As he arrived at Nottingham's Crown Court, cameramen rushed to snap that ever-elusive photograph but the van's windows had been blacked out. Sams was wearing a smart, well-pressed blue suit for the occasion, and to give himself a studious appearance, he wore gold-rimmed spectacles.

After Mr Justice Igor Judge settled on his bench, the clerk rose to her feet to read the indictment:

> *Members of the jury: Michael Benneman Sams is charged on Count One of this indictment with murder, in that on a day between the 8th and 20th days of July 1991, he did murder Julie Anne Dart.*
>
> *On Count Two of this indictment, he is charged with*

*kidnap, in that between the 8th and 11th days of July
1991, he did unlawfully, and by force or fraud, take or
carry away Julie Anne Dart against her will.*

*On Count Three of this indictment, he is charged
with blackmail in that on the 12th day of July 1991,
with a view to gain for himself, in a letter post-
marked Huntingdon, the 11th of July 1991, and
addressed to the Leeds City Police, he made an
unwarranted demand of £140,000 from the police
with menaces.*

The other charges were slowly read out, with Count Four
being the second blackmail attempt against the police
contained in a letter dated Monday, 22 July 1991, and Count
Five being an attempted blackmail of British Rail. Sams
pleaded 'not guilty' to all counts.

The judge spent all of Wednesday, 7 July, summing up the
overwhelming evidence against Sams. He told the jury that
Sams was not to be convicted of one crime simply because he
had admitted his guilt in another. Urging the jury to use their
common sense, he said:

*The defendant's case is that another man was the
criminal. He does not have to prove it … you are
entitled to say that this account of an unidentified friend
is untruthful fiction, designed to deceive you, to enable
the defendant to avoid responsibility for the crimes. But
on the other hand, if you believe his account, then you
must acquit him …*

The following morning, the judge spent ninety minutes finishing his summing up. He brilliantly encapsulated the entire case with the words: ' ... and the question may be: is he hiding someone else, or is he hiding himself?'

At 11.42 a.m. the jury retired to consider their verdict: three-and-a-half hours later they walked back into court and returned guilty verdicts on all counts of murder, kidnap and blackmail. As Sams stood in the dock, not a flicker of emotion crossed his face when the judge told him:

> *You are an extremely dangerous and evil man. The jury has convicted you of murder, a murder in cold blood. You deliberately strangled her [Julie Dart] and beat her to death when your kidnapping went wrong because she saw more than she should. You tried to turn her death to your advantage. You were heartless at the grief you had caused. It was misplaced pride and callous arrogance.*

The judge, who had remained dispassionate throughout the entire trial, was now allowed to show his contempt towards the criminal in the dock: 'The letters that you wrote make chilling reading – no qualms, no remorse.'

Referring to Stephanie Slater, the judge remarked:

> *I have not the slightest doubt that she was in desperate and mortal danger for the first two or three days of her captivity. If it seemed necessary to you, she, like Julie Dart, would have been murdered in cold blood. Her survival was entirely due to her remarkable moral courage and the unostentatious display of qualities of character.*

The ordeal which you inflicted on her is something the rest of us can only imagine. The reality must have been far worse. You are, for an indefinite future, a menace to the community. There is an urgent necessity to protect the public from harm by you.

Mr Justice Judge then imposed four life sentences – one for each kidnapping, one for Julie's murder and one for Stephanie's unlawful imprisonment. Sams was also sentenced to ten years for each charge of demanding money with menaces – all these sentences were to run concurrently, which means that one day Michael Benneman Sams might limp painfully back to freedom.

So, what did Teena Sams make of all this?

It has to be stressed that there is no suggestion whatsoever that Teena had the slightest inkling that her husband was committing such atrocious crimes, and, of course, she has *not* seen the scenes-of-crime photos of Julie lying decomposing in the farmer's field as I have done. Neither has she read the hundreds of police documents, all of the extortion letters Michael wrote, nor did she hear the first-hand evidence given by Stephanie Slater.

Nor has Teena had access to the material that police recovered from the hard drive on his computer as I have. Indeed, on that last night of his freedom, there they were, sitting watching *Crimewatch UK*, and she didn't even bat an eyelid when there he was, *her husband*, photofit, voice and all, staring straight back into her face from the TV screen. However, she had learned of the judge's scathing sentencing remarks, so one might have thought that having suffered so much spousal abuse and knowing about Mr Justice Judge's strong words, she would have never, *ever*, been in contact with this evil, sick and murderous man again. Yet what was to follow almost beggars belief.

* * *

Following his arrest, Michael Sams spent some time on remand in three of Her Majesty's prisons but enjoyed the confines of HMP Winson Green, Birmingham, above all, for almost as soon as his cell door was slammed shut he spent long hours writing to Teena, decorating each letter (all fifty or so which I later obtained) with quite competent drawings of roses coloured with crayon. It makes one want to cringe.

Having accessed his prison file, I confirm that Sams was locked away under Rule 43 (protective custody) because it was thought that the other inmates would treat him like scum or worse. It was his claim to me that the officials placed him in protective custody of their own accord, which is incorrect: an inmate has to apply to be placed into this segregation before it becomes active. The truth is that he was terrified and begged to be put someplace safe and that's the truth of it! Nevertheless, this despicable man wrote to Teena that he was constantly being offered £5.00 for his signature and that the other prisoners treated him like a lord.

Sams's earlier letters *indicated* a desire to help his wife with the obvious financial problems – all of his own making – that she was encountering during her husband's incarceration. In other words, having indifferently and completely wrecked her life, he was now callously suggesting how *she* could sort out the God-awful mess that *he* had left behind. He advised her to change her name and open a different bank account. Then, in almost the same breath, he asked her to make sure that he received the *Star* and the *Sunday People* newspapers, along with the monthly *Railway Magazine*, which, in happier days had been his favourite reading. These subscriptions she was to pay for at £6.50 a month – about £214 today. Time and again, he would demonstrate his love for figures and calculations, at one point going to perhaps extreme lengths to work out his prison sentence in terms of years and months, with time off for good behaviour. Yet, NOT ONCE in all of his letters did I find *a single* word of contrition or remorse for what he had done to his wife, or for the suffering he had caused to his two female victims, their families and friends.

What with the excellent food (which Sams claimed he ate too much of, all specially cooked for him by the prison's chefs), the sweets, listening to football matches on the radio and the long hours of 'peace and quiet' in a place he called 'home', seemingly, Sams had little else to complain about in his so-called 'Life of Riley', except how ' ... I suffer the most by the time delays in getting to trial'.

Page after page, his letters contain little more than sentimental and untruthful drivel about his undying love for Teena. This was somewhat balanced by descriptions of his busy prison life – the hours of sleep and rest, excellent medical treatment, hot food 'served on time' three times a day, to the last of which he added cynically, 'Yes, Teena, three times a day *is something you should learn to do* when I am released and back home.' Then there were his new inmate friends; how they wanted his autograph and how his fellow cons cheered him every time he walked out to meet them – all from a man who had literally got down on his one good knee to beg to be placed under Rule 43 Protective Custody. And, for a time, he immersed himself in writing poetry, with one particular piece of literary work beginning:

> At the end of the day, I just sit and pray.
> I say thank you Teena for being my love today.

Even after eating his prison breakfast of porridge, Sams was capable of bursting into rhyme:

> Did you remember what I did say.
> That you eat your porridge every day.
> For just each day to gain that extra pound or two,
> More if you want but a pound will do.

As his trial approached, Sams's feeling towards Teena underwent a mercurial sea change, for a woman named Victoria Vinchelli had been writing to him and love was in the air.

The *Star* newspaper would later describe forty-one-year-old 'Vicky' as 'Sams' Bit on the Side' and his 'Lonely Divorcee Pen Pal'. Sams would spitefully tell Teena that 'V' – as he called Vicky – was the best-looking woman he'd ever seen.

As their relationship deepened, Vicky would visit Sams at Winson Green. Once, as Teena arrived at the prison gates, she recognised 'V'. Callously, Sams refused to see his wife, preferring instead to sit with his new admirer.

This was a woman I simply *had* to interview during the research for *Unmasking Mr Kipper*, and without wishing to be crude, let's say that on meeting her I found that she was all that the *Star* had described her to be. Nevertheless, 'V' showed me the many 'love letters' written to her by 'Hot Mike'; how he lusted over her figure, bragged about how other inmates treated him like a prison overlord and gloated about the 'happiest days of my life', when he'd held Stephanie Slater captive. He also freely confessed to cruelly beating two of his three wives.

In mitigation, Vicky later told a growing band of paparazzi that she had felt 'sorry' for Michael Sams, whom she had originally believed to be innocent. She was 'lonely', and he seemed as if 'he needed someone to love him'.

Now here is something that one doesn't get to do every day as a criminologist, but it all comes down to learning something new once in a while. Out came the photograph albums showing her posing in a variety of revealing outfits. Her council flat was reached via a flight of concrete stairs, and during my visit our 'Miss Lonely' unsuccessfully tried to sell me me some of Michael's letters, blowing me sly kisses as I made a very rapid exit.

Perhaps Vicky did feel sorry for Sams; perhaps she felt 'lonely', although it has to be said that it didn't appear that way as she did some heavy breathing during the number of telephone calls she took while I was there. Maybe she felt sorry for herself now that the *Star* and *Sunday People* had exposed her in racy headlines to her neighbours. And, to be fair to this sad soul, she later claimed that she was 'horrified' by Sams's chilling crimes and regretted the 'relationship'. Yet this did not prevent her from selling her story to the press, with revealing photographs of her across the front pages. She soon had another complaint: she was forced out of her council flat for fear of reprisals – not from the men, I hasten to add, but their wives. She now lives in London at a secret address.

* * *

All that aside, once a relationship has disintegrated, it should *stay* disintegrated. So by now the reader might have expected that, at long last, Teena would have realised that her relationship with Michael was over and her love for him well and truly rejected. But no. Although she still continued to profess her love for this monster, this cowardly murderous scumbag, his correspondence to her became increasingly vindictive.

He wrote that he'd previously bedded a former Miss Venezuela while she was staying in England in the early 1980s. (The woman in question has categorically denied such a relationship ... and I can believe her, because at the time she was dating some sort of bronzed *Baywatch* hunk, so I can hardly imagine that a one-legged tool-mender would have held much attraction.) He also claimed in his letters to the still besotted Teena that he had been fortunate to escape this Venezualan's clutches: 'Luckily, I went to Thailand the next day on business,' he said. His employers at that time – Black & Decker – told me that he was never sent abroad on business for them; however, my examination of his passport did reveal that he had gone to Bangkok on holiday in December 1981 – at a time, incidentally, when Miss Venezuela was about 17,346 km further west. YET, in all of these letters, almost as titbits to keep Teena onside,

Michael continued to swear his undying love for her – sort of keeping her on her toes, if you will.

* * *

Who am I to judge Teena Sams? – for we *all* have to make our way through our lives as best we can. That said, what I do find utterly reprehensible are those women who knowingly court the attention of evil monsters such as Michael Sams. Have they no conscience, no soul; are they as cold-blooded and as indifferent to the pain and suffering caused by the likes of Sams as the killer himself; are they plain stupid; or are they a combination of all those? I think that maybe they are – either that, or they are amoral idiots who truly do need to get a real life, instead of existing in a fantasy world where killers are somehow absolved of responsibility for their crimes.

Here is the endnote: after I had been been 'gifted' Michael's Suzuki Love scooter and his orange Metro by Teena, with her claiming that the car was attracting unwelcome attention parked up in her front garden, some years later she demanded their return – the drift of which, I gather was, Michael wanted the scooter and the car sold so that he could have some funds.

A bit late in the day, I wrote a most courteous letter to him:

Dear Michael aka Mr Lettin. Long time no hear. Hope all is going great for you in prison. The Metro was a runner for a short time but I couldn't MOT it because the police cut out the seat belts. I scrapped it. The colour of the moped was not quite suitable for my exacting requirements: blue, yes, but not ever plum. I scrapped that too. Please inform Mrs Teena Sams. When you are not too busy, please say hello to John Cannan from me. Thank you. Christopher.

I never received a reply from Sams, and not a squeak out of John Cannan, either ... I wonder why?

Sandy Fawkes v. Paul John Knowles
(USA)

There is nothing glamorous about the Michael Sams case; nothing in the entire sordid affair that resonates with 'The Sunshine State' of Florida. Nor does the awkward figure of Sams resonate with the tall, broad-shouldered young man with gaunt good looks, reddish-gold hair and a moustache to match – he being the rangy twenty-eight-year-old Paul John Knowles, aka 'the Casanova Killer', with whom we will now acquaint ourselves.

Unlike Teena Sams, whose marriage to a killer left her with nothing, there are women who do sleep with the enemy and who *do* come out ahead, as was the case with the British journalist Sandy Fawkes (1929–2005). First, to set the scene for what could have become a very real fatal attraction, the date is Thursday, 7 November 1974. The location is a darkened bar in the Holiday Inn, Atlanta, Georgia. Sandy, aged forty-five, was on a working holiday from the *Daily Express* newspaper in London, and had just flown in from Washington on an assignment for the *National Enquirer* – an American tabloid anxious at that time to recruit British journalists.

Much earlier, in 1949, Sandy had married Walter 'Wally' Ernest Fawkes, a British-Canadian jazz clarinettist, political cartoonist (usually under the pen name 'Trog') and author of the cartoon strip *Flook* that ran for thirty-five years. Sadly, the marriage did not survive the death in infancy of one of their four children, and they divorced in the early 1960s. In that decade Sandy was a fashion artist for the *Daily Sketch*, the *Observer*, *Vogue*, *Vanity Fair*, and then in the 1970s, a feature writer for the aforementioned *Daily Express*.

Weather-wise, that Thursday in November 1974 had been a typical Georgia day; but by evening the the afternoon high of 25 degrees C had dropped to a cool 13 degrees. For Sandy, divorced and single, this trip to the USA was a great opportunity, but to meet a handsome, rich American would be even nicer. She picked a bad apple in the shape of Paul John Knowles, who murdered at least twenty people in 1974, and boasted of taking the lives of thirty-five. Sandy only just escaped with her life.

Upon spotting Sandy through the smoky gloom, Knowles moved in quickly. The hotel's bar was full of the usual collection of big, beefy men in open-necked shirts – all very much alone and seeking female company. He asked her for a dance; she refused, saying that she had to visit the local newspaper offices, the *Atlantic Constitution*, that evening to look up some information for a story she was working on. Knowles seemed fascinated in her job, and with that she left promising to return later. When she did, they went for a meal.

Wearing a soft suede jacket and flowery shirt with matching tie, perfectly fitting trousers and patent leather shoes, Knowles told Sandy that his name was 'Daryl Golden' and that he was in Atlanta to sort out a court case concerning a local woman who had had an accident in one of his father's restaurants – none of which was true. After that, Knowles said that he would be going to Miami while she said that she was soon about to fly to West Palm Beach, Florida. Knowles now made his next move – he offered to drive her there, so she could see some of the beautiful countryside.

The meal was great and when 'Daryl' paid the bill Sandy looked away politely, so as not to see the cost. For this reason she failed to see the signature on the credit card slip – it wasn't in the name of 'Golden', it was 'Knowles'. However, now feeling relaxed with this handsome younger man, she agreed to accompany him back to his hotel provided there were no strings attached. 'After all ... ' she joked, ' ... you might be another Boston Strangler for all I know.' She sealed the joke with a kiss, drawing back hastily because his moustache was so bristly. Nevertheless, they drank and danced until the early hours and when they went to his room he gallantly shaved off his moustache. This gesture so charmed her that she agreed to spend the night with him. But their lovemaking was disappointing: that night her 'Daryl Golden' was sadly impotent – it was the drink seemingly.

I am going to be killed. Soon. It might be two days or two months, I don't know when.

> Paul John Knowles: to Sandy Fawkes,
> night of 7/8 November 1974.

He didn't know it, but Knowles would be shot to death by a police officer on Wednesday, 18 December 1974, while attempting to escape from custody.

With Sandy still intending to fly out to Florida on her own, Knowles repeated his offer to drive her and added an intriguing proposition. He told her that he would like her to write a book about him, as he did not have long to live. He told her that he would soon be killed for something he had done in the past. He went on to say that he had recorded the events that would lead to his death. The taped confessions were safely locked away in his lawyer's office in Miami. The attorney was called Sheldon Yavitz.

Upon hearing Knowles's words, Sandy's ears pricked up because these were bound to appeal to her journalistic impulses and against her better judgement she accepted his offer. So early next morning, the pair set off from Atlanta on the long drive south of about ten hours covering 662 miles. True, there was plenty to see but Sandy was already starting to regret her decision. Her companion remained silent, broody and mysterious for most of the journey, refusing to give her any further details about his alleged sensational past life. Before long, she was convinced that she'd been conned, but as an inquisitive journalist by nature and profession, Sandy Fawkes *should* have spotted a number of giveaway clues about who this Daryl Golden *actually* was. There was a recent story about a gruesome double murder in Midgeville, Georgia, which he had torn out of a morning newspaper. Then there were his fancy clothes – the silk shirts and the brocade jackets – which did not seem to fit with the sleeping bags and the jumble of belongings in the back of his car.

Finally, there was the childish Micky Mouse watch, which he gave her as a present, fastening it around her wrist.

By the time they reached West Palm Beach, Sandy was becoming anxious to disentangle herself from this younger man, but it would not be so easy. To start with, he insisted on joining her when she went to meet her new colleagues on the *National Enquirer* who were staying at Hotel Fontainebleau, even though he was hopelessly out of his depth amongst the boisterous crowd of reporters. He also drove her across to Miami, where, ironically, given that she had a serial killer by her side, she interviewed William Saxbe, the then Attorney General, about the US parole system.

That night, Knowles and Fawkes stayed together at the Fontainebleau, the most renowned hotel in Miami – a great curved building overlooking the sea and furnished with the utmost luxury. Incidentally, exactly a week after they stayed there, on 20 November, John Thomson Stonehouse, the British Labour MP and former cabinet minister (1925–88), staged a 'disappearance' from the beach in order to escape pressing financial difficulties. Leaving a pile of clothes on the beach, it appeared that he had gone swimming and had either drowned or possibly been killed by a shark. I can testify that he neither drowned nor was eaten by Jaws, for he was found completely dry just over a month later in Australia. Charged with embezzlement, he served four years in prison.

At last, the time came for Sandy and 'Daryl' to say goodbye. On the afternoon of Wednesday, 13 November, she told him that she had to start organising her return to London and thanked him for looking after her so well during the past week. As she watched his white Chevrolet Impala glide away from the hotel's car park, she heaved a sigh of relief, now very pleased to see the back of him. However, the next day she learned to her shock and horror that he had returned to the hotel later that evening while she was out – he had intended to kill her.

At 2 p.m. on Thursday, 14 November, a call came in for Sandy at the offices of the *National Enquirer*. Detective Sergeant Gabbard at West Palm Beach police station was anxious to speak to her. He refused to discuss anything over the telephone so Sandy assumed that her lover's premonition had come true – perhaps he had crashed his car or committed suicide? The truth, however, was far worse than even she could have imagined for while Knowles was waiting for her to return to her room the previous night, as fate would have it a couple of her colleagues recognised him from the reporters' get-together, and presumed that Sandy had stood him up. Jim and Susan Mackenzie took pity on this lonely-looking character and invited him to stay with them overnight. The next morning, Knowles offered Susan a ride to the hairdresser's and she happily agreed, but on the way he pulled out a gun and demanded sex. Fortunately, Susan had her wits about her – she struggled free and was rescued by someone in a passing car.

Sandy was stunned when she learned of this, and her confusion mounted when the police showed her a file card from their criminal records. Underneath the photo of her handsome young lover 'Daryl' there was an unfamiliar name – 'Paul John Knowles'. When pressed, reluctantly she had to accept that she had spent the week with a man described as a petty criminal who had jumped bail in Jacksonville, in the north of the state. Stumbling over her words, Sandy related the story about the tapes and the mysterious attorney in Miami, but the police casually dismissed her account as nonsense and allowed her to leave ... they'd soon be talking to her again.

Later, at 9 p.m., the cops were back and took Sandy to be interviewed again, but this time they were openly hostile, for during that afternoon, Knowles had wormed his way into the home of a woman confined to a wheelchair and had abducted her sister, Barbara Tucker. Worse still, the police had received word from the Georgia Bureau of Investigation (GBI) that Knowles was under suspicion for the Midgeville murders. This case was still seen as the work of two people and it rapidly dawned on Sandy that she was no longer being regarded by the law as just a gullible, eccentric foreigner – oh God, she was being interviewed as an accessory to a double murder.

* * *

With its population of around 15,500, the city of Midgeville is in the county seat of Baldwin County, just northeast of Macon, Georgia, and, in 1974, it was the home of Carswell Carr, his wife and their fifteen-year-old daughter Mandy.

In the crisp early autumn morning of Wednesday, 6 November, Mrs Carr returned home from her nightshift at a local hospital to find that her neat and tidy home had been ransacked: the furniture had been overturned and ornaments smashed on the floor, the curtains and upholstery slashed to ribbons. Terrified, she rushed to her husband's den where he sometimes slept on the divan, but when she found him there, he was not asleep – Carswell was naked, covered in blood, face down with his hands tied behind his back. He was dead.

Mrs Carr then rushed upstairs to Mandy's room. Here, she found her teenaged daughter lying face upwards on her bed. Her hands were bound behind her back, a knotted nylon stocking was around her neck and another stocking had been stuffed down her throat. Police were called after Mrs Carr's screams alerted her neighbours. However, what follows – revealing just how close Sandy Fawkes came to a terrifying death after sleeping with the enemy – is not for the faint-hearted.

The investigating officer, Assistant Police Chief Charles Osborne, was shocked by the scene he found at the Carrs' home. In his part of the world most of the murders he dealt with were either the result of domestic fights or of too much 'moonshine' – the rough alcohol distilled illegally in them tha hillbilly hills. Indeed, if the reader thinks back to the 1972 movie, *Deliverance*, starring Burt Reynolds, Jon Voight and Ned Beatty, that is backwoods Georgia in a 110-minute scare you shitless cinematic summary. Nonetheless, the medical examiner pronounced that the murders had taken place at some time between 11.30 p.m. the night before and 3 a.m. that morning. Mr Carr had twenty-seven shallow wounds that appeared to have been inflicted with scissors. Osborne could not be sure whether the father had died from his multiple stab wounds or from a heart attack brought on by the assault. With that said, it was the ME's opinion that the scissors had been used to torment the victim for the killer's pleasure rather than to wound fatally. The killer was a sadist.

Of Mandy's cause of death, there was no doubt. She had been strangled with tremendous force. Indeed, the pathologist had difficulty extracting the stocking that had been stuffed down her throat – it took him fifteen minutes. He also discovered that she had been raped, although no semen was present.

No fingerprints of any evidentiary value were to be found, but certain items had been stolen from the house. These were mostly distinctive clothes from Carswell Carr's wardrobe – evening suits with brocade matador jackets, flowered shirts with matching ties, cashmere polo-necked sweaters, elegantly cut blazers in flamboyant colours, patent leather shoes and belts, and a mottled brown leather briefcase with a matching shaving bag. Carswell Carr had met his future killer in a local gay bar. After a few drinks he'd invited Paul John Knowles back to spend the night with him.

Furthermore, among the items taken from Mandy's room was a digital clock, and her killer had also removed her Micky Mouse watch from her wrist – the very same watch that Knowles had given to Sandy Fawkes as some kind of perverse, sick trophy.

* * *

The reader will be relieved to learn that, although the hunt for Paul John Knowles rapidly gathered pace, Barbara Tucker was found unharmed on Friday, 15 November. He had simply trussed her up and stolen her car. Any relief, however, was short-lived as it soon became apparent that two further hostages had been taken. State Trooper Charles E. Campbell had vanished near the Florida border, as had a James E. Myers, whose blue Ford Gran Torino was being used as the getaway car.

The hunt for Knowles involved helicopters, as well as large numbers of police on the ground. At a roadblock, Knowles smashed the stolen Gran Torino into the barricade and fled into the woods. It was a member of the public – a bespectacled, bookish-looking David T. Clark, who finally captured him. Clark, a Vietnam veteran, saw Knowles emerging into a clearing at the bottom of his garden and challenged the fugitive with his shotgun. Trooper Campbell and Mr Myers were found tied to a tree; both had been killed with a shot to the back of the head.

Paul John Knowles was shot dead on 18 December 1974 by Special Agent Ron Angel of the Georgia Bureau of Investigation (GBI), as he and Sheriff Earl Lee were transporting the killer to the maximum-security jail in Douglas County. Ron had been manacled to Knowles for all of his court appearances and while his charge was throwing his head back and forth and laughing for the cameras, Angel had always kept his shaven head bowed. He was a taciturn man who made no secret of his loathing for the media circus surrounding Knowles. In the sheriff's car, Knowles had picked open his handcuffs and reached forward to the front seat to take Lee's pistol from its holster.

Knowles died aged twenty-eight, and is buried at the Jacksonville Memory Gardens, Orange Park, Florida, where a small bronze plaque marks the grave. The Baptist minister who conducted the funeral service refused to include the words, ' ... and may his soul rest in peace.'

In 1977, Sandy Fawkes published an account of her involvement with Paul John Knowles. Entitled *Killing Time*, the book became a bestseller and was translated into nine languages. In it she disclosed 'intimate details' about the time they spent together – detailing a few nights of attempting to have sex with a young hunk, who was, by her own admission, 'impotent'. She said in later interviews that she had written so explicitly about Knowles's sexual inadequacies because of the: ' ... assumptions people often make about violent criminals having voracious sexual appetites'. To give Sandy her due, at the end of the day she did come out on top after sleeping with the enemy, for her experience was, as she once said: 'The True Crime Story of a Lifetime'.

Well, maybe yes, maybe no. Sandy Fawkes's account of how she had an 'intimate relationship' with Knowles without realising that he was a depraved sadosexual serial killer is not the only one of its kind, because in our next chapter we turn to Ann Rule *v*. Ted Bundy – so it seems that sleeping with the enemy can be, with a great deal of 'Thank God he didn't kill me' hindsight, a very profitable exercise after all. Damn it – the closest I have come to such an experience was a proposal of marriage from serial killer Rose West, which I politely declined.

Ann Rule v. Ted Bundy (USA)

I suspect that everything there is to know about Ted Bundy is already known, so there is no need for me to go through his life and his crimes here. But his relationship with Ann Rule fits well with this book.

In the 1991-released movie, *Sleeping with the Enemy*, Julia Roberts plays the wife of a millionaire investment counsellor-cum-psychopath, played by Patrick Bergin. The film critic Roger Ebert described the couple as: ' ... presumably having a place in town somewhere, but all their domestic scenes together are spent in their luxurious summer home at the beach where the husband ... institutes a reign of psychological and physical terror.'

There is a lot of fancy cinematography going on in this film, but deep down Bergin's character epitomises one of those narcissistic men who sees his wife as both a possession and a servant. To him she is 'arm candy' to show off at parties because this supports his underlying fragile ego, but at home he lashes out at her if the towels are not perfectly straightened in the bathroom, or the tins of food are not lined up on the shelves with military precision. Yes, of course this is star-spangled Hollywood-land, not rural Eaves Cottage, Barrel Hill, Sutton-on-Trent, we understand, but can we see some the parallels in spousal abuse between Bergin and Sams? I think we can, because like Teena Sams, Julia Roberts is allowed no will of her own, and when her husband strikes her for the first time, this scene sends an equally brutal impact into the minds of the audiences. Nevertheless, at the end of the day, whether one likes the film or not, *Sleeping with the Enemy* is more about domestic abuse than waking up one morning to have the police barge in to arrest one's husband because he is a serial killer – which Bergin's character in the film was not.

> *Yet, in reality, Ted loved things more than he loved people. He could find life in an old abandoned bicycle or an old car, and did feel a kind of compassion for these inanimate objects, more compassion than he could ever feel for another human being.*
>
> Ann Rule: *The Stranger Beside Me:*
> *The Shocking Inside Story*

American crime expert and author Ann Rae Rule (1931–2015) had an intimate three-year relationship with Robert Theodore 'Ted' Bundy. In her 1980 autobiography, *The Stranger Beside Me: The Shocking Inside Story*, she tells the reader not only of how Bundy had previously been a work colleague whom she considered a friend, but also of how she learned to her shock and horror that he was one of the most heinous sadosexual serial killers in contemporary criminal history. Nevertheless, during this three-year period, Ann says that Ted was always charming, kind, and considerate towards her and, as far as she could judge, 'he was polite and pleasant to others'. Of course, the Bundy who Ann Rule encountered was the blandly handsome and purely sociopathic serial murderer who was not content to only kill his victims but to make them suffer and degrade their remains in hauntingly inhuman ways.

Ann was an ex-cop who had become a crime correspondent for *True Detective* magazine, writing lurid tabloid accounts of crime stories from Oregon to the Canadian border, but it was when doing some voluntary work for a suicide hotline called the Crisis Clinic (an American equivalent of the Samaritans), that she came to encounter college student Ted Bundy as a colleague.

Ann developed a motherly affection for Ted. In her book, she describes her first meeting with him: 'He looked up and grinned. He was twenty-four then, but he seemed younger ... I liked him immediately. It would have been hard not to, even though there was a big age difference.' She also recalled: 'We had callers who became unconscious from overdoses many times ... but we always managed to keep the lines open ... if, as many people believe today, Ted Bundy took lives, he also saved lives. I know he did because I was with him when he did it.'

In 1974, Ann, then aged forty-two and a divorcee, was commissioned to write a feature on two unsolved crimes – murders later attributed to Ted Bundy.

* * *

Eighteen-year-old Joni Lenz (born Sharon Clark) shared an old-fashioned clapboard house with a number of other university students. When she failed to appear by mid-afternoon on 5 January 1974, friends went down to her basement bedroom to see if she had overslept. They found Joni unconscious, her face covered with blood. She had been hit over the head with a metal bar that had been wrenched from the bedframe. She had not been raped but the bar had been thrust into her vagina, causing lacerations. After more than a week in a coma, she recovered, but was unable to provide police with any useful information. The attack left her with brain damage.

Lynda Ann Healy, aged twenty-one, was seized by Bundy on Thursday, 31 January 1974. A tall, slender young woman with long dark hair and blue eyes, she worked as a weather forecaster for Northwest Ski Reports. Her body was found on Taylor Mountain, Washington State, on Monday, 3 March 1975.

Then, in July 1974, came the double murders of Janice Ott, aged twenty-three, and Denise Naslund, aged nineteen – both of whom disappeared from Lake Sammamish Park – and these killings caught Ann Rule's attention. King County Police, armed with a detailed description of their suspect and his car, posted fliers throughout the Seattle area. A composite sketch was printed in regional newspapers and broadcast on local television stations. Elizabeth Kloepfer, Ann Rule, a DES employee, and a University of Washington (UW) psychology professor all recognised the profile, the sketch and the car and all reported Bundy as a possible suspect. For her part, Rule became suspicious – this man sounded oddly enough like her friend Ted Bundy. The suspect, however, had driven a VW and, as far as she knew, Bundy did not possess a car so she decided to ask a police officer friend to check it out for her. It turned out that Ted Bundy did indeed drive a bronze VW 'Beetle'. Ann Rule now realised that her suspicions about her former work colleague had been well founded.

To be absolutely accurate, during the time Ann Rule intimately knew Bundy he was not out and about abducting, torturing and killing young women. Nevertheless, it came a chilling shock for her to suddenly realise that she had had what the tabloids call a 'steamy affair' with a monster metamorphosing inside of him. How she herself felt, when she learned of the true evil that was Ted Bundy is best described in her own words. What follows is an extract from *The Stranger Beside Me* (W. W. Norton, 1980, and subsequent revised editions), as Ann describes how she felt when she spoke to Bundy in jail for the last time:

> *I had long since managed a degree of detachment when dealing with photographs from homicide cases. They no longer upset me as they once did, although I make it a point not to dwell on them. By the time I stood in Shirley Lewis's office, I had seen thousands of body pictures. I had seen pictures of Kathy Devine and Brenda Baker in Thurston County, but that was months before it was known that there was a 'Ted'. Of course, there were no bodies to photograph in the other Washington cases, and I had had no access to Colorado or Utah pictures. Now,*

I was staring down at huge colour photographs of the damage done to girls young enough to be my daughters – at the handiwork of a man I thought I knew. That man who only minutes before had smiled the same old grin at me, and shrugged as if to say, 'I have no part of this'. It hit me with a terrible sickening wave. I ran to the ladies room and threw up.

For some additional reading, I strongly recommend *The Only Living Witness: A True Account Of Homicidal Insanity*, by Stephen G. Michaud and Huge Aynesworth. For any true-crime buff, the title of this definitive book truly does live up to its cover blurb – 'the book that tells all about murderer-rapist Ted Bundy – including his own horrifying words' – and I can tell you why.

Many years ago, while making the twelve-part TV documentary series, *The Serial Killers*, I travelled the 'Bundy Trail', from Seattle through to Utah ending up in Tallahassee, Florida, where Ted was finally arrested then executed in Starke Prison's electric chair at 7 a.m. on Tuesday, 24 January 1989. During my road trip, I met many of the principal players involved with Bundy's arrest and his trial, and they included attorney Larry Simpson. He allowed me to handle the original denture casts taken from Bundy that confirmed, through forensic odontology, that they exactly matched the bite marks found on the buttocks of Margaret Bowman, aged twenty-one, murdered at the Chi Omega sorority house in Tallahassee, Florida, on Sunday, 15 January 1978.

One final question remains: could, or would, Bundy have killed Ann Rule? The answer is obviously that he 'could

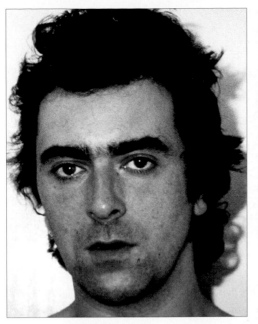

Top left: John Cannan, currently still in prison for murder, rape and abduction, and a suspected serial killer.

Top right: Suzy Lamplugh, the twenty-five year-old London estate agent who disappeared in July 1986 after arranging to meet a Mr Kipper for a viewing in Fulham. Police consider Cannan to be the prime suspect in the abduction and murder of Suzy.

Below: Police searching the area near where the decomposed body of Bristol businesswoman Shirley Banks was found, some six months after Cannan had abducted and murdered her.

Top left: Michael Benneman Sams – kidnapper, blackmailer, killer, amputee, tool repairman and railway enthusiast. His wife Teena was watching TV next to him when he appeared on *Crimewatch UK* over the murder of Julie Dart.

Top right: Stephanie Slater, the young estate agent whom Sams abducted and then released when her company paid him the ransom; he even drove her home.

Below: Eaves Cottage in Sutton-on-Trent, Nottinghamshire, where Michael and Teena Sams made their home, and where he was arrested in February 1992.

Left: October 1979: Kenneth Bianchi, 'the Hillside Strangler', is escorted by police officers after being brought from Bellingham, Washington State, to Los Angeles to be arraigned for the murders of five women there.

Right: Paul John Knowles, 'the Casanova Killer'. Arrested after a police chase in November 1974, he died while being transported by a sheriff and Special Agent Ron Angel of the GBI, who shot him after he tried to seize the sheriff's gun, 18 December 1974.

Left: Sandy Fawkes, the British journalist who had a brief fling with Knowles in Atlanta, Georgia, in November 1974, from which she was lucky to escape with her life.

Left: Theodore 'Ted' Bundy, a notorious serial killer who abducted, raped, tortured and murdered young women in seven US states in the 1970s; he eventually confessed to thirty killings.

Right: Ann Rule, the journalist and crime writer who knew Bundy intimately for three years. She wrote a bestselling book about him, thereby launching a very successful career as a crime writer; Bundy was executed in the electric chair on 24 January 1989.

Left: Police entering 10 Rillington Place, Notting Hill, London, after the discovery of corpses concealed there, 25 March 1953. The house, and indeed the street, no longer exist.

Left: John 'Reg' Christie, who murdered eight people, including his wife and a young baby, in his house at Rillington Place.

Right: Ethel, the long-suffering wife of 'Reg' Christie – her body was found under the floorboards in the front room of No. 10 Rillington Place. Christie was hanged on 15 July 1953.

Below: Sonia Sutcliffe snapped in London in 1984, three years after her husband had been jailed for life. She was later to win a libel case against the satirical magazine *Private Eye*, although the initial award of £600,000 was reduced by 90 per cent on appeal.

Above: Sonia Sutcliffe with her husband, Peter, later notorious as 'the Yorkshire Ripper'. Until his arrest, his wife was entirely unaware of his secret life as a murderer of sex workers and other women.

Above left: Mary Elizabeth Wilson, 'the Merry Widow of Windy Nook', who despatched four husbands and in 1958 was sentenced to hang for two of those murders. She was the last woman to be sentenced to death in Durham, though the sentence was commuted to life imprisonment, and she died in jail five years later.

Above right: Robert Lee Yates, presently serving a full life sentence for the murders of three women. His wife Linda and their four children were woken by investigators in the early hours of 18 April 2000, when Linda learned to her shock that her husband had been arrested for murder.

Below left: One half of 'the Ken and Barbie Killers' – Karla Homolka, also known as 'the Schoolgirl Killer'.

Below right: Homolka's husband, Paul Bernardo: 'between them they killed three or four women and committed some thirteen rapes between March 1986 and April 1992.'

Left: Police investigators outside the house in St Catharines, Ontario, rented by Homolka and Bernardo, 19 February 1993. The Canadian couple were convicted of several murders, but Homolka served only ten years after a plea bargain; Bernardo is serving life.

Right: Gary Ridgway, 'the Green River Killer', one of the most prolific serial killers in US history. In 2003 he was convicted of the murders of forty-nine women, and is serving a life sentence without parole.

Below: Rader's daughter, Kerri Rawson, was only fourteen when an FBI agent informed her that her father had just been arrested as a notorious serial killer.

Above: 'The BTK Killer', Dennis Rader, is escorted into the El Dorado Correctional Facility in Kansas, 19 August 2005. He was convicted of ten murders between 1974 and 1991, and is currently serving ten life sentences.

Top: In 2007, Rader's house in Park City, Kansas, was razed to the ground. His wife, Paula, had been granted an emergency divorce in 2005, and has never spoken publicly about her marriage.

Below left: Colin Pitchfork, the first murderer to be convicted and jailed using DNA evidence. He was handed a minimum thirty-year sentence in 1988 for the rape and murder of two schoolgirls, and was released on licence in 2021. Having breached the conditions, however, he was returned to prison in September that year.

Below right: 'The Werewolf' – Mikhail Popkov, the Russian former policeman convicted of raping and murdering fifty-nine women between 1992 and 2010, though the true figure is higher. His wife, Elena Popkova, still believes him to be innocent.

have', but I say that he 'would not have', simply because Ann, who was many years older than he, did not fall into his victimology type. By this I mean that Bundy had a 'preferred' victim category – one that he *never* strayed from – and this can be confirmed by the reader studying most of the young women's photographs, which are easily found on the Internet.

So, in one sense sleeping with the enemy certainly paid off big time for Ann Rule. The *Stranger Beside Me* (1980), was followed by *Lust Killer* (1983), *The I-5 Killer* (1984), *Small Sacrifices* (1987), *If You Really Loved Me* (1991), *Everything She Ever Wanted* (1992), *Dead By Sunset* (1995), *Bitter Harvest* (1997), *And Never Let Her Go* (1999), *Every Breath You Take* (2001), *Green River Running Red* (2004) and *Too Late to Say Goodbye* (2007).

Sadly, on Sunday, 26 July 2015, Rule's family and her publisher, Simon & Schuster, announced her death, which had occurred the day before, as a result of congestive heart failure. She had been moved to hospice care the day before she passed away, aged eighty-three.

God bless you, Ann Rule, for bringing millions of readers to your most excellent books – in part because you once slept with the enemy.

Ethel Christie v. John Reginald Halliday Christie (UK)

The price you pay for waltzing with the devil is residing in hell.

LORRAINE HEATH: *IN BED WITH THE DEVIL*
(*SCOUNDRELS OF ST. JAMES*, BOOK 1, 2008)

There are many folk unknowingly sleeping with someone who has murder most foul on their minds, and it is not always *another* person they intend to kill – for it could be *you*. One's partner is, for most of the time, acting normally; they do all the normal things around the home, their work ethic seems just fine. One might sense deep down that there is an unusual mood swing here or there, but can one even begin to imagine that one's death could be a heartbeat away – of course not!

In most cases where the secret plotting of murder is afoot, there are two kinds of motives: either an affair that has developed into the need to rid oneself of one's partner or spouse, or for monetary gain – more often than not a mix of both. Nevertheless, there are exceptions and one of the most notable and historic cases in the bleak annals of British criminal history is that of balding, bespectacled John 'Reg' Christie (1899–1953).

Immortalised in the book and film *10 Rillington Place*, we find in Christie a case all too well known and well documented to all of us aficionados of murder most foul. (I have covered his crimes, and his sickening psychopathology in some depth in *Talking with Psychopaths and Savages: Beyond Evil* [2019].)

Of particular interest to us is the undeniable fact that 'Reg' murdered eight people – including his wife Ethel whom we will return to momentarily – by strangling them in his seedy home at 10 Rillington Place, Notting Hill, London, during the postwar years of the 1940s and early 1950s. Perhaps more shocking is the tale of the two women he buried in the back garden where his wife hung the washing out to dry, and – wait for it – the story of how the bodies of lodger Beryl Susanna Evans, aged twenty, and her baby daughter Geraldine, aged fourteen months, were deposited in the washhouse right outside the back door.

The Christies had moved into 10 Rillington Place in 1938, when Christie had just turned forty. It was a cramped Victorian house, built on three storeys with a separate flat on each floor. The street was a cul-de-sac, and Number 10 was situated up against the high wall at the far end and overshadowed by an old foundry chimney. By 1953 its exterior was so ugly and depressing that it gave an overwhelming impression of neglect and desolation, made worse by the dirty curtains that hung from windows of Christie's rented ground-floor flat.

Of note: at the end of 1953, the house was put up for

sale for £1,500 – it has long since been demolished and in an attempt to erase the memory of its dreadful past the cul-de-sac was renamed Ruston Close, and later rebuilt as Bartle Road. Nevertheless, back then the house had the look and smell of doom and gloom about it, and its macabre legacy remains. On Thursday, 24 November 2016, Max Benwell of the *Independent* interviewed a seventy-six-year-old man whose home now stands pretty much where 10 Rillington Place used to be. Time to hide under the bed now, for those who like to be scared half to death:

> *I have a bad feeling about this place. The electrics go wrong. The toilets go wrong. The heating goes wrong. I'm going to get an exorcist in. I've had devout Catholics come and I told them to bring holy water. I think the place is cursed. I've had bad luck since I've been here [1978]. My health's gone. Everything's gone.*

How to exorcise most of this haunted gentleman's problems? Ask an exorcist to pop round or issue a complaint to his local council? It's not for me to say, so let's start with the bodies first, shall we?

By 1953, the terraced cul-de-sac, with crumbling stone doorways, had turned into one of the most neglected streets around Ladbroke Grove, and a cheery Jamaican tenant called Beresford Brown had moved into the top flat. At long last, the ground-floor kitchen was finally going to be cleaned up – I think they call it 'remodelled' these days. The date was Tuesday, 24 March 1953 and Christie had moved out the previous day when the owner of the property learned to his dismay that Christie had illegally rented his flat to sub-tenants, a couple called Reilly who had paid Christie £17 13s – three months' rent in advance – and Christie had done a 'runner'.

The landlord promptly told the Reillys to be out by the morning, and had given Beresford Brown permission to use the ground floor kitchen. Here was the chance for Brown to use it as a home, not as the depressing, rubbish-filled slum Christie had left behind. Brown warmed to his task. Over the next few days he laboured away carrying piles of filthy clothes and rubbish into the little backyard alongside the washhouse. The kitchen stank to high heaven – it had peeling walls, it was damp, there was ageing paint and no amenities. Eventually, he cleared away all of the rubbish and was ready to make a clean start.

After wiping his brow, Beresford looked around. He needed a place where he could put up a shelf where he could put his radio, but brackets had to be put in place first. As all DIY 'experts' know, the first thing to do when putting up brackets is to start tapping a wall with one's knuckles to see if it can take some wall plugs and screws. These days they have electronic devices to do just this; back then, however, knuckles was the way to go. I know this because my father did it once, then he pierced an electrical cable.

We now find our Mr Brown humming away while tapping up, down and from side to side along the back wall of the kitchen. Tap, tap, tap ... tap ... tap ... ummm, 'This sounds a bit hollow,' thought Beresford. He tapped again, and then he pulled away a strip of wallpaper. There was no real wall at all, only a papered-over wooden door to an alcove. Beresford poked a hole through it, then, picking up his torch, he shone it into the opening. At first he could not believe what he saw. Throwing down his torch, he ran up the stairs to the second floor to fetch another tenant, Ivan Williams, who with much trepidation took a quick peek himself. They called the police.

Sitting in the alcove on a pile of rubbish was a partially clothed woman's body. She was wearing a white, cotton piqué jacket held by a safety pin, blue bra, stockings and a pink suspender belt. The bra straps were attached to a blanket wrapped around a second body. Behind them was a third corpse covered in an old woollen blanket, tied at the ankles with a plastic flex. All three women had been strangled. They were: Kathleen Maloney, twenty-six, a Southampton sex worker, gassed and strangled in January 1953; Rita Nelson, twenty-five, a sex worker from Belfast, gassed and strangled in January 1953; and Hectorina McLennan, twenty-six, Scottish, gassed and strangled on 6 March 1953. Shortly thereafter Christie's wife Ethel, fifty-five, was found covered with rubble under the front room floorboards, so now the house had to be searched from top to bottom.

Excavation work in the tiny garden revealed two skeletons. Although one of the skulls was missing, medical tests proved that they had been there some ten years. They were the remains of Austrian-born Ruth Fuerst, seventeen, a part-time sex worker who was strangled in 1943, and factory worker Muriel Eady, thirty-one, gassed and strangled in 1943. Beryl and her daughter Geraldine were found bundled up in the outside washhouse. Beryl's corpse was doubled up, wrapped in a dark blanket inside a tablecloth, hidden behind the boards beneath the sink. The baby was found to the left of the door, fully clothed, but with a man's tie knotted around her neck.

* * *

So what can we make of Ethel Christie? What we *do* know is she was most certainly around the house doing all the things expected of her by 'Reg'. Yet, during the period between the murders of Ruth Fuerst and Muriel Eady and her own murder on Sunday, 14 December 1952, Ethel had not, it *seems*, suspected a thing even though the garden was small, and there must have been some evidence of a freshly dug hole. Indeed, at one point she and her husband were photographed standing right on top of the grave, with Christie wearing a maniacal grin – him secretly knowing what lies beneath their feet.

We also know that Christie killed Beryl Evans on 8 November 1949, and her daughter two days later. Ethel might have had some suspicions about her husband going way back, but these uncertainties were confirmed when she realised that her Reg was lusting after the young, naive young Beryl. But then first her husband Timothy suddenly went away and Beryl soon vanished, only to leave her baby behind. However, for us today, it seems almost incomprehensible that, for three whole years – with Ethel using the washhouse several times a day – she could not have failed to have noticed the distinct stench of rotting flesh, nor the baby's little corpse wrapped up just behind the door. Something doesn't smell right here, does it? Needless to say, Ethel can tell us nothing because she has long gone, and time and tide wait for no man. We don't even know where she rests in peace – a long-lost pauper's grave no doubt. Yet her monstrous husband does have a place, for his remains are in the Pentonville Prison

Cemetery, Barnsbury, London Borough of Islington, under Memorial ID: 19712839. However, if we think laterally, it is just possible that Ethel can tell us a little more from beyond the grave about her life with John Christie.

In my earlier book *Talking with Psychopaths and Savages: Beyond Evil*, I examined thoroughly John Christie's psychopathology, his MO, his life and crimes. In him we find one of the most cold-hearted, utterly callous, manipulative sexual psychopaths Great Britain has ever known. Decades later, we seem to forget the enormity of a case that shocked postwar Britain; one that became what the press like to call 'the Crime of the Century'. Of course, back then this country still had hangings, and what better aid to selling newspapers than the bell tolling on the condemned as the traps sent him plunging to his doom?

In many ways, I think that in studying the psychopathology of Christie himself we find many of the clues as to Ethel's mindset, too, for theirs was basically a sexless marriage – one of postwar convenience, I hasten to add.

With a troubled history already behind Christie, he and Ethel married on Thursday, 20 May 1920. A plumpish young woman, then aged thirty-two, placid, passive, she would have already considered herself 'left on the shelf', and Reg was, for her, perhaps a last chance to marry. A year later, it would dawn on her that she had married a crook: while working as a postman he was caught stealing money out of letters and jailed for nine months; nevertheless, Ethel stuck by him.

Two years later, he was in trouble again, although treated leniently. Magistrates bound him over for posing as an ex-military commissioned officer, and he was put on probation for violence. Ethel stuck by him once again. Finally, in 1924, when Christie was jailed for another nine months at Uxbridge Petty Sessions for larceny, Ethel took the opportunity to leave him – or as this moral bigot Christie ripely put it, 'she deserted me'.

Thereafter, Christie continued to drift around. In 1929, he was once again before the justices for attacking a sex worker with whom he was living. The magistrates called it a 'murderous attack' and he was slapped with six months hard labour. Then, in 1933 – after yet *another* spell in prison, this time for stealing a car from a Roman Catholic priest who befriended him – and proving that a leopard never changes its spots – this manipulative, psychopathic creep wrote a grovelling letter to Ethel, asking her to go back to him. Unfortunately, she did.

I can see *some* parallels with Teena Sams here, although this may seem a bit hard for some readers to swallow. The phrases 'over needy' and 'under the thumb' come to mind. Moreover, I think in our more enlightened times, a woman would long ago have kicked the likes of Sams and Christie out of the door for good.

Ethel was last seen alive delivering laundry on Friday, 12 December 1952. Two days later she was murdered – and it comes as no surprise that the washing was never collected. For some weeks afterwards, Christie kept up the pretence that she was still alive, indeed, shortly before Christmas he wrote a letter to Ethel's sister, in Sheffield, claiming she could not write because of rheumatism in her fingers. Across the top, he scrawled: 'Don't worry, she is O.K. I shall cook Christmas dinner.'

It is also interesting to read Christie's own account of why he murdered his wife, for he says that on 14 December he was woken up by Ethel who was suffering from convulsions. He claimed that his now 'elderly wife' was also arthritic. He said that he could do nothing to restore her breathing and decided to, ' ... end her misery in the kindest way'. So, with the very thought of calling for a doctor being the last thing on this evil man's mind, he strangled her to death.

With sickening hypocrisy, he was to write in 1953:

> *For two days I left my wife's body in bed. And then I pulled up the floorboards of the front room and buried her. From the first day I missed her. The quiet love she and I bore each other only happens once in a lifetime.*
>
> John Christie: prior to his execution.

This claptrap goes out of the window when we learn that immediately after putting Ethel under the floorboards he sold most of their furniture, threw out any of the possessions that had once been hers, and lived with his cat and a dog – to whom he said he was 'devoted' – going on to kill three more times before he was finally arrested. Moreover, all of that stuff is somewhat contradicted by another of his statements:

> *When I murdered my wife I removed the one obstacle which for ten years had apparently held me in check. After she had gone the way was clear for me to fulfil my destiny.*

Thinking back to the time when Teena Sams sat on the couch alongside her husband Michael to watch the TV programme *Crimewatch UK*, and there *he* was: an almost exact photofit, his *real* voice, his railway lapel badge and a full description of the orange Metro – now parked just outside Eaves Cottage – yet Teena just sat there quietly, not suspecting a thing. Then after Michael had entered the prison system, she still kept writing to him; buying magazines and visiting him – all the while he still treated her like dirt by openly boasting of his relationship with Victoria Vinchelli.

They say that forgiveness is a virtue, and I am almost reluctant to quote Matthew 6:14–15, but I am obliged to here:

> *For if you forgive other people when they sin against you, your heavenly Father will also forgive you. But if you do not forgive others their sins, your Father will not forgive your sins.*
>
> Matt. 6:14--15 (NIV)

Well, I feel that Teena Sams and Ethel Christie did a bit *too* much in forgiving the monsters they were sleeping with, for where did it get them? There *has* to be a limit to forgiveness – as in 'one strike and out'.

Before we close, however, I ask readers to remember the Latin aphorism '*De mortuis nihil nisi bonum,*' which translates as 'Of the dead [say] nothing but good,' because they are unable to justify themselves. Well, it almost pains me to say so, but are we truly to believe that Ethel didn't have a clue about what her husband was up to? As we have seen, she was in any event a very forgiving person, so it is almost inconceivable that she was so unaware of what was around her to live in such manifest ignorance, too. I believe that she would have done anything to keep her Reg from abandoning her, to leave her destitute, back on the shelf once more. After all is said and done, Christie was the arch manipulator. In my opinion, as Ethel started to realise that things were getting out of control, and living with her husband was no longer an option, she had threatened to leave him – possibly, at long last, inform on him to the police – and that was why he killed her. For her, it was never a case of her truly loving him; it was one of her *needing* him.

Sonia Sutcliffe v. Peter William Sutcliffe (UK)

They are all in my brain, reminding me of the beast I am …
Just thinking about them all reminds me what a monster I am.
PETER WILLIAM SUTCLIFFE (1946–2020):

ON HIS VICTIMS

Well, thank you, too, Mr Sutcliffe, for reminding us that you *are* a 'beast', and a 'monster'. However, you will not need to remind millions of people worldwide that you most certainly *are* one of the worst serial killers in the depressing history of British crime.

Peter Sutcliffe aka Peter William Coonan aka 'the Yorkshire Ripper', died aged seventy-four, almost blind and serving a natural-life sentence, having been convicted of killing thirteen women and attempting to murder twenty others between 1975 and 1980. Cause of death was SARS-CoV-2, pneumonia, diabetes and heart disease (SARS-CoV-2 is essentially the same as Covid-19 infection). On this occasion, however, it is not the killer himself we are so much interested in, but his former wife Sonia, born Friday, 10 August 1950 as Oksana Szurma. She provides us with an intriguing state of affairs, indeed, for unlike Michael Sams, it was not 'the Yorkshire Ripper' who wore the trousers in the family home. In consequence, some of Sonia's back history is well worth a brief summary here.

In 1947, Sonia's Polish/Ukrainian parents, Bohdan and Maria Szurma, left Czechoslovakia and arrived in Bradford, where Bohdan found work in a mill as a yarn tester. Sonia, their second daughter, was just sixteen when, defying her father's orders, she went to a disco in the function room of the Royal Standard pub at 22 Manningham Lane in Bradford. It was here that she met a somewhat suave, well-groomed Sutcliffe who was four years older than her. They seemed to have an almost instant mutual attraction, for they were seen kissing and cuddling in a corner.

The schoolgirl had spotted the same 'introversion and hauteur' that other girls had detected in Sutcliffe, and she quickly steered him away from his pals in the 'gravediggers' corner of the pub. On Sundays, the couple sat on dining chairs at the back of the sitting room of Sutcliffe's parents' home, lost in their own conversation. Sonia said the family would speak to others only when it was absolutely unavoidable although Peter's father, John, described her as 'a very beautiful girl, very soft spoken', for her part, Sonia said that the family held her in contempt.

In 1969, when Peter Sutcliffe learned that his bride-to-be had a secret boyfriend, he was devastated. Later that same year, he carried out his first known attack – he hit a sex worker over the head with a stone in a sock following a row over a £10 note in Bradford. Back then, Sonia was working at a local primary school, while Sutcliffe was a gravedigger, a furnace-man and eventually a lorry driver.

Following what might be called a tortuous courtship, they were married five years later on Saturday, 10 August 1974, to live the next three years with Sonia's parents in Taunton Crescent, in the Clayton area of Bradford. But three years before their wedding Sonia had suffered a nervous breakdown while taking a teacher-training course at the Rachel McMillan College, Deptford. She suffered from schizophrenia, and had a reputation for being prickly and demanding.

Sonia once told a treating psychiatrist that she had heard the word of God. Following her husband's arrest, she said to her father-in-law, 'Peter pulled me through my troubles so I am going to pull him through his.' In many ways, Sonia was the dominant partner in the relationship. I stress here that throughout their life together Sonia at no time had any knowledge of her husband's murderous activities.

Sonia had suffered several miscarriages over the years and the couple were subsequently informed that she could not have children. But she was able to resume her teacher-training course and when she qualified in 1977 and began teaching, the couple used the salary from her job to buy an upmarket three-storey detached house in Garden Lane, Heaton, Bradford. The price then was £16,000, and they moved in on Monday, 26 September 1977. They were still living there at the time of Sutcliffe's arrest on Friday, 2 January 1981. It was a house where Sutcliffe's parents claim they never felt welcome, while

Peter's brother, Michael, and Sonia certainly made no secret of their personal dislike for each other. It was a house holding many other secrets, as it does to this very day.

Given the background of the Sonia *v.* Peter relationship, the question remains, after being raised thousands of times: why in God's name did Sonia stick by her former husband for so many years? It seems inconceivable, does it not, that having slept with this totally evil serial killer for fourteen years – and under the same roof for something over three years – and knowing precisely what her monster of a husband had done to so many women, she did not drop him like a hot brick as soon as he was found guilty at trial and locked up for good? Perhaps if Sonia had visited a few of the crime scenes, looked at the gruesome post-mortem photographs and talked to the grieving next-of-kin, she might have done just that; however, I rather think not. Moreover, I simply *cannot* get my head around the fact that knowing that *his* hands – the blood-drenched hands that had smashed a hammer into heads and brains; the hands that plunged a screwdriver or blade many times into living, breathing women – were the same hands that held her intimately close in their bed, she was able to tolerate him a second longer. Just because Peter had 'stood by her' while she was in the throes of a nervous breakdown, telling a shrink that God was whispering in her ear, does it make it all right – as in morally acceptable – to still love a beast from the bottomless pit?

And yet, let's hold our horses here for a moment, shall we? Maybe, just *maybe*, we are peering at 'Planet Sonia' through the wrong end of a telescope, and should perhaps focus more closely on what has been going on behind the scenes. If 'behind the scenes' is the right phrase, because it has all been reported in the national press as if this is some kind of macabre soap – one of those shows that you could not make up if you tried.

According to an article in the *Mirror* written by Kerry Harden and Kaisha Langdon, which appeared on 9 June 2019: 'Yorkshire Ripper's ex-wife STILL lived in the house she shared with serial killer'. That's a headline-grabber for you, and this despite the fact that she had divorced Sutcliffe and, up until 2017, she was still visiting him in the secure Broadmoor Psychiatric Hospital, bringing along all sorts of goodies and legal papers for him to sign. Unbelievably, Sonia had remained married to 'the Yorkshire Ripper' until 1994, *thirteen years* after he was jailed, and furthermore, told the *Sunday People*, 'I feel compassion for him.' So what the hell is that all about?

To help clarify matters, let's examine what happened after their relationship formally ended. In 1997, Sonia met and then married a hairdresser called Michael Woodward. Her father, Bohdan, had already passed away by now, and so her mother, Maria Szurma, moved into the Garden Lane property and stayed there until she died of cancer in 2003. Sonia moved with Mike to a flat in a converted mill next to the River Aire, a few miles away in Saltaire, West Yorkshire. The couple had met at a local Bradford salon, 'Stage Door 2', and their wedding reception – at which the new Mrs Woodward wore a white and gold dress – was postponed for six months because of fears that hostile crowds would ruin the event. Yet even then she continued to visit her previous husband, the sadosexual serial killer in prison; he had even created an Elvis Presley statue for her during one of his 'weekly ceramic sessions'.

The *Mirror* also reported that new hubby, Michael, ' ... has reportedly refused to move into the home [that Sonia once shared with Sutcliffe], and instead lives alone in a flat 15 minutes away.' Sonia's sister, Marianne, told the *Mirror* that Sutcliffe was 'the only man in the world for her and always will be'.

However, in 2017, 'the Ripper' was said to be 'furious' that Sonia had not visited him in two years and blamed her new husband, Michael. Sutcliffe said: 'I have been ringing Sonia but Michael tells her off if I speak to her or leave messages,' adding, 'He acts like a spoilt brat and should get over his jealousy and accept we are friends.' All this despite the fact that he was now locked up in HMP Frankland, County Durham.

Perhaps inheriting qualities from her parents, who made a new life in this country after the Second World War, Sonia is a person who, although being a tad testy at times, has certainly kept her head on her shoulders very much intact. Just *maybe*, albeit a very small *maybe*, there was an alternative motive for not divorcing Sutcliffe much earlier – money.

Looking at this through the impartial eyes of a solicitor, or even a bank manager, it would be fair to say that half of that house in Garden Lane was hers. Indeed, it was solely because of her financial status – *not* Peter's – that they were able to get a mortgage in the first instance. Furthermore, it was not she who was running amok killing sex workers and other women, it was he. So in all fairness to Sonia, let's at least take this under some consideration, for was she a victim of sorts too?

* * *

As an aside, over many years long gone by, I freelanced for the *Mail on Sunday*, when Jonathan Holborow was editor. Those were the days when editors had what Jonathan called 'a war chest': bundles of cash used specifically for scoops up for grabs if the opportunity arose. Indeed, it was Jonathan who sent me over to Thailand, then to Singapore, to cover the execution of a British serial killer, John Martin Scripps aka 'the Tourist from Hell', at Changi Prison, Friday, 19 April 1996. I have previously written about Scripps in books and I got to know him quite well. I witnessed his hanging between two Thai bandits. I watched as his head was almost ripped off because he refused to be weighed for the 'Long Drop', and I witnessed his cremation at Sin Ming Drive. I was even more delighted when Detective Superintendent Gerald Lim (Homicide) presented me with a late birthday gift as I left Singapore – a mug with a design of a man hanging from a gallows, which I treasure even today.

So the *Mail* and Associated Newspapers, their journos and correspondents I have much time for. And although I have never met or corresponded with Paul Bracchi and Sue Reid, their 29 May 2010 piece for the *Daily Mail* and the *Mail on Sunday* on Sonia Sutcliffe resonates with me.

Titled: 'Reunited with the Ripper: What's drawn Sonia Sutcliffe back into her evil husband's shadow?' it begins: 'Her once flowing jet-black hair is now greying and unkempt. The smart wardrobe – and trademark designer sunglasses – replaced by scruffy clothes, lines under her eyes and unflattering tracksuit bottoms.' Bracchi and Sue Reid are not inclined to pull their punches if this is the way it was back then.

The feature also asks whether Sonia had any friends. There were none to speak of. Family? Ditto (apart from a sister on the South Coast). Neighbours? She doesn't talk to them either, nor they to her. One neighbour said that her husband gave Sonia a nod and an '"All right?" when we first arrived here [Garden Lane], but he got no response, so we didn't bother any more.'

Of particular interest to me – perhaps for you, too – is Bracchi and Reid's next line: 'How do you start a conversation with Sonia Sutcliffe?' This is followed up with: 'Under different circumstances, we might have some sympathy for a woman who had the misfortune to be married to Peter Sutcliffe, the "Yorkshire Ripper". After all, she has, in one way or another, served her own life sentence for his ghastly crimes, which have found a chilling echo in the terrible events now unfolding in his old killing ground.'

I've eaten some of her ... that's part of the magic.
Stephen Griffiths: to police on
Suzanne Blamires.

The 'terrible events' to which Bracchi and Reid are referring is the 24 May 2010 arrest of forty-year-old criminology student Stephen Griffiths on suspicion of killing Suzanne Blamires, aged thirty-six, who had last been seen alive on Friday, 22 May. Her remains were found in the River Aire in Shipley. He was also suspected of killing Shelley Armitage, aged thirty-one, and mother-of-three Susan 'Susie' Rushworth, aged forty-three. Armitage, from Allerton, Bradford, had been missing since 26 April; Rushworth, from the Manningham area, had not been seen since 2009. The police were also investigating possible links to the case of Rebecca Hall, aged nineteen, a sex worker in Bradford who was murdered in 2001. Her body was found in the Allerton area of the city. Stephen Griffiths aka 'the Crossbow Cannibal' was jailed for life at Leeds Crown Court in late December 2010.

* * *

Bracchi and Reid's article went on to ask further questions about Sonia: ' ... Hadn't Sonia tried to move on with her life? Wasn't she now known as Sonia Woodward – not Sutcliffe – after remarrying several years ago?' Here, the article is tapping into our own hopefully decent moralities in a subtle, almost subconscious sort of way, but then comes the bottom line: 'Several disturbing facts, however, undermine the ex-Mrs Sutcliffe's rehabilitation from "Mrs Ripper", as she was nicknamed, to an ordinary member of society – and any version of events that casts her in the role of a victim.'

The first point is that Sonia was officially Sutcliffe's next-of-kin and according to the reporters' sources, she was visiting him regularly in Broadmoor. Furthermore 'she had returned to her former home.' It was understood by Bracchi and Reid that Sonia's name was given as Sutcliffe's 'next of kin' in legal papers required during a recent controversial legal bid to secure his freedom. This was a neat juggling act because it would mean that any assets he may have had could pass to her, instead of his two surviving brothers. Well, he had said that he didn't get on well with them anyway.

The second issue is that she and Sutcliffe still jointly owned the former marital home. Bracchi and Reid appear to

149

have seen the deeds of the house filed at the Land Registry, because they stated that the Sutcliffes' names are there 'in black and white'.

A third reason, according to the two reporters, is that Sonia's home was: 'neat and tidy as usual' when they visited on 28 May 2010. 'The wooden-framed single garage, where he kept his grisly arsenal of hammers, knives and screwdrivers, was also the same.' Ramping it up a bit, there is 'the kitchen where he would wash his bloodstained clothes – the same. The garden where he burned other incriminating evidence – the same.'

'It's my home', Sonia allegedly told a friend at the time. 'Nothing bad has ever happened to me here.' Which is a fair point.

'But there is a legal reason why Sonia is bound to the house and to Sutcliffe – not that she needs a reason – of course', the reporters wrote. The Legal Services Commission (LSC), the body administering Legal Aid, claimed that it was owed money by Sonia. This appears to relate to a civil case in relation to the couple's legal separation, the LSC told the reporters. The Commission had, back then, placed a legal charge on the property, worth about £260,000. This meant that the LSC effectively owned a share of the house and would automatically be entitled to a part of the equity, should it ever be sold.

Yet here I have to ask myself, is Sonia right in saying, 'It's my home. Nothing bad has ever happened to me here,' and while I think that some may vehemently disagree, the fact of the matter is that Sonia had worked damned hard to buy her 'dream home' in a country that had given her parents refuge, and, later, her and her sister a home, following the Second World War. It is not as if the Szurmas were social leeches, living in the UK on benefits, for they were solid, hard-working people. It is true that young Sonia was a feisty teenager, but there are millions of young women like her, and it cannot be held against her. Indeed, it was Sonia who was pursuing an honourable profession while her husband was dancing from menial work to menial work, earning whatever he could, when he could.

Because Peter Sutcliffe was such an evil man, one might easily assume, with hindsight, that he was the dominant husband, 'Sonia, the put–upon housewife', as Bracchi and Reid suggested. However, in his remarkable 1984 book, *Somebody's Husband, Somebody's Son*, journalist Gordon Burn of the *Sunday Times* outlines evidence that often Sonia would slap her husband down in front of his own family. 'Peter', she would say pointedly, and he would stop whatever he was doing. At other times, according to the Burn, she was prone to 'unprovoked outbursts of rage', which resulted in her husband having to 'contain her physically by pinning her arms to her side'. But, then again I ask myself: so what? Does any of this make Sonia a social pariah?

With all of that being said, ' ... indeed an almost autistic insensitivity is [Sonia's] defining trait,' write Bracchi and Reid, adding, ' ... she once told a journalist that, even though not all of Sutcliffe's victims were prostitutes ... they were behaving like prostitutes,' and in the eyes of most people in this country that would have been a statement cruel enough to cast her out. Not that she would really give a damn one way or the other, one might suggest.

If that's justice, I'm a banana!
Ian Hislop: editor, *Private Eye*, 24 May 1989

In what is known as a 'landmark case' for British justice, the then Sonia Sutcliffe found herself thrust into the public spotlight when she sued the satirical magazine *Private Eye* for libel. The magazine had claimed that she had 'attempted to profit' from her connection to her husband, and had accepted £250,000 from the *Daily Mail* for an article detailing their life together.

It was claimed that there had been a 'squalid race' to buy her story, and that she had negotiated with various publications in order to get the greatest sum possible for this 'exclusive', something that Sonia's lawyers vehemently denied, even though they said it would not be unreasonable for her do so in order to fund the start of a new life, away from the media attention and the opprobrium of neighbours.

Private Eye lost the case, but what had got right up Ian Hislop's nose more than anything else was the amount of the damages awarded to Sonia, which was, by any stretch of the imagination, remarkable, and quite frankly an insult to common sense – £600,000, some £100,000 more than any other previous award in a British libel case. As infuriated as he was, Hislop was spot-on when he pointed out that this amount was a hundred times more than the damages awarded to three of her husband's victims. Nevertheless, this huge sum would have put *Private Eye* in severe financial difficulties and its future threatened. Fortunately, the magazine's readers donated generously to the 'Bananaballs Fund' that had been set up to save the magazine from extinction. Sonia Sutcliffe was awarded £25,000 of the damages immediately, the remainder held over pending an appeal by *Private Eye*. This was partly successful and the sum to be paid was reduced to just £60,000. Furthermore, the magazine scored a PR coup by donating the surplus of their 'Bananaballs' fund to the victims of Sutcliffe's families. Sonia might well have made a similar goodwill gesture – but did not do so.

* * *

In concluding this chapter, I hark back to the question as to why Sonia still wishes to live in the house she once shared with 'the Yorkshire Ripper', and as she has said, 'It's my home. Nothing bad has ever happened to me here.' I get where she is coming from, for the following reasons.

It is no fault of hers that she unknowingly married then slept with a man who turned out to be a monster, so, in this respect, and as I hope as this book proves, Sonia is not grotesquely unique in this regard. As for the killings committed by her husband, she played no part in any of it at all, so, we can say that Sonia Sutcliffe was an innocent victim albeit to a much lesser degree. Indeed, I will go further by suggesting that, knowing what little of her that we do, I dare say that if she'd even got a sniff that he was hurting *any* woman, sex worker or otherwise, she would have given him the hiding of his life and turned him over to the police in a heartbeat. She was not a woman to be messed about with for we know this much – Sonia is a tough cookie.

The other issue crossing my mind is the simple fact that although a serial killer had *once* lived in the house in Garden Lane, it was *never* a place to which women were enticed to be sexually used, abused, tortured then killed. This was not like the long since demolished locations of No. 10 Rillington Place, or of No. 25 Cromwell Street in Gloucester, where Fred and Rose West tortured, killed, dismembered and buried some of their victims.

Nor does it recall another location, this time in America: 8213 West Summerdale, Des Planes, Chicago, where serial killer John Wayne Gacy once lived and where he tortured and raped thirty-three lads and buried most of their corpses in the waterlogged crawl space beneath the property. The building was razed to the ground in April 1979 when investigators searched for the bodies. For years after, the 60-by-144-foot lot had sat vacant, overrun by high weeds and littered with empty bottles and cans, with the locals complaining about rats and infestations, until June 1988, when backhoes started moving in to dig deep holes. Yes, a new place was being built and now the same neighbours were accusing the new owner of being macabre and spouting, 'Who'd want to live on a plot of land that is haunted?'

I am also mindful of 112 Ocean Avenue, in the upscale village of Amityville, Long Island, the home where, on the night of 13/14 November 1974, Ronald 'Butch' DeFeo, shot to death his entire family of six as they slept snug in their beds. That allegedly 'haunted house' has been the subject of numerous horror movies, yet still it stands today with many subsequent owners having lived there without incident. See also 23 Cranley Gardens, London, the former attic flat of the notorious British serial killer, Dennis Nilsen, where he murdered young men and kept their naked corpses 'close to him' for a few days. That flat has recently been remodelled and sold by a local estate agent, with the new owner apparently thrilled with the purchase. Ghosts, indeed?

So, you see that there are thousands of houses and flats and condos and hotel rooms across the world where murder most foul *has* taken place and other people continue to live in them. Yet no murders took place at the Sutcliffe home, a property still shunned by local residents simply because a monster *once* lived there. Really, it all seems a little hysterical to me, even more so to envisage Sonia selling up with new people moving in because not much will change – it will *always* be the house where 'the Yorkshire Ripper' once lived, and that will never change, either.

Perhaps Sonia Sutcliffe has been less than diplomatic over the years, perhaps also a bit too self-serving, perhaps injudicious with several ice-cold and off-hand comments or more. Maybe she does have a chip on her shoulder – and wouldn't any of us when, completely out of the blue and to one's utter shock, one learns that one's spouse has been arrested and revealed as one of the most heinous sex-crazed serial killers of all time, and all with the world's media and paparazzi literally camping outside one's front door. So maybe she is a near-recluse, but let us not forget that *she* is serving her own life sentence for unknowingly sleeping with a serial killer, so maybe it is time for some understanding.

It is now the time to turn the tables and see what happens when the men are on the receiving end, for when it comes down to the guys who sleep with the women with murder in mind, the female can certainly be more dangerous than the male – big time.

John Knowles, John Russell, Oliver Leonard, Ernest Wilson v. Mary Elizabeth Wilson (UK)

For the female of the species is more deadly than the male.
RUDYARD KIPLING (1865–1936):
'THE FEMALE OF THE SPECIES' (1911)

Kipling's famous adage is often applied unfairly, but not so in the case of the 'Black Widow' Elizabeth Wilson, for deadly she certainly was. You would have thought that one look at her matrimonial record would have deterred any suitor, yet we will soon learn what this nursery rhyme-dubbed 'Merry Widow of Windy Nook' saw in a Mr Knowles, a Mr Russell, a Mr Leonard and a Mr Wilson – *their money*, of course. But if she benefited, at least four of her husbands didn't, simply because any accounts of their lives have been reduced to scraps of yellowy paper and faded ink – they are all long dead and in their graves.

Nevertheless, in 1958 our 'Merry Widow' was only convicted of two of the four murders, to become the last woman to be sentenced to be hanged in Durham. Yet fate smiled upon her; the ultimate punishment being commuted to life imprisonment, she peacefully popped her clogs in HMP Holloway in 1963, aged sixty-nine, or she might have been seventy – it seems that no one is quite sure.

The term used to categorise these 'Black Widow' serial killers comes from the black widow spider of the genus *Latrodectus*, whose deadly female often eats their partner *after* sex – with this, I guess, at least being some sort of a plus for the male. Some females of our *Homo sapiens* species act out their anger, sociopathic tendencies, or desire for financial gain, by killing their husbands or partners, athough fortunately, their fatal bites are extremely rare. Actually, black widow spiders are interesting creatures in the grand scheme of things. The females live considerably longer than their partners because after one bonking session her suitor gets cannibalised. Quite why this happens no one really knows expect Ms Spider, I suspect. It could be that by eating him he provides a fast, nutritious post-sex meal, which helps nourish her leading to healthier offspring, or that she doesn't want him spreading his genes around the community. The other possible theory for this seemingly bizarre nuptial meal is that he is so exhausted by the sex act he dies on the job, or shortly thereafter, so it's a simple case of waste not want not. There is some obvious good science behind the latter; namely, that she is four times larger than he, and is therefore the dominant partner.

I fear I have digressed, but there are many examples of

these human black widows who have exacted revenge on abusive husbands and partners, making a profit from their brutal crimes, or committed cold-blooded killings for other twisted reasons, with Mary Wilson being one of them. Perhaps curiously, though, while some of her 'marriages' lasted only a few short weeks, it was enough time for this cunning creature to establish herself as the rightful heir to their estates, thereby inheriting hubby's money after each death.

So it is fair to say that it was *not* surprising that some people started to get suspicious of this supposedly grieving widow who was both garrulous and displayed a penchant for dark humour at the funerals. Indeed, once she asked an undertaker if she qualified for a discount. At one of her wedding receptions, a friend asked, 'What shall we do with the leftover sandwiches and cakes?' to which our merry widow breezily replied: 'We'll keep them for his funeral.' Unsurprisingly, having now more-or-less advertised herself as being a killer, the police cottoned on. The bodies of the deceased were exhumed and found to contain high levels of insecticide, so what the doctors had originally certified as being the cause of death of her four husbands in *two years*, God only knows.

* * *

She was born Mary Elizabeth Cassidy in the mining town of Stanley, County Durham, on 11 June 1889, and christened into the Roman Catholic faith. When she was twenty-five she married her first husband, John Knowles, in around November 1914, the fourth month of the First World War, and they settled in a house in the village of Windy Nook, near Gateshead. At some point she had taken a lover, John

Russell, who eventually moved in with them, the threesome now living under the same roof.

As Knowles was the first man on Mary's marital itinerary, it is perhaps not surprising that he would be the first to die, obligingly doing just that in 1955. Giving herself a moderate amount of time for mourning, hand-wringing and faux weeping, Mrs Knowles waited all of five months before marrying the aforementioned John Russell – who died in 1956 or 1957 – no one is quite sure about that date either – leaving his entire savings of £42.00 to Mary, with the attending physician declaring that both men had died of 'natural causes'.

Mr Oliver Leonard was a retired estate agent. Somewhat pretentious, a little on the portly side, with rosy cheeks and a bulbous nose equally as rosy, for he was often in drink, he married the now Mrs Russell in June of 1957, to live a mere twelve days before he too died, leaving in the now Mrs Leonard's grasping hands the sum of £50.00, while freeing her up to smartly wed a Mr Ernest Wilson.

Ernie's estate was something quite substantial – around £100 in cash, a bungalow and, best of all, a life insurance policy as well. However, this time around, although it also proved to be the last time around, not only did she not bother with the inconvenience of attending her late husband's funeral, she didn't even consider the consequences of having a loud mouth, either. Once again the gossip and curtain-twitching started and Mary was arrested. The bodies of Leonard and Wilson were exhumed, their corpses revealing very high levels of phosphorus – used in a beetle poison. With this evidence in the bag, there seemed no need to go digging up Knowles and

Russell, since it was quite obvious they had been poisoned in the same way. Mary Wilson escaped the noose because of her advanced age of sixty-eight.

To try to end this morbid chapter on an instructive note, I think the reader might be interested in what happens to anyone who ingests more than a small amount of this sort of poison. (If you are eating a meal now, I would suggest that you come back later.) The initial symptom will be almost continuous diarrhoea. Then, after twelve to ninety-six hours the victim will suffer a blood pressure problem. Up goes the heart rate, you are racked with muscle tremors, your liver is packing up, you feel weak and your heart also begins to fail. It's going to be an agonising death I can assure you, one that will make you wish you had never been born.

Michael Wallace and David Castor
v. Stacey Ruth Castor (USA)

I never thought for one second that my own mother would try to take my life in return for her own safety.
ASHLEY CASTOR: STACEY CASTOR'S DAUGHTER

This will take some swallowing – car radiator antifreeze, that is – with yet another 'don't try this at home' advisory note heading up a chapter, for the role of the mother is to love, to protect, to nurture. But Stacey Castor wasn't a proper mother by a long chalk – she was a predator who fatally poisoned two husbands, going on to try to kill her own daughter, Ashley, in a wicked attempt to escape justice.

For the reader who, in the dead chill of winter, unfortunately discovers that the cylinder head of their car suddenly explodes leaving a trail of debris along the road, it may be because they have never been to Halfords or some other similar store and bought a bottle of a bright green liquid called 'antifreeze'. For the uninitiated, this is a fluid that one pours into a car radiator, not down one's throat. Therefore, it goes without saying that antifreeze contains semi-toxic chemicals; moreover, if ingested this type of poisoning can be life threatening if not fatal. It typically contains ethylene glycol, methanol, and propylene glycol, but, although the chemicals in antifreeze are relatively non-toxic, the body can and will metabolise them into highly toxic alcohol by-products. Antifreeze was to become one of Stacey's means to commit homicide.

To make this chapter more distastefully interactive for you, the first stage of antifreeze poisoning typically begins between thirty minutes and twelve hours after ingestion. The ethylene glycol in the fluid first affects the central nervous system – the symptoms appearing very similar to someone who is intoxicated by alcohol: loss of coordination; slurred or jumbled speech; dizziness; fatigue; headache; euphoria; nausea, vomiting and seizures leading to coma, but this is only the start of one's problems, for stage two really *does* up the ante.

Specifically for the reader with an avid interest in pH levels, during the second stage of antifreeze ingestion the body continues to metabolise the chemicals into toxic acids which lower the pH level of the blood. Marching on, this leads to a condition called 'metabolic acidosis', so now the sufferer – well, I did state from the start that this book is about suffering, didn't I? – will have an irregular heartbeat, shallow breathing, changes in blood pressure, dehydration, even more fatigue and will become very confused. And wouldn't you, too, for God's sake, because by now the kidneys and liver have crystals in them and they will have given up the will to do anything more to keep you living, so you will die. Which is precisely what Stacey's two husband's did, and what a God-awful, cruel way of killing this was to be, with her motive being financial gain.

> *Mike was larger than life … the life of the party and if you needed something that Mike had, he would give it to you … but he had struggled with drugs and alcohol for a long time in his life.*
> Stacey Castor: to David Muir, ABC News, 2009

Stacey Castor, born Thursday, 24 July 1967, to Judie Eaton and Jerry Daniels from the village of Weedsport, Cayuga County, New York, was not unattractive, although photographs taken at her 2009 court appearances show a tight-lipped, cold-looking woman, her face framed by long hair. Her last prison mugshot proves the damage even a few years of incarceration can do, yet still beneath the gaunt features there is a reminder of how beautiful she had once been before she was found dead, aged just fifty, in her cell on the morning of Saturday, 11 June 2016, following what was put down to heart failure.

In 1984, Stacey, met her first husband, twenty-three-year-old Michael Edward Wallace, when she was just seventeen. They married a few years later and had two daughters: Ashley in 1988 and Bree in 1991. Mrs Stacey Wallace held down a responsible job as an ambulance dispatcher while Michael worked nights as a mechanic, but they were always short of money. It was rumoured that for some time both had affairs, then, as their marriage started to collapse, in late 1999 Michael started to feel ill – dying, aged thirty-nine, with his devoted daughter Ashley by his bedside, in early 2000 following a mysterious ailment which the doctors put down to a heart attack. Stacey had falsely told the doctors that her husband was a heavy drinker, a heavy smoker and a drug abuser, so a heart attack seemed to fit with cause of death. Yet the extent of this man's medical history was that at one time he had suffered from pneumonia and had had a hernia operation. That was it. Period! However, Stacey declined the offer of an autopsy and Michael is buried at the Owasco Rural Cemetery, Skaneateles, Onondaga County, New York.

Following Michael's death, Stacey found work as an office manager with an air-conditioning company. The owner, David Castor, was smitten and, in 2003 they married, with Stacey taking his name, but that's not all she took either – she acquired all he'd *ever* had, all he *then* had, and all he would *ever* have, and it goes something like this.

One afternoon in August 2005, Stacey Castor telephoned her local sheriff. She explained that the couple had rowed the previous day and David had locked himself in their bedroom. He was not answering his mobile phone and as he had failed to turn up at his office for work she was now worried for his welfare. He had been depressed and drinking heavily all weekend, she added, and said he would be sorry if she left him. In what is called a 'wellness check', Sergeant Robert Willoughby of the Onondaga County Sheriff's Department went around to the house, had a quick look-see around, tapped on the bedroom door then kicked it in to find David lying on the bed. Stacey screamed out, 'He's not dead, he's not dead!'

Of course her husband was dead, and she knew it. She had poured enough antifreeze down his throat to stop an

Anchorage-bound Mack truck's engine from freezing in minus 30-degrees. *Of course* he was dead!

> *It's a mess. There's brown vomit everywhere. David's on the bed. He's nude. On the floor was an antifreeze container laying sideways next to the bed and next to it was a bottle of apricot brandy, a cranberry juice container and then there were two glasses. One glass was half-full of a green-coloured liquid. I went into the bathroom which was right off the bedroom and there was a towel bar that was broken off the wall on the floor and there was an open bottle of the prescription Ambien on the counter and there was nothing in there.*
>
> Detective Dominick Spinelli: Onondaga County
> Sheriff's Office

At first, this grim matter appeared to be an open-and-shut case of suicide, so much so that the coroner ruled it as such. These coroners ... Because if David had been opened up, it might just have been noticed that where there should have been red stuff there was green stuff.

Further embroidering her story, Stacey told the police that David had been depressed; however, it didn't take long for a few people to come forward to quietly mention Mike Wallace's death a few years earlier, and that suspicions had been raised when a suggested exhumation was turned down flat by the then 'Stacey Wallace'. Something just didn't fit together. There were a few red flags being hoisted, and another unfurled when colleagues and friends said that David had not been depressed at all. Far from it! Nevertheless,

167

despite Detective Spinelli's insistence that the case *could* be a homicide, the coroner's half-baked report worked against him and the Captain of Detectives ordered that the case be shut down. It was suicide and that was that! Investigating any further would be a waste of time. There were too many other cases to work with, so Spinelli left the captain's office and went and spoke to Sergeant Norton, who had just taken over the Major Crime Squad, and briefed him on what we knew so far. Norton was now convinced this was a homicide, so he went back to the CID captain and after a heated exchange as to whether or not Spinelli was going to close the case, Norton laid it on the line saying: 'You, Captain, can close it but I'm *not* going to close it. And you go write me up, basically, if you want to go that far.' This bought Spinelli precious time to investigate further. Therefore, to avoid upsetting the stubborn Captain of Detectives, over the next few months the two detectives drip-fed evidence up to the crime lab, with the results trickling back and each sample lending credence to the fact that it looked very much like a homicide – not very much like a suicide.

Talking to David's friends and colleagues, the cops learned that he was an outgoing chap who loved venturing outdoors on his snowmobile, hunting and four-wheeling, so they found it incomprehensible that he was a drunk, a depressive who was to lock himself into his bedroom and commit suicide. Then something else lent credence to the non-suicide theory. Police belatedly found a shotgun under the master bed, so if he had wanted to kill himself, it would have been painless to do it with a single pull of a trigger and not die in an excruciating stew.

Talking to a toxicologist, the detectives learned something even more important: there *was* actually a home remedy, an antidote to antifreeze poisoning, this being, in fact, regular, off-the-shelf alcohol that you or I can buy almost anywhere these days. Indeed, if one were to end up in hospital after drinking this bright green stuff, the first thing the doctors should give you is a stiff drink – I kid you not! Whether or not the NHS will allow you to drink a bottle of Scotch while you are at death's door, I can't say. Frankly, if I were suffering the symptoms of 'AGONISING DEATH by ANTIFREEZE', the last thing I would want to see is a bottle of Lucozade and someone holding a bag of grapes.

Nevertheless, Christine Stork, Clinical Director of the Upstate NY Poison Center, takes us through this get-pissed-quick antidote treatment, and it makes for an interesting read – if you are into glycol, that is:

> *The two substances are similar in some ways and they're different in some ways but all-in-all they are both alcohols; one is ethylene glycol the other ethanol and they both are metabolized via a similar system so because of that, they compete with that system for metabolism and ethanol and like the enzyme better, so it would delay any metabolism of the ethylene glycol – the antifreeze.*

That takes some understanding, I agree. Nevertheless, the very notion that David was a drunken mess and then drank antifreeze to kill himself really didn't fly at all because his liver, and a lot of other parts of his body, was already full of off-the-shelf alcohol – the antidote. Because, according to

Stacey, he was as fall-down drunk as the proverbial skunk, or as they say in my neck of the woods, 'as pissed as a newt' – in the US of A, specifically liberal Connecticut, it would be 'chemically imbalanced', I think.

So, let's move on because amongst the items returning from the crime lab was a turkey baster. Yep, a turkey baster, and it had been discovered buried under garbage in a kitchen waste bin. Furthermore, the turkey baster contained traces of green antifreeze with David's DNA on the tip where the liquid would spurt out. This indicated that the baster had been pushed into the dying man's mouth and the liquid squeezed into his throat, *and*, the fact that it had been found in the bin proved that someone else had put it there – *not* David Castor – because he had locked himself into the bedroom, hadn't he?

Now, as all of my loyal readers are true-crime buffs and will know a good detective thing or two about Miss Marple or our late, beloved Lieutenant Columbo, played by Peter Falk (1927–2011), they will, from their armchairs, mutter something along the lines of Sherlock Holmes, whom I quote as saying: 'There is nothing more deceptive than an obvious fact.' In other words: 'What in God's name, Doctor Watson, is this antifreeze doing in a turkey baster? Is that Dave's DNA on the tip? Where did they get a turkey? Gadzooks my good doctor, it's August, and they aren't on sale yet!'

With that being established as fact, of the two glasses found by the bed the one with the antifreeze in it only had one set of fingerprints on it and they belonged to Stacey Castor. Now, please follow me here because the way the fingerprints were situated on the glass proved interesting, too. If you can imagine a glass being in a dishwasher and the way one would grab it to pull it out and put it back on a shelf, well, three of Stacey's fingerprints were upside down on that glass. Further, David had been sweating, vomiting and suffering from diarrhoea; therefore he was a complete physical mess by this time.

On the other hand, the *other* glass with the cranberry juice in it, was a mess, not sparkling clean for it was all smeared with nasty stuff and had all sorts of prints on it and was 'simply awful looking'. This was yet another major red flag because the detectives realised that if David had drunk from the glass containing antifreeze, why was it that it was in pristine condition with only his wife's fingerprints on it?

The detectives then asked Stacey Castor if she knew anything about antifreeze. 'Yes, I know it's a poison,' she bluntly replied. 'David and I had been watching a TV show about a woman who had killed two husbands using antifreeze,' so the cops decided to track that case down. It was one out of Georgia, in which a Lynn Turner's husbands – a policeman and a fireman – were killed five years apart by her feeding them antifreeze. And if two partners die of antifreeze poisoning that certainly sends up a few red flags – don't you think?

NOTE: I refer to the Turner case after this chapter because the similarities between both cases are chilling.

Realising that the only beneficiary of David's estate was his wife (she had actually forged his will), and that she'd previously benefited from another dead man's estate, the cops placed her under surveillance twenty-four-hours a day, and a wiretap was placed on her phone in case she made, or received, any suspicious calls. There was nothing. Added to which, they placed a camera close to where David was buried, side-by-side with her previous husband at her request. However, this callous woman did not visit the graves even once. So now any chances of successfully prosecuting Stacey Castor were slim, but then she panicked because the police were now visiting the graves. The cops reasoned that if Michael couldn't speak to them, his body might still be able to communicate, so, on Wednesday, 5 September 2007, work began to exhume his body. After autopsy, the medical examiner telephoned Detective Spinelli, and said: 'Guess what, Wallace is loaded with crystals just like David Castor, He was killed by ingesting antifreeze.'

Although the evidence had mounted against Stacey Castor, the case was well short of a slam-dunk. If she'd kept her head down and her mouth zipped up tight, and had had the intelligence to realise that visiting her husbands' graves might have been a good idea – even if was purely for a phoney show of mourning – she might have well got away home free. What, however, was a fact was that while her twisted psychopathology had financially served her well previously, it would be her sociopathic mindset that would quickly see her come undone. It was the cold-blooded, evil, cunning brain inside her head that subconsciously she could not control, for in many ways this mind had a mind of its own. In other words, the sociopath/psychopath is wired up to be devoid of compassion, remorse and warm feelings towards others, and where there *should* be a conscience there is just a black hole. Externally, and wearing a fake mask of normality, the likes of people such as Stacey Castor, and others of her dreadful ilk, appear as normal as anyone else, most especially to their partners, their loved ones, work colleagues and friends, and haven't we already seen much evidence of such sociopathic aberration in this book thus far?

We hopefully 'normal people' have, or should possess, compassion towards others. We *should* feel genuine remorse when we make mistakes, and we have a conscience, do we not? These form our social checks and balances weighing up what is right and wrong to make healthy judgements when the time arises, thus we are able to behave in a decent, lawful way. Stacey Castor had none of these psychological attributes, and, if we had looked into her heart, metaphorically it might have seemed to have been made out of stone. This black widow had ice in her arteries and veins while her husbands had antifreeze in theirs.

With Stacey Castor now believing that she was caught between a rock and a hard place, she came up with what Baldrick, in the TV series *Blackadder*, would call 'a cunning plan'. Yes, why not frame her daughter, Ashley? After all was said and done, was it not Ashley who was with her previous dad shortly before he died in agony? Was it not Ashley who had felt that her dad could have lived if she'd called for medical help much earlier? Oh, yes, what a cunning plan, for how simple it had to be to sacrifice her daughter to save herself. It went like this.

On Ashley's first day back at college in 2007, the cops came to question her about her real dad's death. The cause was not as the doctors had initially thought the result of a heart attack. No, he'd been poisoned with antifreeze; the crystallisation was found in his body. The young Ashley was shocked when

173

the detectives told her that David Castor had probably been murdered in the same way. She called Mom, who later picked her up and drove her back to their lakeside Onondaga village home where they could have a drink together. Stacey told her daughter that they had been through enough emotional upheaval and needed to relax.

> *I am drinking with her [Stacey] and I tell her that my drink tastes funny. So I said 'I'm gonna go lay down' and the next thing I know I'm waking up in a hospital. I remember waking up with a detective saying to me that I had tried to commit suicide and there was a suicide note confessing to my father's murder, my stepfather's murder, and my own suicide. My sister was able to come see me. I remember talking to her saying: ' ... you believe me that I didn't do this. And if I didn't do this, there is only one other person that could have done it, and, it was Stacey'.*
>
> Ashley Castor

Luckily, some seventeen hours after ingestion, Ashley's sister, Bree, found her comatose on her bed and dialled 911. Ashley was rushed to hospital and barely survived. By the grace of God, had Bree not found her when she did Ashley would have died within the hour, for she had been given a drink of potentially lethal painkillers.

So, where was Stacey Castor while Ashley lay dying on her bed? She was out in the garden drinking and partying with friends like nothing was wrong at all.

If there is a ceiling in terms of evil, she [Castor] is at that ceiling.

District Attorney William Fitzpatrick

Almost straight off the bat the police knew that Ashley was innocent, and, indeed, District Attorney William Fitzpatrick became her mentor and offered the terrified young girl comfort; he also promised that he would see her mother tried and convicted. Stacey Castor's vindictive psychopathology and a mountain of evidence had turned against her.

The difficulty in very rare cases such as this is convincing twelve people that a mother is actually capable of committing these sorts of atrocious acts, for this wasn't a case of whodunit – there were only two suspects: Stacey and Ashley, and both of their fates were in the hands of a jury of complete strangers, so we can imagine that this put Ashley into a very difficult, emotional and confusing mental space.

When she was accused of poisoning her daughter and typing out the suicide note, Stacey Castor looked firmly into the eyes of the prosecutor and replied with a categorical 'NO!' The prosecutor said, 'You ARE LYING Mrs Castor', with her responding: 'I was concerned that they [the police] would be able to see through her [Ashley's] lies and that they would doubt me.'

Putting into words the sickening evil this woman possessed is best left to the trial judge when he sentenced her.

In my thirty-four years in the criminal justice system as a lawyer and as a judge, I've seen serial killers; I've seen contract killers. I've seen murderers of every variety and

175

stripe, but I have to say Mrs Castor you are in a class by yourself. What you did to David Castor can only be described as premeditated torture. And what you are not being held accountable for here I must say that what you did to Michael Wallace was also premeditated torture.

Premeditation is something we do not often see in the criminal courts but it certainly is present in both of these instances; now as bad is that is, what you tried to do to your daughter Ashley is simply something that I find I almost cannot comprehend. I've seen a lot of defendants come through this court system, including some whose parents tried to take the blame for what they [their children] did, but I've never seen one who was prepared to sacrifice their child to shift the blame away from themselves.

You know I listened carefully to the testimony of both your daughters and I have daughters too. They're older than yours but they have a similar gap in their ages, and I listened not only to the wonderment of your daughter Ashley as she tried to comprehend what you did to her, I also listened to the horror your daughter Bree experienced in finding her older sister almost dead.

You not only deprived those children of their fathers but you were prepared to deprive them of one another. I'm certain that your daughters, like my daughters, like most children who have siblings, expect and are comforted by the knowledge that when their parents pass on they'll at least have each other to grow old and share life with.

You almost succeeded in murdering one child and orphaning the other and that ranks in my judgement as one of the most reprehensible things I think I've seen in the criminal justice system. I know you maintain your innocence, but I'll tell you it is my view that the evidence of your guilt is overwhelming. Unlike many defendants who pass through my courtroom, you are not just a danger to the general public, you are a danger to the people who love you and who are closest to you, and I believe that the sentence I'm about to impose will remove that danger once and for all.

Upon your conviction for murder in the second degree, the murder of David Castor on Count One of the Indictment, it's the sentence and judgment of the Court that you be sentenced to a minimum of twenty-five years to a maximum of life in the New York State correctional system.

Upon your conviction for attempted murder in the second degree of your daughter Ashley Wallace on Count Two of the Indictment. It is the sentence and judgment of the Court that you be sentenced to a determinate sentence of twenty-five years in the New York State correctional system to be followed by a five-year period of post-release supervision … I direct that that sentence run consecutively to the sentence I've just imposed on Count One of the Indictment.

On your conviction of offering a false instrument [forging David's will] for filing in the first degree on Count Three of the Indictment, it's the sentence and the judgment of the Court that you should be sentenced to a minimum of one and one-third years to a maximum of four years in the New York State correctional system and I direct that sentence to run consecutively to the *sentence I have imposed on Counts One and Two of the Indictments … there is a $275 surcharge Mrs Castor and you have thirty days with which to appeal a sentence and judgment of the Court.*

We are recessed.

Judge Joseph Fahey: sentencing Stacey Castor,
Thursday, 5 February 2019

Under New York State sentencing guidelines, Castor would have to serve just over fifty-one years before she became eligible for parole – at her age, effectively a life sentence. She died in prison in June 2016, to leave *all* couples with some great advice: if your partner suddenly starts bringing home containers of antifreeze, especially during the summer months, go out and stock up on hard liquor.

Glenn Turner and Randy Thompson v. Julia 'Lynn' Turner (USA)

There is no fury like an ex-wife searching for a new lover.
PALINURUS (AKA CYRIL CONNOLLY, 1903–74),
THE UNQUIET GRAVE, 1944

This case is an interesting game play of: 'which came first – the chicken or the egg?' As we have seen from Stacey Castor's claim to detectives that she had learned about the effects of antifreeze poisoning while watching a TV documentary with David about the case of Julie Lynn Turner, née Womack, so with no expense spared I have done a little research here of my own. We will call her 'Lynn' because she liked that more.

In 1991, Lynn, a twenty-three-year-old 911 operator, met Cobb County, Georgia, police officer, Maurice Glenn Turner. They married in August 1992. Because of her spending habits, their marriage started to fall apart, to end up with them sleeping in different bedrooms and with her starting an affair with Forsyth County firefighter, Randy Thompson. Although Maurice was unaware of his wife's infidelity, by 1995 he had already started to plan leaving her and filing for divorce. Then, on Thursday, 2 March 1995, he fell ill and went to the emergency room at a local hospital complaining of flu-like symptoms. After being treated, he felt better and returned home. When Lynn arrived back the next day, she found him dead. Cause of death was ruled 'natural causes' due to an irregular heartbeat. He left Lynn $153,000 in his will as well as his pension.

Thus, as far as Lynn was concerned, all was tickety-boo even though the late Maurice Turner would now be thinking otherwise. But, not one to allow grass to grow under her feet or too much of it to grow over his grave, almost immediately after Maurice's 'passing' Lynn and Randy Thompson bought a house between them and had a son and a daughter. However, just like her previous marriage, marital bliss didn't last too long, and as before, it was her extravagant spending habits that far outstripped their joint incomes that were the cause of the problems. Randy, like Maurice, decided to leave her and move out.

On Sunday, 21 January 2001, thirty-two-year-old Randy had reported flu-like symptoms, and he too went to a hospital emergency room for treatment. He had a severe stomach ache and was constantly vomiting. Upon his arrival back home, Lynn made him some Jell-O desert – the next morning he was stone cold dead. Somewhat disappointingly for Lynn, Randy's $200,000 life insurance policy had lapsed due to non-payments of the premium, so this black widow only received a mere $36,000. Cause of death was an irregular heartbeat, the same cause as her previous husband, Maurice.

To cut a long story short, Lynn Turner was arrested on Friday, 1 November 2002, and charged with double homicide. She was tried for Maurice's murder in 2004 and found guilty. Later, in 2007, she went on trial for murdering Randy Thompson and was convicted. She had killed both men by placing antifreeze in their food. She received life sentences for both crimes – narrowly escaping the death sentence for the murder of Randy Thompson.

While serving her time at the Metro State Prison, DeKalb County, Georgia, she intentionally accumulated enough prescription medication to cause an overdose. Aged just forty-two, she committed suicide on Monday, 30 August 2010, and she is buried at the Holly Springs Cemetery, Marietta in Cobb County, Georgia.

The timelines of all four homicides here may be of some interest to the reader, as being:

- 3 March 1995: Maurice Turner dies.
- Early January 2000: Michael Wallace dies.
- 22 January 2001: Randy Thompson dies.
- 1 November 2002: Lynn Thompson is arrested and this is much covered by the media.
- August 2005: David Castor dies.
- September 2007: Attempted murder of Ashley Castor.

There have been many who say that Stacey Castor's two antifreeze killings were copycat murders of the crimes committed by Lynn Thompson, but this cannot have been the case because Lynn's homicides did not come to the public's attention until she was arrested in 2002 – Stacey had poisoned her first husband *two years* earlier in 2000.

As a twisted endnote: Stacey Castor had placed her two murdered husbands side-by-side in the same plot, with the headstone and the plot leaving room for herself in the middle. However, David Castor's family rightly objected to this everlasting eternal remembrance, and the whereabouts of *her* remains is unknown.

Linda Yates v. Robert Lee Yates Jr (USA)

*Do you know why you killed these women? I want to
know like anybody else. And how could you have done this
and still be married to me?*

LINDA YATES: TO HER HUSBAND AFTER HIS ARREST

ON TUESDAY, 18 APRIL 2000

I have to admit that I don't know whether Linda Yates
received answers to those questions.

Nevertheless, inmate WDOC #817529 YATES, Robert
Lee Jr. is presently on death row at the Washington State
Penitentiary in the 'Evergreen State'. However, with that
said, on Thursday, 11 October 2018, the Washington
Supreme Court ruled the death penalty violated the State's
Constitution, so at least for the time being all executions
are on hold, Yates having been convicted on Wednesday,
19 September 2012 of murdering Melinda Mercer, aged

twenty-four, in 1997, and Connie LaFontaine Ellis, aged thirty-five, in 1998, in Pierce County, Washington State. His not so neighbourly neighbours on 'The Green Mile' are:

ELMORE, Clark Richard: Convicted Thursday, 6 July 1995 of one count of Aggravated First Degree homicide and one count of rape and the murder of Christy Onstad, aged fourteen, the daughter of his live-in girlfriend on Monday, 17 April 1995 in Whatcom County, WA.

GENTRY, Jonathan Lee: Convicted Wednesday, 26 June 1991 of fatally bludgeoning Cassie Holden, aged twelve, on Thursday 13 June 1988, in Kitsap County, WA.

DAVIS, Cecil Emile: Convicted Friday, 6 February 1998 of one count of Aggravated First-Degree homicide for the suffocation/asphyxiation of Yoshiko Couch, aged sixty-five, with a poisonous substance after burgling her home, robbing and then raping her on Monday, 25 January 1997, in Pierce County, WA.

CROSS, Dayva Michael: Convicted Friday, 22 June 2001 for the stabbing deaths of his wife, Anouchka Baldwin, aged thirty-seven, and stepdaughters, Amanda Baldwin, aged fifteen, and Salome Holle, aged eighteen, on Saturday, 6 March 1999 in King County, WA.

CONNER, Michael Schierman: Convicted Monday, 12 April 2010, of four counts of Aggravated First-Degree murder in the deaths of Olga Milking, aged twenty-eight; her sons Justin, aged five, and Andrew, aged three; and her sister, Lyubov Botvina, aged twenty-four, on Monday, 17 July 2006, in King County, WA.

GREGORY, Allen Eugene: Reconvicted Tuesday, 15 May 2012 of First-Degree Aggravated Murder for the rape and murder of Geneine 'Genie' Harshfield on Friday, 26 July 1996 in Pierce County. Originally convicted and sentenced to death on Friday, 25 May 2001, his case was overturned by the Washington Supreme Court on 30 November 2006. The original charge was upheld in a retrial and the death sentence was reissued on Friday, 13 July 2012.

SCHERF, Byron Eugene: Convicted Thursday, 9 May 2013 of Aggravated First-Degree Murder of Correctional Officer Jayme Beindl on Monday, 29 January 2001, while she was on duty at the Washington State Reformatory Unit of the Monroe Correctional Complex in Snohomish County, WA.

So can you imagine having one of these monsters living next door to you and never suspecting a thing, yet, his loving wife Linda not only had Robert living under the same roof, he was cuddled up tight to her almost every night – when he wasn't out and about raping and killing, that is!

* * *

Born Tuesday, 27 May 1952, in Oak Harbor, Spokane, Washington State, to Robert Lee Yates and Anna Mae Yates, Yates Jr. was sentenced to death but then this punishment was commuted to a natural life term of 408 years for the killing of *at least* eighteen women, mostly sex workers, between 1975 and 1998.

There is nothing in his formative years to suggest that Yates was ill-treated by his parents. He was raised in a middle-class family that attended a local Seventh-Day Adventist church. His schooling was without incident, him being a model pupil who graduated from Oak Harbor High School, on Wildcat Way, in 1970.

Aged twenty-three, he applied for a job as a corrections officer at the Washington State Penitentiary, Walla Walla. Little did he know back then that this Mother-of-all-Prisons would eventually become his permanent home, however, his first stint in one of the toughest supermax facilities in the US lasted a mere two years.

In 1975, Yates enlisted in the National Guard, and it may come as something of a surprise to learn that he became certified to fly helicopters and civilian aircraft – quite an achievement in anyone's book. He was stationed in Germany, later Somalia and Haiti during the UN peacekeeping missions of the 1990s. He was awarded Army Achievement Medals, three Army Commendation Medals and three Meritorious Service Medals. All-in-all he served almost nineteen years without a single stain on his character, yet underneath this mask of military and religious rectitude was a deviant sex pervert, and no one in the world had a clue that a monster breathed quietly underneath this well-polished veneer – a beast that was about to become one of the most heinous serial killers in the state's history.

* * *

Yates married Linda in 1976, and they had four children: Sonja, Michelle, Sasha and Amber. Early in the morning of Tuesday, 18 April 2000, police officers raided the Yate's family home. Linda and the children were ordered out of their beds while investigators searched for evidence. To her utter shock, she was told that Robert had been arrested on multiple counts of homicide. With nothing except the clothes on their backs, and to avoid the media who were literally camping outside, they went into hiding.

During one interview, Linda was asked: 'How could you not see the signs [that Robert was killing]?' to which the tearful woman replied: 'But, see, you're so close to somebody you *don't* see it.' Then, after some reflection, Linda added: ' ... maybe I suspected something. Especially when he was going hunting, and he was all dressed up nice and had cologne on ... you don't go out hunting with cologne on.'

Yes, Linda, your husband *was* going out hunting and he *was* dressed for the particular type of stalking he had in mind – human prey. She also told police that she had confronted him when she found evidence that indicated he was having extramarital affairs. However, being the sexual psychopath Robert Lee Yates had metamorphosed into, devoid of conscience like all of his ilk, he always had a very convincing excuse and as she said: 'He always had answers to everything already planned in his mind, I think.'

Can we now see the disturbing similarities between the conniving, manipulating mental trickery being played out again with Yates Jr., and all of the other killers we have met throughout the pages thus far? Of course we can because we are starting to know that when the red flags pop up we most often know what they might indicate.

Of course, Yates Jr. was a monster, for who else could bury one of his victims in the yard *right outside* of their bedroom window? What sort of sickening thrill must this man have felt while Linda slept warm, cosy, with a body decomposing close by? What sort of moral bankrupt would bury a body where his children played? 'They [police] called me at work and said, "We've found a body in your yard." And I said, "Oh my God", and I turned ice cold,' she explained.

Linda Yates also mentioned that her husband was a very 'moody person', adding, 'he could be real easy going, and go into a room and come out and be a totally different person for no apparent reason.'

Yes, we have seen these sudden, unexplained mood changes in our previous cases; where the woman becomes confused, anxious to know what is wrong and tries to placate her partner only to make matters far worse. Part of the reason I think why this occurs is because the female partner is not a sociopath *and the man is* – for not even the best psychiatrists and psychologists in the world can truly understand the true mind workings of people like Robert Yates. So, perhaps some readers have experienced these sorts of sudden unexplained mood swings in a partner, and yet their other half is so convincing – because their warped psychopathology is so deeply embedded – that these highly dangerous people, usually men, actually believe *that they are* right, so much so that *they convince you* that *you* are at fault and that it is *you* who are in the wrong.

In Yates's case, like so many others I have examined, corresponded with, or with the serial murderers I have interviewed face-to-face, these killers are *addicted* to the thrill of hunting and trawling for prey. If, for whatever reason, they are being restricted in their movements, they, like any other type of addict, become agitated, angry, and I have written about this type of behaviour many times before – without any criticism either, thus far.

As for other red flags in this case – some came up when Linda started going through the family accounts. For years this had been her household chore, but in late 1999 she found her spouse throwing credit card statements into their fireplace. It was only then that she noticed charges for 'Al's Spa Tub Motel', a seedy joint at 1421 N. Division Street, Spokane; a place she had never been to, more specifically where 'clients' pay by the hour. I am led to believe that they call them 'short time motels'. I am also led to believe there may be a relatively clean room, a relatively clean mattress, a washroom and little else. However, with this shaggers' motel bill shoved under Robert's nose, his excuse was this: 'Don't EVER accuse me of taking women there. I used the motel's hot tub to soothe my aching muscles after a twelve-hour shift': he worked at the nearby Kaiser Aluminium plant, and yeah, right, with circa 2,000 employees it seems that he was the only smelter or whatever they do in these plants, who frequented 'Al's Spa Tub Motel'! As a side note, if you feel compelled to pay this place a visit – just for a hot tub, obviously – don't bother because it has closed down.

And more red flags? Oh, gosh, there were so many more of them popping up week after week, too. For instance, Sonja found her father's address book one day and called the numbers of women whose names she did not recognise. 'Do you know

Robert Lee Yates Jr.?' she asked the women. Each woman denied pointblank knowing him. When confronted with this, daddy explained that the women were selling car parts for his many vehicles. And, it was around this time – with women disappearing from the streets of Spokane and elsewhere and with all of this reported by the media – Linda noticed that the family was running out of money. She complained to her husband about his frequent withdrawals from ATMs when she had not enough cash to buy decent food or petrol for her own car. Then to cap it all, the morally repugnant bigot that he was, told her for the first time in their twenty-six-year marriage to get a job, while he spent the family's money on sex workerss and seedy sex joints where the drinks were seven times the price of those bought in bona fide bars – not including the 'lady drinks' costing as much for just a glass of water and a spoonful of sweet honey – 'my honey'.

Red flag: Robert Yates stopped having sex with his wife. He told her that he was becoming impotent – a likely yarn that was too. He talked about using Viagra. Bless her, the loving, trusting Linda, said: 'It's okay, Bob. You're probably tired, and I am tired too.' Sick and tired of his lying ways I expect because can one imagine what this poor woman was going through back then? But, Holy Moly, she then found a horde of sex magazines featuring orgies and lists of people interested in group sex. When she asked him about this he replied: 'Have you ever fantasised about making out with another woman?' 'I don't believe in THAT stuff,' Linda curtly replied.

Red flag: Linda also noticed that when they went to parties together, Robert's former military colleagues always seemed surprised that *he actually had a wife*. He would drink heavily, moon over other women and bullshit – saying that he was actually like a real James Bond. What a donut!

Nevertheless, having suffered such incalculable psychological abuse over a lengthy period, Linda's troubles were far from over after his trial because not only had her husband been the breadwinner, half of the family's biggest asset was their two-story home on Spokane's South Hill. It was valued at $113,000 – not a small amount back then – sadly their liabilities totaled $475,000, and one of the creditors was a Christine L. Smith; a woman who had survived an attack in 1998. She had filed a lawsuit against Robert Yates as soon as he pleaded guilty to attempted first-degree murder in that incident.

As an endnote: much earlier in their marriage, Linda had left her husband for a month when she discovered he had drilled a hole in an attic wall so he could watch a couple having sex in an adjoining apartment. Although they reunited, she felt that the romance was gone, but she felt guilty about splitting up the family. 'The kids loved their dad and I just kinda suffered through it. I didn't love him like a wife should. He killed that,' she said, using an unintended pun.

Yes, Linda, and our hearts go out to you and your children and we wish you well for the future. However, as is this is *my* book, I *will* end this on a much less compassionate note for your ex-husband. Having spent some time in the Washington State Penitentiary where I interviewed the sadosexual serial killer, Kenneth Alessio Bianchi aka 'The Hillside Strangler', and having seen the gallows and having stepped onto the trap, as God is my witness I would have loved to have had the opportunity to have pulled the lever on Robert Lee Yates Jr. – having seen some of the horrific post-mortem photographs of his victims. Watching this creep being strapped terrified to a support board *would* have *truly have made my day*, for while he has been given a 'reprieve' of sorts as the state re-juggles his constitutional rights in a renewed effort to top him, I have to ask myself, what about the 'constitutional rights' of his victims, *and yours*, Linda Yates?

> *I am wicked in many ways.*
> Jessica Spotswood: Born Wicked
> (Cahill Witch Chronicles, 2008)

To end this chapter, let's examine what happened in 1977 after one mother (name removed for legal reasons) noticed severe behavioural changes in her husband, James Carson, and who consequently packed her bags and left with their daughter Jennifer.

With his wife out of the way, Carson fell in with Susan Barnes, a divorcee with two teenage sons. They married and became involved in illicit drugs and mysticism, and while stoned out of his head for most of the day and night, he decided to change his name to 'Michael Bear', telling his daughter in a letter that God had given him the new name. Thereafter, Susan became known as 'Suzan Bear'.

After a twelve-month trip to Europe, in 1980, the Carsons, he now aged thirty and she now aged thirty-nine, returned to the USA and moved into the Haight-Ashbury neighbourhood of San Francisco, where they continued their involvement with drugs and the counterculture. However, by this time his former wife had become so afraid that he would harm her and snatch her daughter away, she moved numerous times and even cut off any contact with mutual acquaintances.

The 'Holy War Against Witches' murder spree committed by the Carsons involved at least three awful homicides before they were arrested in 1983. On Tuesday, 12 June 1984, they were convicted of their first murder, that of twenty-three-year-old aspiring actress Karen Barnes (no relation to Suzan), and were sentenced to twenty-five years in prison. Subsequently, the bewitched were also convicted of the murders of thirty-year-old Jon Charles Hellyar and farmworker Clark Stephens, for which they received sentences of fifty years to life and seventy-five years to life, respectively.

If you are inclined to take a peek at inmate #314101 Carson, you can find him by doing an inmate search of the Arizona Dept Corrections website, at once noting that he has a projected release date as of 13 December 2021, but we can be assured that he will not be going anywhere until he leaves prison in a pine box.

As for Suzan Carson, dubbed by the media 'The Witch Killer', she is no longer in jail. It was initially thought that she had acquired a broomstick and flown away, but then I learned that because of prison overcrowding she was released under emergency laws. In an even more bizarre twist, Michael was also offered parole but he turned it down, saying there was no chance of him being let out because he still thought the murders were right. The pair, who described themselves as Muslims and mystics, had once told reporters, 'Witchcraft, homosexuality and abortion are causes for death.' Suzan claimed to have 'yogic powers' and said she could see the future.

Unlike Linda Yates, James Carson's first wife escaped her marriage before her husband started killing, but she remained fearful of him – a feeling all too familiar to many of the wives and partners of such killers.

Monsters Sleeping
with Monsters

All that we are is the result of what we have thought.
The mind is everything. What we think we become.
ATTRIBUTED TO GAUTAMA BUDDHA: PHILOSOPHER;
MENDICANT; MEDITATOR AND SPIRITUAL TEACHER
(C. 5TH–4TH CENTURY BC)

Isn't it chillingly, morbidly fascinating to try to understand what makes these evil psychopaths' or sociopaths' minds tick, for they have no moral compass, no conscience, and no socially acceptable values whatsoever. Can one even begin to imagine being like that ... devoid of any warmth at all – unless it suits them to give it, that is! They are cold, calculating, 'me, me, me' people. They are only in it for themselves: selfish, greedy, hurting, robbing and exploitative; raping and killing with as much compassion as one would thwack an annoying fly – and, of course, most of them are extreme narcissists, which really goes without saying.

But what if we have two of these human monsters of any mix of sexual orientation, sleeping together? Well, there are plenty of examples of this, taking the British psycho-sadistic sexual serial killers Myra Hindley (1942–2002) and Ian Brady (1938–2017), or Rosemary West (1953–) and Fred West (1941–95), to name four names that are all too familiar to us true crime aficionados. Can one imagine what they must have talked about while cooking dinner or in bed for the night – not their love of humanity or any form of religious belief, that's for sure! However, before we move onto several of the most appalling specimens and look a little closer into their psychopathologies, I want to move off track for a moment or two to refer to what I call 'The Blame Game'.

* * *

Over my years of interviewing and corresponding with many of these God-awful types, I have learned, while trying to suspend my disbelief, that they are *never*, *ever* to blame. They are all innocent, you see. And, if you were to write to any homicidal psychopath behind bars, they will, with few exceptions, tell you exactly the same thing – as having been 'fitted up'!

'The Blame Game' takes many forms and trying to understand the mechanics of these is a complex business. Yet here is some good news; I think that we can get a bit of a head start with this 'blame shifting' aka 'transference of blame' stuff, in a 'Not me, guv' sort of way.

Perhaps a more technical way of putting this is called 'psychological projection'. At its most basic level, this is a defence mechanism people employ – either subconsciously or overtly consciously – in order to cope with difficult situations, feelings or emotions. The theory of psychological projection was developed by the 'Father of Psycho-analysis', Sigmund Freud, and the psychiatrists-cum-'trick cyclists' will call this 'Freudian projection'. During my interviews with killers, I have noticed – as Freud did during his sessions with patients – that they sometimes accuse others of having the same feelings they themselves were demonstrating. A sort of mirroring if you will and, by engaging in this behaviour, the subject was better able to deal with the emotions he or she was experiencing. Sounds a bit complicated doesn't it, but it isn't, trust Christopher on this one, please – allegedly.

A classic example of Freudian projection is that of a woman who has been unfaithful to her husband – or vice versa – but who accuses her husband of cheating on her. If you are an avid TV watcher, you might have seen the USA victim reality series *Cheaters*, in which you would recognise another aspect of Freudian projection – 'denial'. This is when the cheater literally gets caught with his trousers, or her panties, pulled down, yet they vehemently deny any guilt – even when it is staring them straight in their faces, and even when all of their naughtiness has been captured on hidden cameras for millions to watch on TV.

Another aspect is the distortion element, inter alia: changing the reality of a given situation to suit one's needs. Of course, there are many positive types of Freudian projection, but for the purposes of this book, we are looking specifically at the 'blame game' and projecting the blame for one's criminal acts and weaknesses and shortcomings onto someone, or something, else.

Some of the best examples of transference of blame can be found during criminal trials – in cases where a defendant attempts to mitigate, or present extenuating circumstances, in other words 'excuses', for his, or her, unlawful behaviour, using their pathological distortion of reality. One can attend any criminal trial in the UK or the USA and watch an accused person's legal team use any mitigation ruse known to mankind to get their client off the hook so to speak, even when it is as clear as day that the person standing in the dock is as guilty as sin.

For example: 'the Word of God' ordering a person to commit rape and homicide is a well-worn try-on that never works, yet attorneys still try to pull off this excuse even to this day. In the UK we had Peter Sutcliffe hearing it, allegedly telling him to kill sex workers, while he was digging a grave. But of course Sutcliffe didn't only kill 'working girls', did he, so this mitigation fell on deaf ears.

Years ago, I interviewed the US serial killers, Harvey 'The Hammer' Louis Carignan and Arthur 'Art' John Shawcross (aka 'The Monster of the Rivers'), in their respective prisons. Both of them at one time used this divine mitigation, while Kenneth Alessio Bianchi aka 'The Hillside Strangler' – whom I have also interviewed – blamed all of his crimes on 'Stevie', a purely invented, and thus fake, multiple personality (MPD; see page 278).

Specifically in capital cases, another category of attempting to mitigate a lighter sentence, i.e. shifting the blame onto someone or something else, is an issue that truly does stick in my craw – that of psychological mitigation. Here, an offender might argue that he suffered an abusive childhood: he was badly potty-trained; he fell down a flight of steps and bumped his head; he was forced to wear diapers until he was eighteen years old; he was only allowed to drink green top milk instead of blue full cream; he was under the influence of drugs wrongly prescribed by a doctor; he was temporarily insane at the time of the killings, and, therefore, was not responsible for his or her actions; or he even demanded a retrial because his original public defender was as drunk as a lord and had never before tried a homicide case. Some of these claims may have been true, but so what? Does it excuse a person for stalking, raping, torturing and killing innocent men, women of all ages, even kiddies – NO IT DOES NOT, period. Indeed, the reader can watch any criminal trial on YouTube and listen to the utter bullshit these 'mitigation specialists' so often dish out ... In the USA they have to, because they are paid by the defence team to come up with any crap that might sway a half-awake jury in their 'client's' favour. I have extensively covered this very same issue in my bestseller, *Talking with Psychopaths and Savages: A journey into the evil mind*, in which I uncovered a terrible truth – that some of the so-called 'experts' who have examined and psychologically mitigated some of the most heinous killers at their trials have more in common with the mental state of the defendants than one would ever have expected, with head-shrinker and 'client' both being completely off the wall.

Having got that off of my chest, back to the subject in hand – blame it all on one's partner-in-crime – with another tried and tested Freudian denial/distortion of the facts scenario, as in the sort of blame game typified by 'He [or She] made me do it', or 'I was led astray'.

In British criminal parlance, 'grassing your accomplice up' means to become a 'snitch', a prosecution witness hoping to get a lighter custodial term in the nick, or 'the pen' as they say across the pond. In the USA's criminal justice system, police and prosecutors *will* bend over backwards to cultivate a defendant who 'grasses up' an accomplice just to gain a solid conviction when the evidence is so paper thin one could roll a cigarette in it. They might blame corrupt cops; in appeal proceedings they will argue that their previous legal representation was slack if not useless, that the attorney was hand-in-glove with the judge – which is quite often true, because many judges and cops in the USA are so bent they cannot even lie straight in bed. So transference of blame does have its place in criminal proceedings – but whether or not a jury can see through the smoke and mirrors is another matter entirely.

* * *

Do you fancy watching about nine plus hours of YouTube? If you are nodding affirmatively, please try the trial of Jodi Arias for the stabbing/shooting murder of her ex-lover, all-American hunk Travis Alexander, on Wednesday, 4 June 2008. Here, one can see 'mitigation' plastered everywhere: memory loss; it was all Travis's fault that dear, sweet Jodi, went berserk and painted half of the first floor of his house with his own blood. If you have the stomach for it, take a peek at the scenes-of-crime photos on the Internet and you will see her defence, of acting in self-defence, shot completely to pieces.

Better still, and a lot shorter time-wise, is the murder

trial of Oscar Pistorius for the 2013 murder of his girlfriend, Reeva Steenkamp; one which highlights again this mitigation issue of transferring blame onto something or someone else. This narcissistic, self-absorbed, up-his-own-backside piece of work had picked an argument with Reeva on Valentine's Day. She had been amiably chatting to a male friend on the telephone ... it was all completely innocent, too. Although the bigoted Pistorius was having affairs left, right and centre while Reeva was totally in love with Oscar and as faithful as anyone can be, this man with a profoundly fragile sense of self-esteem had the damned nerve to accuse her of cheating on *him*. They argued, and she became so terrified she ran to the bathroom and locked herself in. What did this monster do? He picked up a heavy-calibre pistol and fired several shots through the locked door and literally blew this beautiful woman's head apart. Pistorius's mitigation was, essentially, that he *thought* that there was an intruder who had locked himself into the bathroom. He *thought* that the burglar might have a firearm. He *thought* that when he fired his gun loaded with dum-dum rounds, that Reeva was downstairs at the time making a cup of tea, or something. I mean, one could not have made this up if one tried. So watching his trial on YouTube makes *for very fascinating viewing* – far better than any TV soap, I can honestly testify to that, too!

Yes, yes, I know that Pistorius was known as the 'Blade Runner' on account of him being a Paralympic sprinter and stuff, so we can't take that away from him, but imagine if it had been *your own* daughter whose head had been blown apart, with bone and brain and blood splattered all over a wall. Please, just think about it for a moment. Hold this terrible thought in your mind. Think how Barry and June Steenkamp feel, when every hour of every day they look at the silver-framed photos of their ever so precious daughter and grieve at her passing. Look up Reeva on Wikipedia. Now imagine being Barry and June and witness some well-paid assholes of shrinks and lawyers trying to get that scum piece of work off the hook. Even today he *still* holds court and whines, bitches and complains that his sentence is too harsh.

* * *

The subject of 'couples who kill' is equally as interesting as their individual psychopathologies. One might reasonably ask whether or not Myra Hindley or Rose West would have become involved in serial homicide without the influence of their respective partners. I think not. However, this can be *no* mitigation in any court of law because each woman was as guilty as the man, of this there can be no doubt. Had either of these women had any moral compass whatsoever they would have walked away long before the crimes began, not slept with their respective accomplices until they were arrested for murder most foul.

Dubbed by the media as 'the Ken and Barbie Killers', Paul Kenneth Bernardo (1964–) was married to the very attractive Karla Homolka, aka 'the Schoolgirl Killer' (1970–). Both Canadian, between them they killed three or four women and committed some thirteen rapes between March 1986 and April 1992. Three of their victims were minors: Leslie Mahaffy and Kristen French, plus Homolka's own sister

Tammy, who was raped and killed. For her part, and using the defence that she was forced into the rapes and killings by Bernardo, Karla copped a plea bargain deal with prosecutors for reduced manslaughter charges and sentenced to a mere twelve years in prison. However, to prove just how corrupt the system of justice can be at times, this woman – who knowingly slept with 'Bernie the Sex-Craved Monster' – had videotaped some of their crimes which surfaced after their sentences had been confirmed. These tapes demonstrated that she was not by a long chalk the 'Miss Innocent' party at all. She had been a very enthusiastic participant throughout. As a result, the deal that she struck with prosecutors to shift all the blame onto Bernardo was dubbed in the Canadian press 'the Deal with the Devil'.

Homolka was released from prison in 2005 having served just ten years. She remarried, and the couple have children, despite an order that she should not come into close contact with children ever again, *and* despite the most vehement protests from scores of parents. At the time of writing she works part time at a children's school, taking kids out on day trips from time-to-time. This Christian school says that it is well-aware of Homolka's criminal antecedents while blandly turning a deaf ear to any complaints.

Now, I am all up for the reformation of character ... giving the chance to those who commit crime to learn their lessons, even to settle down into our communities – but allowing Karla Homolka to interact with young children again is going too far, I think. Can you imagine if in this country we had allowed Myra Hindley out of jail after a mere ten years behind bars ... or Rose West, for that matter,

203

permitting these two morally defunct homicidal monsters to take kids out for the day?

But, finally to nail this case, despite the original charges of kidnapping, aggravated sexual assault, unlawful confinement and first-degree murder ... yes, yes, yes ... topped up with torture and dismemberment, Homolka being the 'seat of evil' was evaluated by psychiatrists as having every chance of rehabilitation. For his part, Bernardo is presently incarcerated at the Millhaven Institution, Bath, Ontario. One can watch his previous police and prison interviews on YouTube – all real-life true crime brought right into *your* front room, or even *your* own bedroom if you want a nightmare, so enjoy.

Now, how about another couple of monsters: Cynthia Lynn Coffman and her lover, James Marlow, who were found guilty of raping then killing four women and a thirteen-year-old girl in October and November 1986. Both killers were sentenced to death, with Coffman's mitigation being that, although they were always out of their tiny minds on methamphetamines she was battered, brainwashed and starved so she did not run and inform the police and tell all. Why? Because she says that she suffered from 'battered wife syndrome', none of which prevented her from having 'Property of the Folsom Wolf' tattooed on her backside. Nevertheless, she did earn the notable distinction of becoming the first woman in the State of California to receive the death sentence since its reinstatement in 1977. Of course the jury never believed a word of her mitigation – this blaming everything on her lowlife partner.

At present, Cynthia is sitting on death row in the Central California Woman's Facility. She had been charged with the following: murder in the course of flight; kidnapping; kidnapping for robbery; robbery; residential burglary; forcible sodomy; and unlawful possession of firearms. Her appeal in the Supreme Court of California – 'PEOPLE *V.* COFFMAN' – can be found under 'Findlaw' on Google. It makes for fascinating reading.

Claudia Kraig Barrows, Marcia Wilson, Judith Mawson v. Gary Leon Ridgway (USA)

He made me smile every day. I had the perfect husband,
perfect life. I absolutely adored him.
JUDITH MAWSON: ON GARY RIDGWAY

How *can* the 'perfect husband' be the archetypal spawn of Satan at the same time? That's a question begging to be answered as we now turn our attention to perhaps one of the most heinous serial killers in US history. It is probable that Gary Ridgway's body count exceeded that of Ted Bundy's – for even today the precise number of Ted's killings is unknown.

Ridgway certainly committed murder more times than John Wayne Gacy, or our Victorian 'Jack the Ripper', or Peter Sutcliffe aka 'The Yorkshire Ripper'. Not even the sadosexual serial killing duo, Kenneth Bianchi and his half-cousin Angelo 'Tony' Buono, came close to the forty-eight confirmed killings committed by the man dubbed by the media as the 'Green River Killer', who was active from 1982 to 2001, yet he confessed to even more slayings: seventy-one. However, as Judith 'Judy' Mawson would testify, 'Gary was the perfect husband'.

During their nineteen-year manhunt for the Green River Killer, the very elite of US law enforcement were at such a loss as to identifying the offender that the FBI went and interviewed Ted Bundy on Florida's death row to seek his help in trying to profile the man they were seeking. It all bears similarities to the plot of *The Silence of the Lambs*, with rookie FBI Agent Clarice Starling interviewing Dr Hannibal Lecter in the grim dungeon scenes we have come to know all too well. Of course, none of this implies that US law enforcement was slack, incompetent or anything else, but what this *does prove*, beyond a shadow of any doubt, is that Ridgway so perfectly wore the mask of normality that for almost two decades no-one had a clue that beneath his socially acceptable façade breathed a sex predator of truly monstrous proportions.

This mask of normality issue is a subject upon which I have written extensively in many of my books, including the international bestsellers, *Talking with Psychopaths and Savages*, and its sequel, *Talking with Psychopaths and Savages: Beyond Evil*. It is a mind-bending subject, indeed it truly is, for as we have seen thus far in this book, the women who marry these types of monsters have *no* idea whatsoever that they are sleeping next to vicious beasts and the sadistic behaviour of their partners goes completely unnoticed.

I was crying. No, it can't be him.
Judith Mawson: after Ridgway's arrest

According to Judith, during the entire thirteen years of their relationship they lived a completely normal life – going to work then on weekend camping trips, etc. – but there were one or two red flags that raised mild suspicions. When she visited Gary's home while they were dating, she found no carpet – only a mattress and box springs on the bare floor. His excuse was that his tenants had ruined the carpets and an ex-girlfriend had taken the bed away, so, with no reason to doubt him, she believed him. Little could she have known that he'd removed the bed and carpet because they were soaked in the blood and urine of his murder victims, whom he had strangled, and then dumped their bodies like so much garbage in the forest and at other desolate locations, sometimes returning to have sex with the rotting corpses. How could she have suspected such a God-awful thing – no woman ever would have, that's for sure.

Matthew Ridgway remembers his father as a 'relaxed man who never yelled', as a pa who took him camping at weekends, alternating between Washington and Oregon, who taught him to play baseball near the sixty-five-mile long Green River and who always attended school concerts and soccer practices. 'Even when I was in fourth grade, when I was with soccer, he'd always be there for me,' Matthew (then twenty-six and a US Marine stationed at Camp Pendleton, near San Diego) told investigators on Saturday, 1 December 2001, the day after his truck-driving father's arrest for four murders. 'I don't think I ever remember him not being there,' he added. However, during the years when his father was taking Matthew on bike rides along a Green River trail, to stop to eat Hostess cakes or play in a park, he was also terrorising the South Sound by killing women and dumping their corpses in deserted areas in King County. Indeed, as a matter of fact, Matthew played an unwitting part in the serial killing; after his arrest, Gary Ridgway told cops that he sometimes showed a photograph of his son, or one of his son's bedroom, to women to put them at ease. One example of this twisted ruse was in July 1982. Ridgway had picked up a woman with his son in their car, killed her in nearby woods and then told Matthew that the woman had decided to walk home. On another occasion, he had sex with the dead body of one of his victims while Matthew slept in his car, about thirty feet away.

* * *

Born in Salt Lake City, on Friday, 18 February 1949, Gary Ridgway was the second of three sons: Gregory was born in 1948, their younger brother Thomas Edward in 1951. Gary's formative years were somewhat troubled: he was dyslexic, and a bedwetter until he was thirteen. According to relatives, Mrs Mary Ridgway, a saleswoman at J.C. Penney in Renton, was a domineering woman and he witnessed occasional fights between matriarch and patriarch. His father was a bus driver who often complained about the presence of sex workers near their home; he was a nasty man who frequently beat his sons badly with either a stick or a leather belt. Later, Gary told defence psychologists that as an adolescent he had conflicting feelings of anger and sexual attraction towards his mother and fantasised about killing her – which seems to stem from experiencing his mother washing his genitals after every bedwetting episode. But he also had a violent side to him.

Aged just sixteen, with an IQ in the low eighties, he led a six-year-old boy into woods, where he stabbed him through the ribs and into his liver. The kid survived.

On Monday, 18 August 1969, now aged twenty, Ridgway joined the US Navy, was sent to Vietnam where he served on board a supply ship, frequently enjoying the services of sex workers – especially Filipinas – from whom he contracted gonorrhea and, although this upset him greatly, he carried on using these women without protection.

We can now turn to Ridgway's female partners – his first wife being nineteen-year-old Claudia Kraig Barrows whom he married on Saturday, 15 August 1970. They had met in a bar, with frequent outdoor sex in a car marking the high points in the young couple's courtship. They favoured a wooded area in Seward Park and a dead-end street off Military Road South – one of the many South King County side roads Ridgway knew all too well. However, soon after that they moved to San Diego, Ridgway set out on a six-month tour. While he was gone his young wife had an affair – she was living with a female friend and a male roommate. Meanwhile, overseas he had a fully blown extramarital affair, so it will come as no surprise to learn that his marriage to Claudia lasted until 1972. In the interim, during the summer of 1971 Ridgway returned to Seattle. Court records show that Claudia followed a few weeks later. He was discharged from the US Navy on Friday, 23 July 1971, returning to his former job with the Kenworth truck-manufacturing company.

It is fair to say that, at first blush the couple did try and save this botched-up marriage, but the effort, like their marriage, was brief. Initially, they lived with Gary's parents, then in an apartment near Sea-Tac Airport, then in August, Claudia left for San Diego and moved in with a boyfriend whom she later married. On Thursday, 2 September, five weeks after leaving the Navy and one year after marrying Claudia, Ridgway filed for divorce, which was finalised in January 1972.

Next up was Marcia Winslow. Around the middle of 1972, Ridgway met a woman who was 'cruising the Renton loop'. Marcia says he pulled her over in what she described as a 'police-like-stop'. With his short hair and military manner, she thought he could have been a cop. He wasn't, and he and Marcia started dating; during their first sexual encounters he called her 'Claudia'.

They married in December 1973, yet throughout this period he spoke often about his bitter divorce from Claudia in racially charged terms, at once claiming that Claudia, although he still loved her (allegedly), had moved in with several men and had become, or resumed her career as, a sex worker, which might well have been true.

During Ridgway's marriage to Marcia, he introduced her to his favourite South King County haunts – the same places where he'd taken Claudia for outdoor or in-car sex trysts along back roads and wooded dead-ends in Maple Valley, Enumclaw and North Bend. All a bit seedy, perhaps, but one can easily find these locations on Google Maps, all obscure, untended turnoffs along Highway 18, shady spots near Star Lake and along the banks, of the ... *yes*, of course, the Green River.

'He was a scavenger,' Marcia would later tell investigators. 'He picked through the refuse at dump sites, searching for items that might be worth selling.' Indeed, this habit stayed with him. Buying and selling at garage sales and swap meets was a hobby throughout Ridgway's life, according to neighbours and co-workers.

It is also interesting to note, that by the time of his marriage to Marcia, Ridgway was well established at Kenworth's Seattle plant, for he had risen in seniority and salary, then having moved to the new Renton factory, opened in 1993. 'This was Ridgway's domain,' said Martha Parkhill, one of his colleagues. 'He was a truck painter and good at it. He was meticulous. He had a steady hand, an attention to detail, a natural ability to transfer the intricacies of a blueprint to the expanse of fiberglass,' she said, adding, 'He wanted to do a good job. Some designs are very complex, and you have to have the left side and right side of the cab perfectly match. It takes a lot of patience.'

What a fascinating psychopathology Ridgway has. There he was out scavenging for stuff to sell, searching for various antiques or cheap materials he could use to improve his home, while breaktime at work was his Bible time. He was sociable, a friendly guy who knew everyone enough to say 'Hello'. He often wore jeans and Western-style or button-down shirts. He carried a squirt bottle and comb to keep his hair and moustache in place. Yet, with all of this, Parkhill sensed something a bit creepy about her fellow cab painter: 'He'd come up behind me and massage my shoulders. He did that to several women down there. I'd try to shrug away from him. I never wanted to make him mad, just for him to stop,' she later to detectives.

It has to be said that within this marriage there were infidelities on both sides, and the marriage was sometimes stormy, with Marcia claiming that Ridgway had once tried to choke her. Returning home from a party where the couple had been drinking, she stepped out of their van and stumbled toward the door of their house. Suddenly she felt hands around her neck, squeezing tighter and tighter. She screamed and fought, not immediately realising it was her husband, who finally let go then darted to the other side of the van while trying to convince her someone else had done it. If this wasn't a red flag, I don't know what is. In addition, he liked to sneak up and scare her, she said. 'He would see if he could walk up noiselessly,' which she says he could.

In 1982, seven years after the birth of their son Matthew, Ridgway started committing sexual homicide.

* * *

If one were to look up the term 'priapic' in an online dictionary, one might imagine Ridgway's face staring back. According to the women in his worthless life, he had an insatiable sexual appetite. His three wives and several ex-girlfriends told police that he demanded sex from them several times a day, which echoes precisely the sex drive of the now executed Connecticut serial killer, Michael Bruce Ross, whom I mentioned in an earlier chapter. Ridgway's preference was for sex workers, about whom he admitted he had a fixation coupled with a love/hate relationship. And, ever the moral bigot, and just like his own father, he frequently complained about them working in his neighbourhood. So, here, once again, we find a man with three masks – a so-called devoted family man torn between his sexual deviancies and his apparently staunch religious beliefs.

Despite being married to Marcia, Ridgway also played around behind her back, and unbeknownst to her, in early 1981 he joined a 'Parents Without Partners' group and started dating three women we shall call A, B and C.

Not wasting any time, he met his first bit-on-the-side, Miss 'A' that May, and soon slyly moved into her West Seattle home. Patterns from his prior relationships materialised – the couple had sex outdoors in many locations. Twice, he tied up Miss 'A' without her consent. Their relationship was almost exclusively physical and many times she told Ridgway to back off from his constant demands for sex. He had no personal friends and she assumed that he was 'dominated by women'. In December 1981, she'd had enough so she ordered him out of her home, but by then Ridgway had met Miss 'B'.

Ridgway started dating Miss 'B', but they didn't visit his usual locations, they either went to her house or his place on Military Road in SeaTac – a place he had bought in 1981 and had lived in for seven years. This was a quiet neighbourhood where everyone minded their own business, so Ridgway minded his, too. 'His house was always closed up – it seemed very private although the yard was always messy,' said Debbie Roselieb, who lived near by. She recalled that, 'If I was walking by, I'd say "Hi", But he'd just ignore me and walk past. It was more private than rude. It was like he just wanted to be left alone.'

Miss 'B' had met Ridgway at about 11 p.m. on Christmas Eve 1981, at the White Shutters Inn, in SeaTac, for a Parents Without Partners function. During the conversation, he told her that he had nearly killed a woman, and she thought he meant a sex worker. As one might imagine, this relationship would soon fizzle out like a damp squib, and whilst still seeing 'Miss B' he started dating Miss 'C'.

On Tuesday, 11 May 1982, police arrested Ridgway on suspicion of soliciting an undercover King County vice cop disguised as a sex worker, and Miss 'C' would later tell police that Ridgway regarded sex workers as 'things to be used'.

> *When they mentioned the name, I thought, 'Gary Ridgway. I hope that's not the Gary Ridgway I knew.' I told my wife, 'That was my neighbor. I went to school with this guy.' It was really sad. He never exhibited anything like an oddity that way toward women or anything that I would see that would make me suspect him of having that type of personality. The picture I keep getting in my mind is of a somewhat smallish kid – 5 feet 7 or 5 feet 8, 145 pounds, with wispy hair. Nondescript.*
>
> Gilbert Mendiola: The News Tribune,
> 16 December 2001.

In 1975 she gave him a son, whom they named Matthew. Around about this time Ridgway underwent something akin to a religious conversion. He began to preaching door-to-door around his neighbourhood, he always had the Bible with him, even when at home watching television, and would regularly read it aloud, even at work; he kept exhorting his wife to follow the strict teachings of their pastor and would weep after sermons or during Bible readings. Yet despite all of this, he continued to solicit the services of sex workers and wanted his wife to have sex outdoors, sometimes even in places where his victim's bodies were later discovered.

According to the women in his worthless life, he had a voracious sexual appetite. His three wives and several ex-girlfriends all told police that he demanded sex from them several times a day. His preference, however, was for sex workers, on whom he admitted he had a fixation. And, ever the moral bigot, and just like his own father, he often complained about them working in his neighbourhood. So, here, we find a man with three masks – an apparently devoted family man torn between his sexual deviances and his pseudo staunch religious beliefs. Marcia would later tell police that he became 'fanatical' about religion, before his churchgoing gradually tapered off.

During this time, even more red flags were being hoisted. Marcia told detectives that her husband began to come home from work later and later without explanation, often returning to the house dirty and wet. Another thing she noticed more and more: he had no personal friends throughout their entire marriage. Eventually, Marcia filed for divorce in May 1981 and this included a restraining order. The spiteful Ridgway countered with one of his own, with both saying they feared the other would become violent.

Ridgway would also meet his third wife, Judith Lynch, at a 'Parents Without Partners' event in 1985. They married in 1988, and bought a home on South 253rd Street in Des Moines. They lived there until 1997, during which time he radically changed, becoming an extrovert who went out of his way to talk to his neighbours. He also took an almost obsessive interest in gardening, neighbours said. 'He kept his house well and he kept his yard up well,' said Mike Welch. 'He seemed to be a model neighbor. If Ridgway had a fault, it was that he was a little overly friendly.'

So let's leave this chapter with the words of Judith (from an interview with *Serial Killer Magazine*):

I was shocked that day when I heard someone driving up in the driveway and, I couldn't believe it. I still can't believe it but it has happened and, oh, it was like a brick wall had dropped in front of me and I didn't know what to do. Everything stopped. It still feels the same way today, as if time is standing still and I can still hear the sounds of police cars coming down the driveway. It's a day I can never forget. He was happy and smiling. He never changed. He made me feel like a newlywed every day.

What I miss the most is the love that I had, and our life, and, he was the best. To me anyway. After his arrest, he was assuring me that everything would be okay — it was painful. He's never raised his hand to me. Never raised his voice, and when he was away from home or late he always had an explanation. He was working overtime at Kenworth, or attending a union meeting. I never saw anything suspicious at all — I was such in total denial.

The penny finally dropped for Judith when she found a stash of condoms in their garage. Police found stuff in the framework of Ridgway's pickup truck and it got worse when they tore Judith's car apart and the crime lab found traces of semen, with cops now telling her that her husband had been using her car to pick up some of his victims.

'Then I suddenly felt the anger that he'd had sex with

someone else that, um, that he'd hurt me, he'd betrayed me,' she later said during a TV interview. 'He said he did not do anything with those women but when I found the condoms and stuff then I realised that he did. So I said to him: "Oh, you son of a bitch, why did you do this to me, why? Why did you put me through all this?"'

> *My heart goes out to all of those families and the victims that he hurt and I can't even imagine what they have been through. I loved the man I knew and I hate them who took him away. Yet now I wish they'd execute him.*
> Judith Mawson: Gary Ridgway's third wife

The locations of Ridgway's body-dumping sites can be found on the Internet: https://storymaps.arcgis.com/stories/e457a96188eb4473b0739463e368e026

As for their killer, WDOC #866218 RIDGWAY, Gary L., is serving a natural-life term at the Washington State Penitentiary (WSP), in Walla Walla, WA.

Juliana 'Julie' Baumeister v.
Herbert Richard 'Herb' Baumeister
(USA)

We were really looking for a house that was somewhere
out there that had some space and kinda away from the city
and so I ran across it at night and thought this is just perfect.
JULIE BAUMEISTER: ON FOX HOLLOW FARM

There is an almost nursery rhyme feel to the name 'Fox Hollow Farm'. In reality it's an eighteen–acre stable, off 156th Street, Westfield, Hamilton County, Indiana, and for the population of approximately 38,700, it's a place of peace and quiet and traditional family lives. A suburb of Indianapolis, it is one of the best and safest places to live in the Hoosier State. Yet the events that took place at sleepy Fox Hollow Farm have become one of the notorious series of crimes in the state's history, and since 1996 the 11,000–square-foot 1977 lavish mock Tudor house with an indoor swimming pool has had various owners who claimed that the place was haunted. They have said that

221

they heard strange noises, feel unsettled and see apparitions – and perhaps there is something eerie and sinister going on, for police would find eleven bodies and over 5,000 human bone fragments buried on the land – up to sixteen murders taking place there – all of which would have remained unearthed until one of killer Herb Baumeister's children found a human skull and human bones. Later, during the 1980s, many other partially naked corpses were found dumped along the I-70 across central Indiana and western Ohio.

Herb Baumeister, aka 'Brian Smart' (1947–96), was one of four children, with an apparently normal childhood. However at the start of his adolescence he started behaving in an antisocial manner, played around with dead animals and urinating over his teacher's desk. Make of that as you will, but in his teens he was diagnosed with schizophrenia. As an adult, he drifted through a number of jobs, and although a hard worker his increasingly bizarre behaviour was a problem throughout.

Things started to look up for Herb when, in November 1971, he married Juliana 'Julie' Saiter. They'd met when she was a sophomore at Indiana University and while preparing to go to the Rose Bowl. At first impression he was great fun to be with and she enjoyed herself, later saying: 'I enjoyed myself more when I was in his company ... it was love and peace and everyone was spaced out on drugs and just talk ... and we never did that ... most of things we did was driving around and getting a Coke there ... we had a great time ... sometimes much better than adulthood.' Then they had three children: Marie in 1979, Erich in 1981, and Emily in 1984, with Julie saying:

When the kids came along we had very family-orientated values, you know we didn't have candlelight dinners and we didn't run off on romantic weekends together, we were much more family loved. We enjoyed life. My kids would go out rollerblading, at night, they could ride their bicycles getting muddy and going tramping through the creek, or playing out in the leaves and just being kids. It was the perfect place, the all-American Dream.

Somewhat remarkably Julie would later say that they had been sexually intimate *only six times* in over twenty-five years of marriage – so, to be a tad on the crude side, one could say that three out of six darts hitting the Bullseye wasn't bad going after all! However, during the 1970s, his father, Herbert Baumeister Sr., had committed Herb-the-Younger to a psychiatric hospital. Julie said that he was 'hurting and needed help', yet he seemed to have fully recovered because in 1988 he founded the successful Sav-A-Lot thrift store chain in Indianapolis. But it all came unstuck when their thirteen-year-old son, Erich, found a human skull and bones.

This was not at all what Erich had imagined finding as he played around in the dirt in his yard. I mean it's not the sort of artifact one digs up every day, *is* it? But Erich was a bright lad – knew a thing or two about the human skeletal system, did our Erich, certainly enough to know that the skull was the part that sits atop the rest of our assemblage of bones. So, he did what any other young teen would do, he called his mum, with: 'MAAAA, look what I've found, it's somebody's head!'

He held the skull out at a respectful distance from his mother, who immediately told him to put it back where he'd found it. She would ask Herb all about the skull when he'd got back home after he'd probably killed someone else. Nevertheless, Herb's bland answer was that the bones belonged to a medical school skeleton once owned by his now late father – and she completely believed this highly unlikely yarn, not suspecting for a millisecond that her hubby was the killer of some twenty, mostly young gay guys, in the Indiana/Ohio areas. Then the skull vanished along with the bones – mysteriously carried off, she presumed, by animals.

Herb Baumeister now started to mentally disintegrate, his behaviour becoming more erratic as time passed. He went through bizarre moodswings, telling his wife that police were falsely accusing him of theft and not to let the cops into their house if they knocked on the door and they did and were sent packing. Eventually a search warrant was obtained and Baumeister fled to Canada, subsequently committing suicide before he could be brought to trial.

So, the question has to be asked: how can a woman live with a man for all those years with him burying bodies on their own land, and yet claim to know nothing about it? In fact, how well does anyone know their spouse? – for Baumeister was bisexual – and a very strange character, as well.

One Mark Goodyear, who narrowly escaped with his life recalls being taken back to Baumeister's home in 1994, and found the place, 'dusty with mannequins all over in different postures.' Now laying it on the line as to his preferred homosexual inclinations, he added, 'I was standing in the pool and he [Baumeister] began to drop hints, you know as what he was into. He placed a hose around my neck ...

... 'This was not an attack ... um, this was him asking if I was into this. He liked to be strangled so he asked me if I would strangle him or to hold his throat, so I did, and … '

' … Well, guess what? He fell unconscious down into the water … but, and here's the thing … within a minute he came to, looks directly up at me and tells me of the rush that he had, the exhilaration of the whole experience for him. That's what is known as sexual asphyxia that does cause a heightened, accentuated sensation when oxygen is deprived to the brain … 'Well, I tried it, and I quite enjoyed it, and I got wet, too. Yeah, I went back a couple of times, then I saw a police poster with this suspected gay serial killer's drawing on it and I thought to myself … um … maybe it's the guy with the pool, maybe it's him … '

Asked what happened thereafter, Mark replied, 'Well, I never went back again!'

* * *

Of course, we should try to reasonable here − horses for courses, and all that. But perhaps the first red flag, aside from the naked mannequins that Herb insisted on having around their home, and one that might have aroused Julie's suspicions, was after her son had found the human skull and bones in the yard. Herb's excuse was that they had belonged to his father and his medical practice, yet Herb was meticulous and he'd actually kept *everything* belonging to his dad in the garage, so why bury these items in the yard, only to throw them away after they were discovered?

The FBI has come to realise that this sort of bizarre behaviour indicates in serial murderers a growing over-confidence. On the other side of the paddock, others will say that this is the killer *subconsciously* wanting to be apprehended and he is leaving clues like a trail, in Baumeister's case, right up to his back door – as in follow the dots. The latter is somewhat of an over-simplification because in my humble opinion – and I have interviewed some thirty killers of all sorts – I've still not yet met one who wanted to be caught, with one exception: Wayne Adam Ford, aka 'The Killer with a Conscience'.

Although I corresponded with Ford, I didn't actually meet him in person, but someone who did was the crime writer Victoria Redstall. She wrote about this serial killer in her excellent book, *Serial Killers Up Close and Very Personal: My Death Row Interviews with the Most Dangerous Men on the Planet* (2001). Thirty-six-year-old Ford was convicted of mutilating and killing four women – one of whose remains are still unidentified – between 1997 and 1998. Ford handed himself in to Humboldt County Sheriff's Department in Eureka, California, on Tuesday, 3 November 1998, with a woman's severed breast in a Ziploc bag in his pocket.

Wayne Ford was sentenced to death by lethal injection on Friday, 26 March 2007. Inmate #F65748 FORD is now on 'Condemned Row' in San Quentin State Prison, California, where I once interviewed Inmate #C63000 CLARK, Douglas Daniel, aka 'The Sunset Slayer' – who, incidentally does *not* have a conscience.

Leaving aside the rare example of Ford, logic tells me to go along with the FBI's line of reasoning because over time serial killers *do* become over-confident. After a while they come to believe that they are immune from arrest, and thus they get lazy and start making mistakes. It is this slack behaviour that leads them to having their collars felt by law enforcement. One does *not* require a Master's Degree in Forensic Psychology to figure that out. Period.

> *I'm the one person who didn't know anything. I wonder why a lot of people didn't say something with all of this going on under my nose and no one said anything.*
>
> *I know a great deal about Herb Baumeister. I know more about him than all the people on the face of this earth put together, but I know nothing about his other side. Nothing!*
>
> Julie Baumeister

Precisely, Julie, well put, and does she not speak for all of the other women or men in this book who have been deceived and betrayed by their partners? Of course she does. Is it a case of turning a blind eye – for Julie Baumeister because of a desperate need to keep her family together – or is there a hidden agenda someplace yet to be discovered? The answers are not always obvious, but, I leave this chapter on an advisory note: if one of your young children comes rushing in holding a human skull that they'd found in the garden, I'd have a very serious word with your partner when he or she arrives back home.

Paula Rader v. Dennis Lynn Rader aka 'BTK' (USA)

I actually think I may be possessed by demons,
I was dropped on my head as a kid.

DENNIS L. RADER

Paula Rader's husband, Dennis, was another serial-killing chameleon-type of expert at living a double life; half of the time a family man, the other half a sadistic murderer who gave himself the moniker 'BTK' (an acronym for his method of binding, torturing and killing his victims).

To those who *thought* they knew our Den, he seemed like your everyday father of two. Living in Wichita, Kansas, with his wife and children he worked as a Park City compliance officer and dogcatcher. He was also a Cub Scouts troop leader, and he and Paula were very much involved at their local church. Yet, little did *anyone* know that he was sneaking out at the night to murder local residents, ten of them in all, including his own neighbours, between 1974 and 1991.

Paula was known for her volunteer work at the Christ Lutheran Church – Den having been elected president of the church council. However, some strange and unexplainable incidents occurred that should have set alarm bells ringing in Paula's head. Perhaps the most obvious red flag was when she discovered a rough draft of a poem her husband had written about killing the sixth of his ten victims, Shirley Vian Relford. When Paula questioned Dennis about the poem, he claimed that it was an assignment for a university class he was taking. Later, to taunt the police he mailed them the same poem, which he called 'Shirleylocks'. News agencies regularly published the BTK notes and at one point Paula even told her husband that his own abysmal spelling was just like the rubbish grammar of the serial killer whom the cops were trying to track down. And she had most likely heard his voice on the news when he left a 911 message to inform police about one of his murders.

It goes without saying that Dennis Rader's sadosexual criminal narrative is well worth further study. He was born on Friday, 9 March 1945, in Pittsburg, Kansas, one of four sons – his brothers are named Paul, Bill and Jeff – and what a rotten apple in an otherwise basket of good fruit Dennis turned out to be. He kicked off at a young age when he started harbouring sadistic fantasies about torturing 'trapped and helpless women', as he later put it. He also exhibited 'zoosadism' by torturing, killing and hanging small animals.

To elaborate a bit more, zoosadism is pleasure derived from cruelty to animals. It is part of the 'Macdonald triad', a set of three behaviours that are considered to be precursors to psychopathic behaviour. The other two forming this triad are: obsession with arson and experiencing persistent bed-wetting past a certain age. Among other online sources, the Wikipedia 'Macdonald triad' entry is an excellent reference guide, a very informative read for anyone interested in the precursors to predictive violent tendencies.

Rader also acted out sexual fetishes for voyeurism, autoerotic asphyxiation and cross-dressing. He would often spy on his female neighbours while dressed in women's clothing, including female underwear that he'd stolen, and would masturbate with ropes or other bindings around his neck. Years later, during his self-proclaimed 'cooling-off periods' between murders, he would take photos of himself wearing women's clothes and a female mask while bound. Yet, as remarkable as this may seem, he managed to adroitly keep all his utterly perverse sexual proclivities well hidden from the whole of humankind.

Many of those who *thought* that they knew Rader regarded him as friendly and polite, while others recalled him as sometimes overzealous and extremely strict, as well as taking 'special pleasure' in bullying and harassing single women; one neighbour complained that he'd killed her dog for no reason. So, when we consider all of this, one might ask: why didn't Paula sniff out any of this twisted, morally bigoted man's character out *before* they were married in May 1971? They went on to have two children – Kerri and Brian – and it is Kerri who remembers 25 February 2005, the day her father was arrested by the FBI.

Aged just fourteen, Kerri was standing in the kitchen staring at a chocolate Bundt cake – of all things – as an FBI officer explained that her father had just been arrested as a notorious serial killer.

'You're going into shock and you don't know what's wrong with you,' she told Anna Maria Tremonti of *The Current*, on 6 February 2019. 'And the room gets literally brighter; it gets dark, it kind of spins. So you're focusing on things like cookbooks, or a purse, because you're going through trauma and you don't know it and you're trying to ground yourself.' Can one even begin to imagine how devastating that can be for an innocent, impressionable teenager?

To Kerri and Brian, Dennis was a normal loving father who built a tree house and taught her all about the great outdoors. Indeed, Kerri's book, *A Serial Killer's Daughter: My Story of Hope, Love and Understanding*, talks about her journey in reconciling those two figures: the father she loved and the killer. She writes that her father taught her to fish, raised her to be wary of strangers, and even taught her to hold her keys between her fingers when walking alone at night. 'He was trying really hard to protect us, but we realised he was also trying to protect us from somebody like him,' she ominously explained.

Moving on, she says that when the FBI came to her home to tell her that her father was a killer, she asked to see their ID. 'My dad had always told me ... make them prove who they are, because he said they can pretend to be somebody else. And my father had gotten into peoples' houses ... just by doing that.'

Maybe there is a brighter ending to such a shocking and evil story as this, something for Kerri to cling on to. Over the years her Christian faith has helped to forgive her father, saying: 'People need to understand when you're forgiving somebody, you're not saying whatever they've done is OK, because nothing is OK about what my dad did to those seven families. I'm trying to forgive what he's done to my family and the betrayal, because I had to let that go because it was rotting in me. It was killing me.'

She explains that she still loves her father as the man she grew up with: 'I want people to understand what it's like for somebody like me, to go through hell ... I lost somebody I loved.' So, I think that this extremely intelligent woman with a heart and soul packed full of human decency and compassion, has good advice for anyone suffering from the same mental trauma as she has done.

There's a lot of shame and guilt from being related to one of these people, or knowing them. You could spend the rest of your life questioning every moment that you had with them, and wondering what did you miss and why didn't you see it. At some point you've got to let that go, because if you don't, it's going to eat you up inside and kill you, too.

Finally, on 26 July 2005, Paula was granted an emergency divorce, which waived the normal waiting period. She has never spoken publicly about her marriage to Dennis Rader who is presently listed at the Kansas Department of Corrections, as: KDOC #0083707 RADER, Dennis L. He has several aliases: El Caverna, Killman, and Bill Thomas. Green eyes, brown hair, height: 5ft 11inches, weight: 171lb. Admission date: 19 August 2015. El Dorado CF-Central.

One will be pleased to note that, with his earliest possible release date being 26 February 2180, by then Rader will be *232 years old*.

Now that's what I call 'Doing Time' – wouldn't you agree?

Darcia Brudos v. Jerome Henry 'Jerry' Brudos (USA)

At this stage in our book, I'd like to go off-beam for a moment and ask you to think about 'shopping online' – yes, I *am* being serious here – and there are two reasons for this:

1. I watched a Channel 4 television documentary called *The Truth About Amazon,* which was first aired in 2020. It offered the fairly obvious conclusion that, given periods of lockdown, Amazon is more-or-less the way to go these days. This was especially true since the onset of COVID-19, when government regulations meant that there was pretty much nowhere to go to shop anyway. Yet this somewhat misses the point that, whenever one shops online, there is the occasional chance that one will end up with fake goods – in other words, 'fleeced'.

2. This TV programme reminded me of a book I

had written a number of years ago called *Murder. com*, for which I had much cooperation from law enforcement agencies in the UK, US and elsewhere, including the Russian Federation, who helped enormously. In a nutshell, the subject was all about the inherent risks involved in meeting complete strangers through online dating agencies – or any kind of dating agency come to that – often resulting in being fleeced of every penny you ever had or will ever have, or, in the most extreme cases, even being raped or murdered. Furthermore, the book discussed 'hybristophilia', which refers to someone feeling aroused by being with a partner who has committed a serious crime. And, yes, there *are* men and women who court convicted sadosexual serial killers and one-off murderers behind bars, and *yes*, many want to marry this pond scum. As mentioned earlier, these morally upended idiots are often referred to as 'murder groupies'.

Now, I beg you to indulge me further, because while Amazon – indeed, any other responsible retailer – go out of their way to prevent marketing fake goods, they simply cannot monitor every seller of the quality of the goods on offer, so most of these large online retailers warn potential buyers to BEWARE!

Much the same applies to any type of online dating agency or in one of the million forums that seem to sprout up each month. The truth is that if one is mug enough to fall in love online with a four-star general serving in the US Army and send him your life's savings, because he says that a zillion-dollar deal property he is buying has been put on hold until he recovers from being shot seventeen times, one shouldn't be surprised to find out that you have lost everything, and that he's actually a grossly overweight, forty-five-year-old shoe salesman, still living with his parents in small town (pop. 28) in, say, rural Indiana. Once again, it is simply a case of 'buyer beware', because you most certainly could end up with a counterfeit husband or partner, as almost all the previous cases in this book prove only too well.

And here, I want to do what I usually do in my books – use a totally non-professional analogy, this time when a guy sets off out with a wad of cash in search of a new car. Well, to start with, we need to see the service history, and the list of previous owners, don't we? Look up *Glass's Guide*, check out other deals for similar models, check out reviews and road-test videos. Next we haggle, get a few floor mats thrown in, then we give the car to our beloved as a surprise present. The same problems can arise with all of this 'love at first sight, he swept me off my feet' stuff when people fail to carry out any prior background research, the kind of research that most of the men and women in the previous chapters failed to carry out. Look into a bit of 'provenance', as they say in the art and antiques trades. Sort of take a test drive if it pleases you, until you are absolutely sure that your intended is all that he, or she, is cracked up to be. For when it comes down to it, psychopaths are the arch manipulators and very good at bullshit baffles brains, period!

Remember Sharon Major at the outset of this book? Yes, it's a hard, matter-of-fact, unintended misogynistic thing to say, but all it took was the oily John Cannan to buy a bunch of roses and she was in bed with him faster than a mousetrap snaps shut, at once completely forgetting that if he, or she, seems too good to be true, they probably are as was the case with Darcie Brudos.

* * *

Jerry Brudos (1939–2006) was aged nineteen when he married seventeen-year-old Darcie in 1961, but if anyone on Planet Earth should have a done even a teeny-weeny bit of background provenance on her intended before they wed and had two children, common sense would have told Darcie that any ideas of a blissful marriage would soon be shipped off in a handbasket to Hell. Her parents certainly swiftly sniffed out that 'Our Jerry' was a wrong-un, but kids being kids, Darcie thought that she knew best – and, oh boy, did she mess up, as in BIG TIME!

The Internet is inundated with details of Brudos's crimes, so there is little need for me to go into his offences here, but it is not difficult to imagine the reaction of Darcie's parents to their daughter's choice of husband, if they knew of his past, which can be briefly summarised as follows:

> *Brudos had fetishes about women's shoes, especially stilettos, and underwear, and even as a child would steal them, or attempt to. As a teenager, he took to stalking local women, knocking them down or choking them till they lost consciousness, then running off with their shoes. In 1956, when he was seventeen, he abducted a young woman, whom he beat and threatened to stab if she did not comply with his sexual demands. After being arrested,*

he spent nine months in a psychiatric ward, and was
eventually diagnosed with schizophrenia and extreme
misogyny, the latter apparently deriving from his hatred
of his mother.

Even so, Brudos graduated from high school and
trained as an electronics technician, settling in Portland,
Oregon, after his marriage to Darcie in 1961.

The above is only a brief résumé of Brudos's life and early criminal career, but it does more or less cover most of Brudos's somewhat chequered history up until he and Darcie married, when things truly began to go wrong. And it is also not unreasonable, I think, to question Darcie's intelligence, because as we read on, we will find someone who seems to have been unaware of what was going on around her.

Nevertheless, the first thing that we *do* have to understand is that for the eight years during which Darcie was married to 'the Shoe Fetish Slayer', she never suspected that anything was wrong at all. It never crossed her mind to call the police when local girls started turning up dead and her hubby just happened to bring home an actual female breast to keep as a paperweight. Of course, he did cast it in resin, so maybe she thought it was a model of a severed boob, regardless of the fact that other not-cast-in-resin amputated body parts were lying around the house.

Furthermore, if you think that this was way off the wall, while Darcie knew – as in *100 per cent knew* – that Jerry was as mad as a March hare, she obeyed his every command, including when he ordered her to stay in their house, and that she wear nothing but high-heel shoes and her birthday suit. I mean, seriously, c'mon, isn't it a bit too much to ask one's new bride to do the housework and some hoovering while starkers in five-inch heels, and take Polaroid photos of her bent over the kitchen sink as she washes the dishes? And this is all true!

So, now let's move to the garage. No red flags popped up when Jerry forbade Darcie from going into her own garage, not even the attic come to that, without her first announcing her presence over an intercom and gaining his permission to enter. Indeed, she could not even go into several rooms within her own house ... never once questioning why the walls were somewhat thicker than normal ... and she never heard even the slightest whisper, or a blood-curdling scream, as her Jerry, dressed up to the nines in lingerie and high heels, suspended girls from hooks in the ceiling, sexually abusing them and strangling them to death.

Yes, of course Darcie knew that Jerry was a cross-dresser, that she turned the other cheek when she caught him developing photographs of naked women, and when he did a bit of nocturnal wandering to slip into sleeping women neighbours' bedrooms and steal their lace knickers and shoes, she suspected zilch. This was *all* going on with a national police search for a man that matched, pretty much precisely, her piggy-eyed husband with his photofit plastered over every newspaper front page – *and* on TV screens most nights of the week.

Jerry Brudos, necrophile, is long dead now. He died on 30 March 2006, aged sixty-seven, of liver cancer while in a psychiatric institution. He is buried in the Oregon State Penitentiary Cemetery, Salem, Marion County, Oregon. However, what he was wearing as they shovelled earth over his remains, remains unknown – a pink, lacy matching bra and panties, suspender belt, stockings and a pair of six-inch stilettos, maybe?

As for Darcie, I would have dearly liked to have come up with some form of psychological evaluation as to how her mind worked. This is probably going to sound very cruel and callous, but I am left with the distinct impression that she lacked *a* mind, at least one of her own, so such an exercise would have been futile, but I have tried, as follows.

Firstly, I tried to find out whether Darcie was 'controlled' by Jerry or not. To be truthful, after reading anything under the heading of 'Controlled by a Partner', and there are pages and pages of more or less the same well-intended advice to be found on the Internet, I have come to the opinion that she may have been pathologically subservient, dim and gullible – but overtly controlled, no! On the subject of whether there was any physical abuse present throughout their marriage, the answer seems to be again no – psychological control in a passive sort of way, just maybe!

My second port of call was to examine 'defence mechanisms', these being psychological strategies used unconsciously to protect a person from anxiety arising from unacceptable thoughts of feelings and guilt, Sigmund Freud knew a thing or two about defence mechanisms, or 'ego defence mechanisms' as he prefers to call them, all of which he referred to throughout his written works. Then his daughter, Anna, developed these ideas and elaborated on them, adding ten of her own. For my part, I have not counted how many defence mechanisms there are, but there are ten commonly deployed by humans, and many more besides.

It is totally inconceivable that this young wife had not a clue as to what her husband was up to. It beggars belief that Darcie's suspicions, as she has claimed, were *never* aroused, and if they were, then she had to be completely docile, dim and naïve to not have figured out that Jerome was most certainly the wrong type of husband and should have scooted off back to her parents *tout suite* – doing the decent thing by calling in at the nearest police station en route. But she didn't! Nevertheless, maybe she does offer something positive to us, after all is said and done. One might think that understanding this issue of defence mechanism plays a role when red flags start to appear in any relationships, but when they do, what do we do about it?

> *But love is blind and lovers cannot see*
> *The pretty follies that themselves commit*
> *William Shakespeare (1564–1616):*
> *The Merchant of Venice*

Many readers will already know that there are scores of self-help articles such as '24 Relationship Red Flags You Should Never Ignore' on the Internet, all of which generally list the same stuff. Indeed, there are plenty of other self-help papers advising you along similar lines when meeting or seeking a new partner. Quite a good one is '10 Relationship Red Flags: Ignore them at your own risk', written by Abigail Brenner MD for *Psychology Today*, posted 29 July 2014. With the great gift of hindsight we might say that *if* all of the women and men who have featured in this book had read that article – or something similar – then they might not have found themselves in the dire pickle in which they ended up. Nevertheless, I very much doubt that any woman embarking on a new relationship is going to be thinking: 'Umm, he seems a real catch, but I'd better take a look see if I can notice any red flags in his behaviour', because in the real world, life doesn't quite work in such a carefully ordered and methodical way. And why? Because it is in our human nature to seek out the best in someone and not, from the very outset, to start off looking for the worst!

According to recent divorce statistics, 42 per cent of marriages in England and Wales end in divorce, with 102,007 couples divorced in 2017 (the most recent year for which official statistics are currently available). In the US of A the stats are slightly higher, for if you get married there, you stand a 50/50 chance of ending up getting divorced – in both countries the divorce rate for subsequent marriages is even higher. What I am driving at, though, is this: whether your lover or spouse turns out to be a monster or not, the odds are about equal that you'll probably begin by regarding marriage as an arrangement by which the two of you started out by getting the best out of each other and end up by getting the worst – red flags or not!

Maybe another issue should be taken into consideration when we look at the relationship between the Brudoses and the other relationships previously referred to in this book. The issue is 'dominance'. Basically, this means that one partner is attempting to limit the other's power. It has been written that 'this is *not* a sign of someone who cares about you', which seems patently obvious, but it does infer that they care about themselves and are attempting to manipulate or control a partner's decision-making, which is unhealthy and emotionally abusive. Perhaps we can see this taking place with the Brudoses and in all of the above chapters – it is emotional dominance, with one overwhelming the other's emotional boundaries and beginning to control what the other is allowed to show, think, feel, and/or how to outwardly behave. As psychotherapist Emily Roberts MA, LPC, explains of the dominant: 'They are often quick-tempered, lack regard for your time and emotions, and often blame others for their feelings and problems, so one sees all of this within the relationship between Jerry and Darcie Brudos, and this is where the manipulation comes into play: a person holding himself in high self-esteem – let's say him being a narcissist – dominating a partner with low self-esteem and thus the latter is vulnerable. Folk with low self-esteem, a sense of low worth, often feel unlovable, awkward. These people see rejection and disapproval even when perhaps there isn't any.

In the interpersonal relationship between Jerry Brudos and his wife Darcie, what we have here is a controlling by default homicidal sexual psychopath, wedded to a woman with a low sense of self-esteem, one whose defence mechanisms are so strong that they apparently enabled her to turn a blind eye to the terrible events within her own home. For her, it wasn't a case of how she loved Jerome Brudos; she *had* to love him and tolerate a monster to survive.

Elena Popokova v. Mikhail Viktorovich Popkov (Russia)

If I suspected something was wrong, of course, I would divorce him. I support him, I believe him.

<small>ELENA POPOKOVA: IN SUPPORT OF HER HUSBAND'S INNOCENCE</small>

I start this chapter by saying that I have adored visiting Russia ever since I was a lad when, in 1962, my parents packed me off on a school cruise aboard the MS *Dunera* ... a Baltic cruise it was, and St Petersburg I recall the best. I remember staying at what is now the Radisson Royal Hotel on Nevsky Prospect, and here with the manager I bartered Biro pens for a small horde of those little lapel badges that many middle-aged Russian men proudly wear by the dozen. Back in the early 1960s the sidewalks were mostly cobbled stone, and you would see the babushkas – elderly women all dressed in drab clothes – stooped over after heaving the stones off horse-drawn carts. And, as our ship pulled away from the

245

dockside, we British kids threw bars of chocolate to our newfound schoolfriends, although those Soviet-era Russian cops stamped all over the chocolate, the miserable bastards.

I fell again in love with Russia when I later watched the 1965-released movie, *Doctor Zhivago*, starring Omar Sharif, Julie Christie, Geraldine Chaplin, Tom Courtenay, Rod Steiger, Rita Tushingham, Ralph Richardson and Alec Guinness. I wanted to go back to Russia, to stumble knee deep through the snow, my beard as white as Santa's and witness St Petersburg all lit up like a Christmas tree, a magical wonderland, for *only* in Russia is Christmas as it *should* be. Moreover, I should add, almost with a tear in my eye, that not until someone has visited Russia will they understand that we peoples are as one worldwide – anxious to please guests and make them feel at home and safe, too.

I have visited many places in Russia, and made many friends: ordinary citizens, mafia, police, and believe it or not they regard the British highly. They'll invite you into their homes and give you the shirts off their backs. I think this harks back to the Second World War, the respect for our small nation fighting off the Nazis, bearing in mind that the Germans then stormed into Russia and Ukraine, slaughtering many innocent citizens as well as thousands of Soviet troops, but failed to win a quick campaign, and so were caught when winter came, plunging the country into a deep freeze and ending Hitler's plan to eliminate the Soviet Union from the war.

In Buzuluk, Orenburgskaya Oblast, a former US oil company city, I was entertained by Igor, mafia boss for the region. It's a place where the water coming out of the taps is orange, and the local river is polluted; where the electricity supply goes off for hours when another company corruptly buys the juice from another equally bent band of crooks. It's a place where one never sees a cop for days on end, then suddenly they are out in numbers, stopping cars, extorting on-the-spot fines – and why? Well, it was the annual Buzuluk police get together, so they needed the money to buy as much vodka as possible, get as drunk as skunks, and fall down in the snow, where some of them will die.

For cop-paid crispy dollar bonuses I gained access to several of Russia's most notorious prisons – actually, they are *all* notorious by Western standards. I visited the small room where the serial killer Andrei Romanovich Chikatilo, aka 'the Butcher of Rostov' (1936–94), was executed with a single shot to his head. Then there was Sablino, a women's prison that I have mentioned in my book *Talking with Female Serial Killers*, where I filmed for the first-ever TV documentary inside such a facility, and where the governor was another Mother Teresa who, if you ask me, also deserves to be sainted.

Then there was Kresty Prison in Saint Petersburg – back then with cells designed for six men, yet 'hot-bunking' twelve. The guards wore paramilitary black uniforms and balaclavas, with vicious dogs straining at their leashes, and in one of these correctional hellholes today we may find Mikhail Popkov, a sado sexual serial killer who assaulted and murdered at least seventy-eight women between 1992 and 2010.

* * *

Born on Saturday, 7 March 1964, Popkov has been dubbed 'the Werewolf' by the media and 'the Angarsk Maniac' for obvious reasons, given the very terrible nature of his crimes. Moreover, this guy didn't mess about during his killing time, for he caused a great deal of bloody mess in doing so. Little is known about his formative years except that he *was* born, and while thousands of Russians must wish he hadn't been, there was one exception: his wife, Elena Popkova, who bore him a daughter they named Ekaterina. More to the point, Elena truly believes, despite all of her hubby's confessions to fifty-nine of the homicides, that he is totally innocent and as pure as the snow atop Dr Zhivago's blue seal-fur shapka.

Seriously, one could not make this up if one tried!

Russian cops get paid very little and this was my reason for mentioning their way of raising some extra cash earlier; most of them moonlight in other jobs just to make ends meet, and who can blame them for that? So it may come as no surprise to learn that our 'Werewolf', at the time of his arrest on Saturday, 23 June 2012, was not only a police officer in the Irkutsk Oblast, but also a security guard at the Angarsk Oil and Chemical Company, and working at another private firm – so what was Mikhail's motive for committing serial murder most foul?

Over the years, I have been asked to compile some form of psychological profile on many serial killers. Alexander Yuryevich Pichushkin aka 'the Chessboard Killer' aka 'the Bitsa Park Maniac' springs to mind, but Alexander certainly was not! Not unlike most serial killers, embedded deep within his psychopathology was the mind of a calculating games player, one who likes to pit his wits against the police. His hunting ground was Moscow's vast 18-square-kilometre Bitsa Park, his initial claim being that he wanted to kill sixty-four people, the number of squares on a chessboard, although he later changed his mind, saying that he would have carried on committing murder indefinitely had he not been arrested. Although Pichushkin's true motives are mixed, variable and do not directly concern us here, he placed his victims' bodies around the park as a chess player moves his pieces on a board: one at a time and waiting for his opponent – the police – to make their next move. In many respects Popkov played a similar 'catch-me-if-you-can' game.

Like many of the monsters we have met thus far in this book, if we were to look inside Popkov's head we will find a case of 'little man with a big ego' syndrome. He's a moral bigot, a control freak, a sexual sadist who could only achieve sexual release by raping, beating, axing, hitting with baseball bats, stabbing with knives and strangling to death his mostly female victims all between the ages of sixteen and forty. There is a single anomaly with his tally of murders: one male police officer, and why he was killed no one – except perhaps Popkov – truly knows.

Popkov's *modus operandi* was not unique. He – like so many of the other killer cops I have documented in previous books – used his uniform and authority to lure his victims into his net. In the main, his prey were sex workerss, or women incapacitated by drink – people whom this disgusting man thought were immoral. But upon whom did he blame his 'problems'? His wife, of course – with the transference of blame game being played out over and over again ad infinitum, and all because he *suspected* her of being unfaithful when she wasn't! So, how can we account for Elena's refusal to come to terms with the most obvious fact that her husband is/was

'The Werewolf', and how can we get our heads around that?

Perhaps the answer lies with the issue of Mikhail being a well-respected police officer, and if law enforcement, the Russian judiciary and prosecutors trusted him, why shouldn't Elena? Of course, he could explain away coming home late, making the excuses that his job demanded it, when in reality he was out and about killing over and over again. How she felt when he was arrested is not referred to in the public record, nor will it ever be, but I'd put many roubles on it that she would have been none-too-pleased.

Capital punishment has been abolished in the Russian Federation and in April 2013 President Vladimir Putin confirmed that the death penalty moratorium will stay in place – hence Popkov will spend the remainder of his days shovelling snow in some hellhole of a prison, after which his dead body would be thrown into a pit then set ablaze. *Do svidaniya Mikhail Popkov. Naslazhdayasya adom!*

Despite this and, since February 2022, the terrible events in Ukraine, I truly do love the the country and its people (well, most of them). And despite the catastrophic political situation since this book was first published, I want to add this: 'Thank you for making my time in your wonderful country feel so safe, so cared for, so loved and respected. Special gratitude goes out to the St Petersburg State Police for their hospitality, mucho vodka, the VIP front seats at a fabulous rock concert, and later all of the high-ranking military officers who treated me in my honour – as a former 'Green Beret' Royal Marines Commando – to a banquet at their top-secret camp deep in the forest outside of Buzuluk, and to my dear interpreter, Tatiana Maksina, for making it all possible.

Carol Pitchfork v. Colin Pitchfork (UK)

The name 'Littlethorpe' means a small village or hamlet. This particular one, located around six miles south of Leicester, has had but one notable resident – a Mr Colin Pitchfork, born on Wednesday, 23 March 1960 in Newbold Verdon. By the time of his arrest for murder, in 1987, Pitchfork was living with his wife Carol and their two children in a pretty semi-detached house in Haybarn Close.

To give the reader an insight into this locality, aroud six miles from the city of Leicester are three closely neighbouring villages:

Narborough is a typical old country village onto which has been grafted a relatively new housing estate. The M1 motorway runs close by. With only two public houses and very little nightlife, there was practically no crime to worry either the residents or the police.

Littlethorpe is a ten-minute walk from Narborough, across

the River Soar, while a twenty-minute walk along Ten Pound Lane leads to the village of Enderby, which has as I recall seven pubs and in the 1980s at least, a more working-class population. Back then, also, the three communities had a total population of some 12,000 people – that is, if one did not include the inmates of the large psychiatric hospital that dominated the area.

Opened in 1904 and closed in 1995, Carlton Hayes Hospital was a sprawling Edwardian edifice. It stood in extensive grounds and midway between the villages of Narborough to the north and Enderby to the south. At either end of the hospital's grounds are two footpaths – Ten Pound Lane to the east, the Black Pad to the west. Indeed, the hospital was to play crucial roles as a murder incident room, a red herring, and a positive clue in what were to become known as the 'Enderby Murders'. We will revisit most of these locations shortly, and for the more thorough reader, Google Maps is a must.

Incidentally, the surname 'Pitchfork' has nothing whatsoever to do with the two- or three-tined farm implement as we know it. No, the name has a long Anglo-Saxon heritage, and it comes from when a family lived in the small village of Pitchford, Shropshire. Quite how Pitchfork derived from Pitchford is anyone's guess, but the village owes its name to the strong, pitchy smell that emanates from a bitumen spring, which leaves an oily residue on the surface of the water in the Row Brook. Hence, the name means 'ford near where pitch is found'.

The second child in a family of three siblings, Colin always thought that he was the black sheep, perhaps because he could not live up to his parents' expectations: his older sister was studying medicine while his younger brother was studying for a degree in engineering. Nevertheless, he left school at the age of sixteen without any formal qualifications and became an apprentice baker and confectioner with the long-established Hampshires Bakery, attending day-release classes to learn the finer points of his trade. Indeed, he made exceedingly good cakes, showing such a flair for decoration that he was featured with one of his creations, a model of a racing motorcycle, in the *Journal*, his local newspaper. Indeed, this quick-fire burst of publicity gave a boost to his confidence. He became a 'Jack-the-Lad', who saw himself as 'the Dog's Dinner' – so much so that he started making unwarranted and crude approaches towards his female colleagues.

During the next few years, the young and good-looking Pitchfork started showing definite signs of a dual personality: by the age of nineteen he had twice been convicted for indecent exposure, a 'flasher' in common parlance. However, he was also interested in doing good deeds. In the summer of 1979, he became a voluntary worker at Dr Barnardo's Children's Home in Leicester, playing with children, taking them for walks and organising outside activities. It was here that he met eighteen-year-old Carol, a resident social worker at the home – known as 'Auntie' to the kids, and who would become his wife.

They started dating in the August of 1979, for she had spotted in Pitchfork the potential for good in him. They became engaged, and started living together, but little could she have known back then what lay beneath the apparently decent façade Colin presented to the world. Soon, the monster would stir.

Life seemed to be going well for the young couple, until Pitchfork was again arrested for indecent exposure and put on probation. However, a probation officer apparently assured him that he would grow out of his urge to expose himself to females. Red flags indeed, especially as he was now twenty-one, but what Carol made of it all we simply don't know. It was at this time that he gave counsellors the clearest explanation of his sexual drives: 'You get that need. You go out sometimes and cover 50 or 60 miles looking for that opportunity. It's the high I needed,' he said without any indication of remorse.

I should explain here that Pitchfork's frank statement tells us an awful lot about his psychopathology around that time. We can see sociopathy writ large, for during that entire interview he makes no admission of regret or remorse. One does not need to be a psychiatrist, psychologist, or any other type of 'ologist', to see that he is well-entrenched in an addiction – that of trawling and 'hunting' for hours in sexual excitement and relief.

The act of masturbation in front of non-consenting witnesses, along with 'flashing' and similar activities, is classified as 'exhibitionism', in which, quite obviously, a person such as the young Pitchfork, derives sexual arousal from the act or fantasy of exposing their genitals to strangers. Exhibitionism, which can progress to 'exhibitionist disorder', is a form of paraphilia, which *Psychology Today* defines as ' ... a condition in which a person's sexual arousal and gratification depend on fantasising about and engaging in sexual behaviour that is atypical and extreme.' At the age of twenty-one, Colin Pitchfork was already in the grip of an exhibitionist disorder; it was as if he had a delusional entitlement to do whatever he wanted, no matter what anyone else thought, to embarrass and shame the person he was doing it in front of: power and control.

* * *

In May 1981, Colin married Carol. They moved into a house in Barclay Street, Leicester. The future looked bright: he still had his job at the bakery and Carol was still working, but then ... oops. They say that a leopard never changes its spots, and nor could Colin Pitchfork, for once again he was caught flashing and sent by the Magistrates' Court to the nearby Carlton Hayes Hospital for psychiatric counselling.

When performing assessments on sex offenders to determine if they are likely to reoffend or potentially escalate their actions, the two key areas of consideration are: the degree to which they are sexually deviant, and their degree of anti-sociality (or criminality). The latter area refers to criminal thinking, criminal behaviour, feelings of entitlement, a willingness to victimise others, an inability to kind of empathise with other people or a deficit in their ability to feel remorse. They want what they want, and it doesn't matter what they have to do to get it. All of which, when combined, bears every resemblance to sociopathy and psychopathy, for which there can be *no* cure. In effect, the writing was now on the wall for the psychiatrists to read and the person making his mark on that wall was an emerging serial killer.

In 1983, our budding 'Mr Kipling' began a course of evening classes studying cake decorating at Southfields College. Carol, now pregnant, was no longer desirable to him. He had an affair with a young college student, even taking her into his wife's bed, and this fling gave him so much excitement with the thought that his wife might catch him, he had what we might call a moratorium: a temporary halt to his vulgar exhibitionist behaviour.

It was perhaps inevitable that Carol would learn of her priapic husband's affair – and when she did, she threw him out. Well done you, Mrs Pitchfork. Well done *you* – but, guess what, within weeks she took him back. Yes, of course we know that she was by then heavily pregnant, but then she was also well aware of his criminal antecedents: his psychiatric counselling, his treatment at Carlton Hayes Hospital, *and* that he'd been screwing a fellow student in the marital bed, so her life would never be the same again.

In August their son was born, and so, to be nearer to Carol's local councillor father who lived in Narborough, the Pitchforks upped sticks and moved to the aforementioned neat little house in Littlethorpe. However, before moving to their new home, Carol decided to throw a 'leaving party' for friends and neighbours. On Monday, 21 November 1983, she set off for her evening class where she hoped to gain qualifications to become a probation officer, which, no doubt, wouldn't have suited her husband one bit. The police, magistrates' courts and probation service were the last busybodies he needed in his life, let alone have one of these officials living with him under the same tiled roof! So, while Carol was about to leave for her evening class, Colin was supposedly about to spend the evening taping records to have music ready for the party.

At about 7 p.m., he drove Carol to her class in his Ford Escort with the baby asleep in his carrycot. Dropping her off, he would return to pick her up at 9 p.m.; however, during those two hours he murdered fifteen-year-old Lynda Rosemarie Mann who was taking a shortcut on her way home from babysitting instead of using her usual route. The official version of events is more-or-less this: that evening Lynda left the family home in 'The Coppice', Enderby, to visit her friend Karen who lived near by. She popped into Karen's home for just a minute or so. It was 7.30 p.m. and the theme music for *Coronation Street* was just starting on the television. Lynda left saying she was going on to visit another friend, Caroline, who lived in Enderby – a fifteen-minute walk which would take her close to the Black Pad footpath. It was a bitterly cold dark night.

Lynda was a typical teenager. She liked clothes, makeup, hairstyles and music. She attended Lutterworth School and was considered a bright student with an aptitude for languages. She was learning French, German and Italian. Her ambition was to travel the world, and friends described her as happy-go-lucky, but now she was walking along the Black Pad and towards her own brutal death.

Her stepfather had reported his daughter as missing at 1.30 a.m., but to the police this was simply a routine missing person's report (MISPER). They reasoned that the girl had probably decided to spend the night at a friend's house, and would no doubt turn up in the morning. She was found at 7.20 a.m. by a porter from the psychiatric hospital on his way to work. Taking his usual shortcut through the Black Pad footpath, he glanced casually through the iron railings bordering the track, and was startled to see what he took to be a mannequin lying in the frost-covered field beyond. He ran out into the street and flagged down a car driven by an ambulance man who also worked at the hospital. Lynda was lying on her back, her jeans and knickers in a heap a few feet away. A scarf had been knotted tightly around her neck and there was blood around her nose. She was stone cold dead. The cause of death was asphyxia due to strangulation. The girl had been brutally raped and the pathologist had noted that there were traces of semen in her pubic hair. A sample of semen was taken and carefully preserved for analysis and this was to become a vital clue, for Colin Pitchfork was soon to become the first British rapist and murderer to be convicted of murder based on DNA fingerprinting evidence, and the first to be caught as a result of mass DNA screening.

In a later police confession, Pitchfork admitted that after dropping off Carol at college he had driven around looking for girls to 'flash' at. He had seen Lynda walking along the street, but when he exposed himself to her, she had run in terror from him into the Black Pad, effectively cutting off his escape route. To all intents and purposes, he was blaming his victim for backing herself into a corner.

'I went up to her and grabbed her and she didn't really resist me,' he said with a smug look. 'The urge hadn't subsided at all. It was just getting stronger. Because not only had she got herself into the situation, she hadn't screamed. She hadn't struggled. If she'd screamed she'd probably have scared me off.'

Pitchfork then described the rape. 'Afterwards, I had to kill her,' he said. 'She knew I was married ... she saw the ring ... ... I also realised I'd got an earring on. And, I'd been losing my bloody hair. She could describe those things ... Almost certainly she would see me in the village ... There was no way out. I was trapped. So I strangled her.'

In the months that followed, Pitchfork became even more restless in his marriage, saying he wanted a better job, a better house. He even told people that he wanted to write a book although he could barely read. By 1986, now aged twenty-six, he was complaining of headaches and insomnia. He was prescribed sleeping pills, and well might he have needed them, for the real underlying problem was that his new mistress, a twenty-nine-year-old, was pregnant. To exacerbate further Carol's own problems and to give her yet another slap in her face, he had told her that he found marital sex 'boring'. To bring excitement into their relationship, he persuaded her to wear white socks, like a schoolgirl. Red flags, once again.

* * *

During the afternoon of Thursday, 31 July 1986, fifteen-year-old Dawn Amanda Ashworth left her home in Enderby to visit a friend's house in Narborough. Several people saw her walking along Ten Pound Lane. Dawn's friend was not at home, so she had to walk back to Enderby. The last person to see her alive encountered her at around 4.40 p.m. when she was about to return the way she had come – along Ten Pound Lane.

Police and volunteer searchers found Dawn on Saturday, 2 August, in a clump of bushes in a field next to the lane. A futile attempt had been made to hide the body with foliage. She was naked from the waist down, her knickers caught on her right ankle and her bra pushed up to expose her breasts. She lay on her left side, in a foetal position. There was blood around the vaginal area. Just as in the previous murder of Lynda Mann, there were no broken fingernails – had there been, it would have proved Dawn had put up a defensive struggle – although she had also been battered about the head. She too had been strangled, and her hair was matted with semen, indicating premature ejaculation. And, just like Lynda, Dawn had the normal teenage interests in clothes and music, but she was a sensible and mature girl. Well known in the village of Enderby, she had a part-time job in a local shop. Her special talent was art: she had a natural gift for drawing and painting.

Of the murder of Dawn Ashworth, Pitchfork told police that he had been riding his Honda motorcycle when he saw a girl walking and watched her turn on to a footpath.

'I parked the bike ... and just walked after her into Ten Pound Lane,' he said.

'Was there anyone around?' a detective asked him.

'Nobody. Nobody ever saw me there. I was in broad daylight ... when I was following behind her I had this gut feeling. It was saying, "No, no, no, no!" but the other side of me was saying, "Just flash her. You've got a footpath. You've got all the time in the world."'

Most, if not all, of the serial killers and monsters I have interviewed over the decades are inclined to blame all of their evil deeds as being the fault of others. It's the transference of blame game, and Pitchfork is no exception. Again he blamed Dawn for the murder. 'There's rules to how I play that game [flashing],' he said. 'They always have room. No matter where I exposed myself they always have room to walk by me. It's the easiest way. You shock them. They walk by you, and then you get your exit route clear.'

With Dawn, he claimed that she did not walk by him or allow him to escape by his 'exit route'. Instead, she ran into a field. He followed her. She had seen his motorcycle jacket and if she reported that, it might lead the murder squad from Lynda's murder to him. 'The same feelings came back. That I was in a trap.' Then the monster who was Carol's husband grinned as he coldly told the homicide investigators, 'One murder or two – the sentence is the same.'

* * *

In January 1987, Pitchfork's mistress gave birth to a stillborn child. He visited her in the hospital in tears, and shortly afterwards, he confessed to his wife about the affair, sobbing that his baby daughter was dead. Now, fully immersed in his own self-pity, he actually expected sympathy from Carol. He drew a blank.

In June 1987, a seventeen-year-old girl from Oadby had a terrifying experience when she accepted a lift from a stranger. She had spent the evening with friends in Wigston. During their night out she had had an argument with her boyfriend. Angry and upset, she started walking home.

Shortly after midnight a car pulled up alongside her, and the driver asked her where she was going. He offered to give her a ride in the direction of her home, but as soon as she climbed into the front passenger seat, his friendly manner changed. In silence, he drove past the road to Oadby, heading out for the open countryside. Terrified, the girl made a grab for the steering wheel and the car skidded to a halt. Sobbing, the girl insisted that all she wanted to do was go home, so he turned around and drove her to the A6 where he finally pulled over.

The girl leapt out of the car. She had a lucky escape. The driver was Colin Pitchfork.

* * *

Pitchfork was finally arrested at his Littlethorpe home at 5.42 p.m. on Saturday, 19 September 1987. He calmly reacted with, 'Give me a few minutes to tell my wife.'

Later bragging of the girls he had 'flashed' at – more than a thousand of them by his own over-puffed-ego imagination – he only managed to name half a dozen with whom police were able to verify his claim. He also told of two indecent assaults he had committed in 1979 and 1985, and the attempted abduction of the girl who had hitched a lift in his car. He was tried, pleaded guilty on all counts and sentenced to life for both murders, with ten years concurrent for the rapes, three years for the indecent assaults, and three years for conspiracy. His sentence was later reduced on appeal.

Colin Pitchfork was an 'emerging serial killer', and there can be no doubt in anyone's mind that he would have carried on committing rapes and murders had it not been for the almost accidental discovery made by a young geneticist who has since revolutionised police procedure. His name was Doctor (now Professor) Alec Jeffreys. Today we know this technique as DNA fingerprinting or DNA profiling (among other terms), used especially for identification (as for forensic purposes) by extracting and identifying the base-pair pattern of a person's DNA.

As for Carol, there were red flags being hoisted almost from the start of the Pitchforks' marriage and throughout. It's a wonder that she tolerated any of his perverted behaviour, yet she did – most especially after the children were born, for it was in her interests at least to give them a decent start in life, and her husband was a breadwinner after all is said and done. A decent, strong woman is Carol, and that cannot be taken away from her.

But I want to leave this chapter with the words of Barbara Ashworth, for Dawn's parents have had to learn to live with the tragic loss of their daughter – it is heartbreaking, it truly is, even more so with what follows:

That night in July 1986 changed not only our future but that of my other two daughters, who had to live without Dawn, and also the grandparents, uncles and aunts, and anyone who ever knew Dawn. She was unable to see her sister develop into a lovely girl or ever set eyes on her other sister's baby son – Dawn's first nephew – and watch him growing up so like his mother.

This gentle, quiet girl was cruelly snatched away from us, and but for Dr Jeffreys, her killer would still be free to rob other families of their treasured children. His discovery of DNA, or genetic finger-printing, has removed the doubts which have in the past allowed guilty people to walk free and continue their evil doings. 'Thank you' is all we can keep saying to Dr Jeffreys for our peace of mind, knowing that our daughter's killer is off the streets, as will so many others be in the future. There are children who will live because of his life's work.

We have had almost seven years of frustration trying to make sense of what has happened to us and why. We could not bury Dawn's poor body for over two months after the murder and no one on earth can say they know how we felt because we went through hell. My husband, Jim, was made redundant in 1984, just before Christmas, and his health has so badly deteriorated since then that he is now registered disabled and we try to survive on very little money. I also lost my job after Dawn's death. We live day-to-day now but our Dawn is always only a thought away.

Obviously we must try not to let our feelings of helplessness overwhelm our daughter [name removed] as she begins to enter the adult part of life. She never had much of a childhood as she had to cope in her own way with what happened to Dawn. We cushioned her as best we could but the media will constantly bring up this case because of the importance of the DNA. We shall always be returned to one of the worst parts of our lives, the part we can never forget but do not want to remember.

Mrs Barbara Ashworth.

Now comes perhaps the most sickening and shocking part in this book, perhaps of anything I have extensively written about in my decades of writing about murder most foul. I would ask the reader to bear in mind the poignant words of Dawn's mother, above.

On several occasions, Pitchfork applied for parole, and as late as Thursday, 3 May 2018, he was 'knocked back'. Nevertheless, in November 2018, while serving time, presumably in the open prison of, Leyhill, he was spotted smugly walking unescorted around Bristol without a care in the world, fit as a fiddle, bald, sporting a white beard, blue T-shirt and trousers, light-coloured windcheater and black trainers with luminescent green trim, having been released for unsupervised days out. Yes, this monster was once again back amongst us, yes amongst *you* and *me* – a really terrifying thought indeed.

Then, in June 2021, Pitchfork was released on conditional licence. Yes, the parole board *thinks* that he poses no further risk to society. Yes, he *may* wear a tag. Yes, this human scum, this 'flasher', was out on life licence, most probably ogling any young girl he set eyes upon. I am not someone who advocates reform for psychopathic killers. Why? Because homicidal psychopaths can never change their spots for their urge is *always* there to rape and kill again.

As luck would have it, however, in November 2021, just as this book was going to press, Pitchfork was returned to prison from his bail hostel, having breached the terms of his licence by 'approaching young women' while out walking, although he had not committed offence since being released. Dawn Ashworth's mother, Barbara, had what I fervently hope is the last word when she was quoted as saying that she was pleased 'he's been put away and women and girls are safe and protected from him now'.

Lynda Rosemarie Mann (1968–83) is buried in Narborough Cemetery, Narborough, Leicestershire.

Dawn Amanda Ashworth (1971–86) is buried in St John the Baptist Churchyard, Enderby, Leicestershire.

God bless them both, and if you happen to be passing by, it would be a comforting thing to do – to place some flowers on their graves. Thank you.

Summary

To write a summary of this book is no easy task, for who am I – or we – to judge the actions and the decisions made by the men and women who unknowingly slept with monsters? However, all of those innocent people, being victims themselves in some way or another, can teach us something. Of course, I am referring to the 'red flags' so frequently raised in each and every one of their doomed relationships. Whether they didn't notice these red signals, as in 'red for danger', or chose to ignore them, or for interpersonal domestic reasons were compelled to tolerate these flags, is all something we *might* learn from, so I will refer now to the issue of 'Three Strikes and Out'.

This is an off-the-wall analogy without doubt, for we are almost wandering into a Utopian world, but in the USA, habitual offender laws (commonly referred to as 'three-strike laws') were first implemented on 7 March 1994, and are part of the United States Justice Department's Anti-Violence Strategy. In a nutshell, these laws require both a severe violent felony and just *two* other previous convictions to serve a mandatory life sentence in prison. The purpose of these laws is to drastically increase the punishment of those convicted of more than two serious crimes. To put this into some sort of perspective: if 'Mr Jimmy Bent' has two previous convictions for relatively minor thefts (shoplifting could be amont them), then clubs a driver unconscious and steals the car – an aggravated felony – the US criminal justice system awards him a prize: life behind bars.

Twenty-eight states in the USA have some form of a 'three-strikes' law. A person accused under such laws is referred to in a few states (notably Connecticut and Kansas) as a 'persistent offender'. For those into sport, the expression 'three strikes and you are out' is of course derived from baseball. In the UK, you might say we are less tolerant because we have the noble game of cricket, a game where someone hurls a red-coloured ball weighing between 155.9 and 163 grams at another person holding a bat, and if the ball hits what is called the wicket, three sticks with bails atop them – which the batsman is sworn to protect – or he actually hits the ball by design or by accident, and someone else catches it, then it is 'one strike and out!' It's a damned shame that the British criminal justice system doesn't adopt the same attitude when sentencing serious offenders instead of giving them bail seemingly at every opportunity.

Persistent offending, is, however, of interest to us insofar as the controlling and bullying behaviour which so many women suffer, in extremis at the hands of the conniving likes of narcissists Michael Sams and John 'Billy Liar' Cannan. In both of their cases, there is abundant evidence of psychological abuse, and in Cannan's case with Sharon Major, physical abuse too.

There is an old saying that goes something like this: 'The person who doesn't make a mistake learns nothing.' Well, I think that with the great gift of hindsight we can see that Sharon, a sensible woman at the best of times, failed to see the red flags right from the get-go. Red roses, yes, and these first blossoms of love shielded her eyes from the obvious – that Cannan was a charlatan, and ultimately a sex monster of truly murderous proportions. One might ask ourselves, why didn't she go and visit this self-alleged car 'sales manager' at his place of work, his office, where she would have undoubtedly been impressed by the efficient way he ran the place? Reeve & Stedeford were no fly-by-night motor dealership outfit. Indeed, it was founded by Sir Ivan Stedeford GBE, after the end of the Second World War, when he went into partnership with a motor dealer called Reeve. The company specialised in limousines and sports cars for the wealthy, and for John Cannan to be the firm's manager would have been a motoring miracle by any stretch of the wildest imagination. Washing the cars, making tea and coffee and selling the occasional secondhand motor was all that he was good for, but Sharon didn't visit Reeve & Stedeford, simply because he steered her away.

We might think it odd that John never once invited Sharon back to his home, and there are several reasons for this: (A) He was married and his wife lived in the place alone with his child after she had thrown him out for persistent adultery;

(B) He had a seedy flat; and (C) When he wasn't at his flat having been evicted for non-payment of rent arrears, he was dossing in a B&B hotel and having sex with any women who looked half decent to him. This doesn't fit at all with sales manager Cannan at all, yet he once told Sharon: 'The life of a car salesman has its advantages, and access to as many cars as I want.' He told her that he enjoyed times with the 'Sutton Fast Crowd' – whoever they were I cannot determine – 'dancing at The Belfry Golf Club' – to which he had no membership – and 'screaming through the back lanes of Sutton in our Jag, TVR and company's demonstrators'. He explained he was a 'factory trained sales executive conversant in finance depreciation, projection, motor engineering and himself personally responsible for six-figure sales turnovers.' Yeah, of course you were, John. We all know what the *Glass Car Guide* is. As for finance depreciation ... you certainly knew about that because you never had a pot to piss into, did you, John? Yet, with all of this BS coming her way, Sharon still allowed flashy Cannan to move into her own home to become a cuckoo in her nest. One might have thought that when she bumped into Mrs June Cannan with John's child, she would have kicked him out instantly. Single, indeed! But the fact remains that she didn't, with very nearly disastrous consequences for her.

* * *

Regarding Teena Sams *v.* Michael Benneman Sams – what a messed-up pair these two were, even before they married each other – if either of these people had actually learned even something from their own disastrous narratives, Teena should most certainly have done so. But she didn't, while going through marriages faster than a canoe plunging over rocky rapids to the most predictable of disasters. Indeed, I've lost count of how many red flags were hoisted in their relationship. I have lost count of how many strikes she suffered and not once did she count him out – even when her husband, the most wanted man in the UK, is peering back at her on the TV show, *Crimewatch UK*. Moreover, I am lost for words in trying to fathom out why she kept chasing him after he was locked away for life, at once with him parading Miss Vinchelli under her nose – the ultimate slap in the face, yet still Teena came back for more.

Therefore, can any female reader come to her own conclusions by imagining that, God forbid, she found herself in shoes similar to those worn by Teena Sams. In those circumstances, would you have continued to suck up to your hubby who, seemingly content to blame all of his shortcomings on you, enables his middle-aged mistress to advertise her 'assets' all over the UK's redtops?

Many will say that I am being cruel. But those are the facts whether one likes it or not, and unwittingly, Teena has educated us in some way – so we might at least thank her for that.

* * *

In the case of Kelli Kae Boyd *v.* Kenneth Bianchi, we find her tolerating his appalling behaviour, his adultery, his blatant lying, and his consummate thieving, and even when she hightailed it from Los Angeles north to Bellingham in Washington State to escape him, she allowed this monster, despite her own parents' pleadings, to move back in with her after kicking him out three times before. There were scores of red flags raised throughout their relationship, yet she chose to tolerate them. It should have been one strike, just maybe two strikes and then out, for good. Was she simply dim-witted? I am inclined to think not, for we have to remember that all psychopaths are arch-manipulators, and if one were even to glance across the pond to the USA, we can find yet another extreme and recent example: Donald Trump who manipulated his way into the Oval Office for four years. Well, let's just say that if a guy like 'The Donald' can convince the American peoples to vote him in as POTUS, we can forgive Kelli Kae Boyd for hitching up with Mr Bianchi – who is, by his own admission, now an ordained priest, a fully-paid-up member of the American Bar Association, and who has married at least twice while behind bars to women whom, I think, exhibit a psychopathology as disgusting as the one he had.

* * *

Sandy Fawkes *v.* Paul John Knowles are a totally different kettle of fish. Here is an attractive and very bright British journalist with a secret desire to meet, then have a randy affair with, an all-American hunk. But once again we see that she noticed red flags almost from the get-go. Yes, Sandy's suspicions were raised, and it was only thanks to a God-given windfall that she didn't return to her hotel room as expected, that enabled her to live to tell the tale in her tale of between-the-sheets sexual disappointment, a book called *Killing Time*, later republished as *Natural Born Killer*. And she made a fortune too. You can probably file the Ann Rule *v.* Ted Bundy relationship under this category, too.

* * *

The case of Ethel Christie *v.* John Reginald Halliday Christie is, perhaps, a much more puzzling relationship to get our heads around. Their relationship existed in austere postwar days, and we find in Ethel a downtrodden woman who tolerated so many red flags that it seems inconceivable that she did not dump Reg Christie pretty soon after they had married. It also appears impossible that she didn't know of some of his murders before he eventually dumped her under the floorboards of their seedy home at 10 Rillington Place.

There will be folk who will argue that Ethel knew nothing of her husband's vile behaviour, and that she lived in ignorance throughout their marriage. However, the facts state otherwise. How could she, for weeks on end, not have seen, not even smelt two dead bodies, stinking and decomposing in the tiny washhouse and toilet which she visited several times a day – with one corpse a baby, no less? Of course she knew Reg was a murderer, and when she had finally had enough, she intended to leave him. That put Mr Christie between a rock and a hard place, so he had to kill her.

* * *

With Sonia Sutcliffe *v.* Peter William Sutcliffe, it must have come as a terrible shock to Sonia when she suddenly learned, out of the blue, that the monster she had been sleeping with for so many years was the notorious 'Yorkshire Ripper'. It is fair to say that one might harbour mixed feelings about her relationship with him following his incarceration, for I would ask any of my readers if they would have continued to correspond, visit or have any further dealings, financial or otherwise, with one of the most reviled pieces of human scum who has ever infested British society? It almost doesn't bear thinking about. Yet, for her own reasons, and I have detailed these reasons as best I can, Sonia has a strong mind of her own. So I should best leave it at that.

* * *

John Knowles, John Russell, Oliver Leonard, Ernest Wilson *v.* Mary Elizabeth Wilson, are cases where men terminally got the wrong end of the stick and fell prey to a calculating, cold-blooded 'Black Widow', as was also true of Michael Wallace and David Castor *v.* Stacey Ruth Castor. One might be mindful of this quote from the Hindu Vaishnava saint and poet, Tulsidas (possibly 1532–1623; his birthdate varies between sources): 'There are three all-powerful evils: lust, anger and greed,' for it fits here like hand in glove.

It's a chilling thought for any of us guys to imagine that your intended wife has been checking through your finances then plotting your murder *even before* the wedding. Indeed, I have interviewed a few of these so-called 'Black Widows' in my time, and I have studied the case histories of many more, and guess what, there is always a life insurance policy tucked away somewhere. In the USA double-indemnity policies are often automatic red flags on their own, especially if one partner insists on the police being drawn up prior to marriage or within five-and-twenty-minutes of warming the marital bed ...

... Rest assured, the taking out of such a policy is pretty much what happens when a 'Black Widow' zeroes in on a rich man's wallet, albeit with countless variations.

* * *

Linda Yates *v.* Robert Lee Yates Jr is one of those cases where there were more red flags than can be counted, for Linda – although suspecting that something was seriously wrong with her marriage – could never have guessed that she was sleeping with one of the most lethal and mentally twisted of sex serial killers in US history. If one re-reads that particular chapter, one might have thought that the penny would have dropped far sooner than it eventually did for Linda, for she tolerated more strikes than most women should accept as tolerable. Was she turning a blind eye, was she gullible, or was she a thoroughly decent woman getting through rocky wedlock as best as she could?

* * *

Monsters sleeping with monsters is a subject in itself for there are countless cases where the likes of Rosemary West and Myra Hindley, become so fixated and indoctrinated that they become tools in their male partner's deadly serial killer's game. They are 'murder groupies' in extremis. I have interviewed several other female serial murderers in my time: Aileen Lee Wuornos, Cathy May Wood and Gwendoline Graham among them, and I have written extensively about women murderers in my book *Talking with Female Serial Killers: A chilling study of the most evil women in the world.* And, here is a strange, perhaps banal thing to say, for while I can almost understand the twisted psychopathology of women acting alone who commit the most God-awful of crimes, the women who sleep and have sex with the likes of Fred West and Ian Brady disgust me the most – they are the stuff of Stephen King nightmares come true.

It is galling that hundreds and hundreds of women worldwide write to these sexual psychopaths who will spend the remainder of the lives behind bars. These women pledge undying love, want to bear these killers' children and send them money. It is chilling to know that one of Keith Jesperson's murder-groupie fans sent him a kiss lip imprint in menstrual blood, other items include damp panties. I truly believe that each one of them should go the same way as Jesperson's innocent victim, Angela Subrize when he tied her up half alive and dragged her for about twelve miles behind the rear axle of his rig. Harsh words, perhaps, but can't these mentally unhinged women find something better to do?

I would, however, be signally failing in my duty as a writer not to mention the male murder groupies, who as far as I can determine, outnumber their female counterparts tenfold. Men seem to be real suckers for this malarkey – big time. There are countless examples of these morons finding an incarcerated female soulmate who is sending him – and dozens of other guys – photos of herself as a glamorous model, when the reality is very different indeed. These criminal women are enterprising. They plead for money and get it. They find out where the guy lives and how much money he has in the bank, along with his social status and if he is worth blackmailing. Then, when the goodies are in the

276

bag, so to speak, she'll send some of her hoodlum buddies around to pay a house call. If he's lucky he may live another day, penniless, and never to post any sort of letter to any con ever again.

* * *

Back to Claudia Kraig Barrows, Marcia Wilson, Judith Mawson *v.* Gary Leon Ridgway, and if ever there was a homicidal wolf in sheep's clothing, Ridgway certainly pulled the wool over everyone's eyes. We recall what his wife Judith said after his arrest: 'I was crying. No, it can't be him', but it *was* him, one of the most heinous serial killers of all time, and she had been sleeping with this Devil's spawn for that unlucky number of thirteen years.

Ridgway's psychopathology gives us all the clues we need to understand precisely how and why he managed to hoodwink Judith for over a decade, so there is no need for us to go searching for any red flags that she might have noticed during what appears to have been the perfect marriage. Indeed, she tells us this much when she stated: 'He made me smile every day. I had the perfect husband, perfect life. I absolutely adored him.' Furthermore, to endorse his ability to cover his tracks, we know that he was able to run rings around law enforcement for sixteen years, reducing the cops to go crawling to the notorious death row inmate Ted Bundy for his professional advice as to the identity of the Green River Killer.

* * *

With Juliana 'Julie' Baumeister *v*. Herbert Richard 'Herb' Baumeister, Julie sums it all up when she said: 'I'm the one person who didn't know anything. I wonder why a lot of people didn't say something with all of this going on under my nose and no one say anything. I know a great deal about Herb Baumeister. I know more about him than all the people on the face of this earth put together, but I know nothing about his other side. Nothing!'

How tragically shocking for this decent woman to wake up one morning to learn to her utter shock horror that effectively she had been sleeping with two different personalities in the same bed – one being her husband and father of her kids, the other a depraved, sadistic fiend. I was considering describing Herb's condition as a 'Dissociative Identity Disorder', previously known as a 'Multiple Personality Disorder', as in being a mental disorder characterised by the maintenance of at least two distinct and relatively enduring personality states. But it would be more apt for one to state instead that here we have two individuals living in the same skin – let's say maybe a Dr Jekyll and Mr Hyde. Indeed, are not all of the offenders listed throughout this book very much of the same ilk – two minds fighting against each other inside the same head, so to speak?

* * *

The case of Paula Rader *v*. Dennis Lynn Rader aka 'BTK', bears similar hallmarks to the case of the Ridgways, and at the risk of repeating myself, here is yet another serial killing chameleon-type of expert at living a double life; half of the time a family man, the other half a sadistic murderer. He is the stuff of nightmares coming true, as Mariah Simpson writes in her self-published poem, *Nightmare:*

> *A dream can keep you awake.*
> *A nightmare can get you scared.*
> *Waking up screaming from a dream you were never*
> *meant to dream,*
> *A murder that never happened, but you were the witness.*
> *To fall forever into the pits of Hell.*
> *You know it's a dream but you can't wake up. Your*
> *mind is on fire, your heart is racing. No one can hear you*
> *in the land of the dead.*

But what if it was all too real? *Real* murder is not like 'As seen on TV' – more often than not, murder most foul takes place in dark places far away from prying eyes and where no-one can hear the screams, as was the case with Colin Pitchfork's sweet, young victims. Can one even begin to imagine the terror those girls went through? Of course we cannot, so can you also imagine being the parent of a beautiful child, and would you want that evil man to be released back into society by some leftie parole board?

Many years ago, I was making a twelve-part TV documentary series called *The Serial Killers* during which I helped clear up the cold-case homicide of a deaf mute called Kimberly Logan – her killer being Arthur John Shawcross (1945–2008). On 19 September 1994, I interviewed Shawcross, aka 'The Monster of the Rivers' aka 'The Genesee River Killer', who was at that time incarcerated at the Sullivan Correctional Facility (NYSDOC), in New

York State. Accompanied by Rochester PD detectives, the ever-smiling Leonard 'Lenny' Borriello and Billy Barnes, I visited the banks of that river, a place where 'Art' strangled many of his victims to death, then cut them open and mutilated their bodies in the most terrible of ways. You can find a few photos of me with those cops, and also me with the Captain of Detectives, Lynde Johnson, on my website: www.christopherberrydee.com.

I went back to that place in the dead of a starlit night. There was a scudding moon, the trees' spindly branches pointing like accusatory fingers to the sky, a slight breeze played amongst the reeds, the water as black as coal. In the distance one could just hear traffic, but it was a long way away, and had some terrified woman tried to scream as Shawcross put his massive hands around her throat and sat his bulk on her chest, no-one on this earth could have heard a thing.

I asked Shawcross to describe his murders down by the banks of the Genesee River and he told me this:

> It was a combination of the quietness of the area, the starlight, an' I got sweating and stuff. I can't control that. I strangled most of them, an' it ain't like on TV where they just drop dead. In real life, they can hold their breath for three minutes, and up to seven minutes before they susscumm [sic]. One woman, well, just as I was strangling her, she said, 'I know who you are.' Then she went limp an' she didn't feel nothing. She just went limp … yeah, an' some of the bodies had bruises on 'em. That's where I knelt over them with my body weight, or I dragged 'em into the rushes down by the

water's edge. I cut 'em open so's they'd rot a lot quicker
that way ... One body I rolled into the water and it sank
and her head come up. She was smiling.

Yet Shawcross had been married to a woman who had known all about his dismal past: that he had previously been a paedophile killer and had served a lengthy prison term, and was released upon the advice of shrinks and an incredibly dumb-assed parole panel. Then he fell in with another woman, Clara Neal, and she was living with him throughout his later killing spree of sex workers. Although she too knew about his criminal record, she hadn't a clue that he was committing serial homicide.

There is a lengthy chapter dedicated to Shawcross in my bestselling *Talking with Serial Killers: The Most Evil People in the World Tell Their Own Stories*. Written with the full cooperation of the Rochester PD, it makes for very grim reading, and contains material not for the faint-hearted. To take one indelicate example: he returned to the frozen body of thirty-year-old June Stott, hacked out her vagina with a pocketknife, thawed it under his car heater, gnawed at it and ' ... threw the other bits away', after which he went to a Dunkin' Donuts stall where he says he 'chewed the fat with the dumb fuckin' cops who told me what sort of guy they were looking for.'

As mentioned above, Shawcross had a longtime girlfriend called Clara Neal. Even knowing of the enormity of Art's crimes, Clara told me on camera that should he ever be released she would marry him and make sure that he ' ... kept taking the pills to stop him from killing again.' For his part,

Arthur asked me to be his best man at their wedding, which took place in July 1997 – I didn't attend.

Whoever said that criminology is *always* a serious subject is misguided, because it can be extremely amusing at times!

* * *

With the next subject, I find myself almost at a loss for words – a rare state of affairs for a writer – because the tale of Darcia Brudos *v.* Jerome Henry 'Jerry' Brudos is, without doubt, unique.

In Jerry we have a certified serial killer and necrophile, while Darcia is one who symbolises the Japanese pictorial maxim, from a seventeenth-century carving, embodying the proverbial principle 'See no evil, hear no evil, speak no evil' to an extraordinary degree. Of course, readers might like to refresh their memories by re-reading the earlier chapter about Jerry Brudos, but to put things into perspective, the Brudoses' home was about the size of a British three-bedroomed bungalow with attached garage.

I am not trying to be sarcastic, but one might have thought that under these domestic circumstances dear Darcia might have noticed at least one red flag. Yet she says that she didn't spot any more of them, simply because she saw no evil, heard no evil, and was totally clueless throughout her husband's murderous spree.

* * *

Welcome to 'Russia with Love' and Elena Popokova *v.* Mikhail Viktorovich Popkov. So sickeningly duplicitous are many of the killers mentioned previously, that we can understand why their wives or partners can live in total ignorance, unaware that their other half is out and about at all hours committing similar murderous atrocities as did Arthur Shawcross, Kenneth Bianchi or Gary Ridgway, et al.

Elena's life, her hope and her dreams were all shattered in a heartbeat when she learned that the man she loved and cherished, an honourable well-respected police officer, was a perverted sex beast. She had invested everything in her man. She gave her soul to him. She gave Mikhail everything because she was proud of him, and she lost everything, for he repaid her with a treachery that is beyond calculation.

Yes, I know Russia very well as I do with so many countries around the world, and just like the Philippines, once the breadwinner has been locked up there is not even a breadline to fall onto, so to end this book, it is appropriate that we recall …

* * *

… Carol Pitchfork *v.* Colin Pitchfork – and please note that this worthless piece of murdering scum, the depraved cake-making sex killer of two teenage schoolgirls, was until recently walking around amongst us as free as a bird, albeit for only a few months. No doubt he was probably leching after any young girl he sets his eyes upon, because, you see, a leopard can never change its spots. Once a psychopath, always a psychopath, for they can never, ever be cured. They do not have a conscience – reformed and safe to be released, be damned – simply because criminal history tells us that's exactly how it is.

... Pitchfork, like all of the other narcissistic bullshitters featured throughout this book – and they are merely the tip of the iceberg – will find another female partner who has *no* clue whatsoever that she's sleeping with a monster. Such is the evil of these beasts, and this former cake-maker could be living next door to *you*.

God bless you all, and no nightmares please.